GREAT LAKES
Steelhead, Salmon, and Trout

0 11557 03583 4

GREAT LAKES Steelhead, Salmon, and Trout

ESSENTIAL TECHNIQUES FOR FLY FISHING THE TRIBUTARIES

KARL WEIXLMANN

STACKPOLE
BOOKS

For Lisa. Thanks for letting me go fishing.

Published by
STACKPOLE BOOKS
5067 Ritter Road
Mechanicsburg, PA 17055
www.stackpolebooks.com

Printed in China

10 9 8 7 6 5 4 3 2 1

First edition

Photography by Jack Hanrahan unless otherwise noted
Illustrations by Dave Hall

Library of Congress Cataloging-in-Publication Data

Weixlmann, Karl.
Great Lakes steelhead, salmon, and trout : essential techniques for fly fishing the tributaries / Karl Weixlmann. — 1st ed.
p. cm.
Includes bibliographical references.
ISBN 978-0-8117-3583-4
1. Trout fishing—Great Lakes Region (North America) 2. Salmon fishing—Great Lakes Region (North America) I. Title.
SH688.N7W45 2009
799.12'40977—dc22

2008047521

Contents

Acknowledgments vi
Foreword vii
Introduction ix

1. Species 1
- Steelhead 3
- Chinook Salmon 11
- Coho Salmon 16
- Atlantic Salmon 18
- Brown Trout 21

2. Seasons 27
- Fall 28
- Winter 31
- Spring 38
- Summer 42
- Great Lakes Shoreline and Beach Fly Fishing 46

3. Reading the Water 55
- Tributary Sections 59
- Fish Location and Tributary Hot Spots 62
- Adjusting to Water Condition Changes 70
- Floating Great Lakes Tributaries 77

4. Essential Flies and Foods 85
- Streamers 87
- Eggs 107
- Nymphs 111

5. Techniques 123
- Sliding a Slinky 123
- Indicator Nymphing 127
- High-Stick Nymphing 146
- Swinging Techniques 150
- Fighting the Fish 154

6. Tackle 161
- Fly Rods 162
- Spey Rods 164
- Reels 164
- Lines 165
- Leaders 165
- Accessories 167

7. Economic and Environmental Issues 169
- Angling Pressure 171
- Access 173

Resources 175
References and Required Reading 176
Equipment and Tackle 177
Index 178

Acknowledgments

I would like to thank all the regional fisheries biologists, technicians, and managers who provided information for this book. Cheryl Peterson, Steve Hogler, and Dennis Pratt of the Wisconsin Department of Natural Resources; Brian Breidert, Lake Michigan fisheries biologist for Indiana; Scott Prindle, James Markham, and Fran Verdoliva of the New York State Department of Environmental Conservation; Jay Wesley, Jim Backer, and George Madison of the Michigan Department of Natural Resources; and Jim Bowlby of the OMNR.

Special thanks go to all the fly tiers and fly fishers who graciously provided their talent, knowledge, and time: Kevin Feenstra, Steve May, Ron McGraw, Gerry Darkes, Mike Schmidt, Greg Senyo, Tom Harris, Matt Supinski, Will Turek, and Alan Carter. Thanks to Dave Hall for his illustrations.

I'm especially grateful to Jay Nichols for pointing me in the right direction with his organizational help and assistance, and to Jack Hanrahan for his world-class photography and the many years of unforgettable experiences shared on the stream.

Most of all, I'd like to thank my family, friends, and fishing buddies for their encouragement and support. To my wife, Lisa, and son, Kyle: thanks for your patience, giving me the space and time to complete this book, and putting up with my weird work schedule. To my Dad: thanks for showing me the magic of fishing and the wonders of the outdoor world. To my Mom: thanks for putting up with dried worms, soaking wet clothes, and kids who disappeared on drizzly April mornings. And to my brother, David, who was with me through it all. To all the people who have given me the privilege of taking them fishing, my appreciation is gratefully given.

In the end, it's more than just the fishing that you remember, it's the people who make the memories: Jim Jakubek landing a huge chromer at dusk. Evan Morse pounding them on the Catt. Randy St. John looking over at me with that sly grin. Elliott Haverlack and Paul Johnson catching their first steelhead on the fly. Tommy Lang's marabou streamers. Glen Schaeffer slamming fish after fish with the two-hander one evening on Conneaut Creek. Ronnie Mount dropping his jaw after seeing a school of steelhead stacked up in a tributary pool. Dwight Hurd getting slapped in the face by a jumping steelhead. Jeff Brausch catching fish between floating icebergs. Lake-effect blizzards with Jack and Rob. These, and the many other people who entered my life to go fly fishing, have shared with me many wonderful experiences.

Foreword

As a young boy growing up next to the magnificent and thunderous Niagara River Gorge, I learned early on in life to have a tremendous amount of respect for the vast volume of water that makes up the Great Lakes and its rivers. It is truly one of the most unique inland sea systems on earth.

Awestruck by its angling secrets and opportunities, and armed with a fiberglass fly rod and Pflueger Medalist, I was determined to conquer its rivers. In particular, I was fond of the shoreline corridor of steelhead rivers from the Salmon, emptying into Lake Ontario, to Elk Creek, which was, and still is, Lake Erie's crown jewel. Everyone called them "rainbows" back then; "steelhead" is a more contemporary term. My dad and I would take weekend jaunts to ply these watersheds, often going fishless. But every once in a while, with good timing and perfectly bad weather (which always produced the best fishing), we'd end up with a few chrome beauties.

We didn't have books to teach us.

I can still recall my first steelhead. I caught it in Clear Creek, a tributary to Cattaraugus Creek in New York where my uncle lived. That fish will forever haunt my dreams, and it gave me the passion to pursue these fish to a point of obsession. Days spent at our family's cottage on Georgian Bay of Lake Huron found me chasing those gorgeous rainbows of the spring-fed Bighead and Beaver Rivers. I'll never forget the fish I caught on a snowy New Year's Eve in the Devil's Hole on the mighty Niagara. At dusk, a very large broad-shouldered steelhead struck my crudely constructed yarn fly. The material for the fly's construction was purchased by my mom at a knitting store. The fish jumped at least a half-dozen times and ran down the vicious waters of the gorge, stripped me of all my line and backing, and broke the last knot holding it to my reel. In the dark, little did I know that if I had chased this fish one more step, I would have been a tragic statistic of the Niagara, having been swept away by its wild currents. Luck and that angel was looking out for me.

Since these rewarding misadventures of my youth, I've written *Steelhead Dreams* and the *Orvis Guide to Great Lakes Salmon and Steelhead.* I relish everything I can read about these fish, and I thought I'd written and read all there is to know. Then along came Karl Weixlmann's *Great Lakes Steelhead, Salmon, and Trout.* It is a breath of fresh air given all that has been written about this subject. I first met Karl when he came out to my Gray Drake Lodge on Michigan's Muskegon River. He was with a good client of mine, Joe Tinko. Being their guide, I was told by Mr. Tinko that Karl was the best steelheader on the Erie tributaries. At first I thought, "Who the heck is this Pennsylvania stump-jumping bushwhacker?" Boy, was I wrong in my first assessment. Karl is a fish magnet. He thinks like a steelhead. His persistent optimism as a guide and angler, coupled with a good sense of humor and adventure, makes it a pleasure to be on the water with him.

Why do I like this book so much? Because it's easy to read, it is simple, and it cuts to the chase of the subject matter. Karl, being an ace of the "steelhead alley" Lake Erie tributaries, has explored all the Great Lakes tributaries, so if you're a salmonid chaser anywhere from Lake Superior to Ontario, this book is for you. I also had the pleasure of showing Karl the summer Skamania steelhead fishery of the St. Joe River in Michigan in the summer of 2008. He was amazed by the incredible leaping and powerful fighting ability of these magnificent silver Washington State transplants.

The chapters are well organized and I particularly like the tributary sections, surface and bottom river structure, and his easy-to-use rigging guides. The fly patterns are the state of the art in Great Lakes fly fishing, featuring nothing but the best fly tiers and innovators in the business. The section on surf fishing and steelhead on the dry fly are a welcome touch. Couple the good writing with the outstanding photography of Jack Hanrahan and you've got a definite must-read for the Great Lakes chrome chaser.

Matt Supinski
Newaygo, Michigan

Introduction

A few years back, a guest of mine, after chasing down and landing a wild, 32-inch-long chrome steelhead, looked up at me and said, "That was better than sex, and it lasted longer." It's still the best excuse I've ever heard to go fly fishing on Great Lakes tributaries. You don't have to take an expensive trip to British Columbia to hook up with a double-digit chrome steelhead, or travel to Tierra del Fuego to catch monster brown trout. You can catch these species, along with Atlantic salmon, Chinook salmon, and coho salmon, all within a four-hour drive of half the population of the United States. Without a doubt, the Great Lakes provide one of the best coldwater fisheries on the planet.

But it wasn't always this way. Before Europeans settled North America, the Great Lakes were the largest pristine bodies of fresh water on the

Michael Checchio calls it taking the pulse of the planet. Electric jolts thump the rod up and down as a steelhead thrashes the surface on a small tributary stream in early fall. JAY NICHOLS PHOTO

The Great Lakes and their tributaries were formed as glaciers retreated during the last Ice Age.

planet. Atlantic salmon swam into Lake Ontario tributaries in what are now New York State and the Province of Ontario, providing sustenance for Native Americans, and lake trout, burbot, whitefish, sturgeon, and herring flourished in the lakes' cold water. However, once Europeans arrived, these species quickly became merely entities of commerce.

Margaret Beattie Bogue wrote in *Fishing the Great Lakes: An Environmental History* (University of Wisconsin Press, 2000) that the history of the Great Lakes fishing industry was ". . . yet another example of a highly competitive, virtually unregulated, and wasteful exploitation of a natural resource for profit that over time seriously eroded its commercial utility." During the 1800s, from the growth of industry and an increasingly urbanized society, industrial waste and inadequately treated sewage ruined water quality, and mill dams blocked returning salmon from reaching their historical spawning areas. By the mid-19th century, native populations of Atlantic salmon were virtually wiped out.

By the late 1800s, the Great Lakes commercial fishing industry provided a living for more than 13,000 people. Regulations begun in 1908 between the United States and Canada did little to protect the fish populations of the Great Lakes, and commercial harvests also increased greatly during World War I. During the 1920s, the herring population crashed as a result of continuing Canadian and American exploitation of the Great Lakes. In the following decades, the introduction of the sea lamprey into the upper Great Lakes would further decrease numbers of coldwater species like lake trout.

Even though "environmental stewardship" was an unheard-of catchphrase during those troubling times of Great Lakes history, fish culturists were experimenting with a new species of trout brought in from the West Coast. At the Caledonia Hatchery in New York, in 1874 and 1875, fish culturist Seth Green incubated the first rainbow trout eggs brought to northeastern North America. In 1878, rainbow trout from the Caledonia Hatchery were planted in Caledonia's Spring Creek and the Genesee River, tributaries of Lake Ontario. These first efforts began a century of stockings from Pacific salmon species such as Chinook and coho, to brown trout, to West Coast steelhead, to attempts to restore the Atlantic salmon that had been depleted.

For Christmas 1975, my father gave me a *Boys' Life* book that included a chapter called "Steelhead: The Rainbow That Went to Sea." The notion that a trout would swim to the ocean and come back to its river of birth, all sleek and silver with mind-boggling proportions, enthralled me and fueled my desire to catch one. I thought often of ancient West Coast rainforests, jagged mountain ranges, and emerald green rivers, not knowing that this magnificent species swam much closer to home.

My first introduction to the wonders of the Great Lakes steelhead fishery came from my Dad and my Uncle Donny, who made yearly trips to several Lake Erie tributaries during the 1970s. Their tackle would seem crude by today's standards—short fly rods and reels spooled with heavy monofilament, two big split-shot crimped on the line, and a square orange sponge impaled on a size 6 bait hook. I would gawk at the specimens frozen in my Uncle Donny's freezer and peel away the

A triumphant Robert Kinkoph raises his rod as the author tails a fish during ice-out.

Fly fishing for steelhead has become a passion for many anglers bordering Great Lakes states. Photographer Jack Hanrahan gets ready to release a mint-bright early fall steelhead on New York's Cattaraugus Creek. KARL WEIXLMANN PHOTO

freezer wrap to glimpse the rose-colored cheeks and silver sides of a fresh-run steelhead.

In the early 1980s, I caught a dose of steelie fever of my own. Living on the east side of Erie, Pennsylvania, put me within walking distance of several Lake Erie tributaries, where I honed my technique with salted minnows and nightcrawlers. Little did I know that I would one day make my living fly fishing for them and the many other fantastic cold- and warmwater species that abound in the Great Lakes. More than 20 years later, the south shore Lake Erie tributaries between Cleveland and Buffalo have become an ever-changing "office" in which to conduct my business. And while we do not have the jagged mountain ranges and rainforests that first captured my imagination, the landscape is no less impressive—rivers and creeks cut ancient gorges, where waterfalls plunge hundreds of feet into desolate canyons, and raging whitewater feeds into placid emerald pools lined with overhanging hemlocks.

This book is the culmination of more than 20 years spent fly fishing Great Lakes tributaries and more than a decade spent guiding on them. I still learn new things every day I spend on the water, and I'm still evolving as a fly fisherman. The pioneers of today's modern Great Lakes steelhead, salmon, and brown trout fisheries have given us a year-round menu of diverse angling opportunities. Without the vision of these individuals, our hands may never have felt the silver elegance of a bright steelhead or the adrenaline rush of a double-digit brown slowly sloshing to the surface.

CHAPTER ONE

Species

The diversity of the Great Lakes coldwater fisheries enables fly fishers to pursue steelhead, salmon, or brown trout for almost 12 months of the year. Some of these species die after spawning, and others are capable of making repeated spawning runs. Species genetics plays an important role in run timing. The many strains of steelhead, for example, ascend Great Lakes tributaries at different times of the year, with fall-, winter-, spring-, and summer-run strains each available in certain Great Lakes regions.

Though most people fish the tribs from September through April, spring runs of steelhead can last into May, summer strains of steelhead can be caught in July and August, and Atlantic salmon can run in June. Pennsylvania's state record brown trout was caught at the mouth of Walnut Creek, a Lake Erie tributary, on July 4, and certain tributaries have runs of Chinook salmon in August.

Above: Steelhead were introduced into the Great Lakes during the late 1800s and have adapted to the habitat well.

Steelhead are the most sought-after Great Lakes coldwater gamefish species, bringing smiles to legions of dedicated fly fishers. Jim Fendler gets ready to release a spring-run steelhead on Ohio's Conneaut Creek.

Steelhead

Perhaps no other fish in the Great Lakes has generated as much passion, reverence, devotion, and dedication among fly fishers as the steelhead trout. From the Knife River on Lake Superior's northern shore to the Salmon River on Lake Ontario's southern shore, catching these captivating gamefish has become a way of life for many fly fishers. First-time anglers are often shocked by their bursts of speed and power, their leaping ability, their sleek, muscular beauty, and blushing rose-toned cheeks. Even after many years of hooking steelhead, your inability to control them is humbling and keeps you coming back for more. Hooking a steelhead is one thing—landing it is another.

Its size and eagerness to take a wide variety of fly patterns and presentations throughout the seasons make it one of the most perfectly designed fly-rod fish. Its willingness to strike a fly in subfreezing weather extends fishing opportunities into the winter, when other species just can't be caught.

Wild, pure strain, God-given steelhead are sea-run rainbow trout, born in the clean gravel of cool, freshwater rivers and streams that feed the Pacific Ocean. Technically speaking, a steelhead is a rainbow trout, found on both the western coast of North America and the eastern coast of Northern Asia, that migrates to the ocean (anadromous). Great Lakes steelhead are potadromous rainbow trout, meaning that they complete their life cycle exclusively in fresh water, and some West Coast purists consider Great Lakes steelhead just another brand of lake-run rainbows. However, Great Lakes steelhead have diverse genetic backgrounds as a result of the many strains of West Coast rainbow trout that have been stocked throughout the Great Lakes Basin, and they are born with the genetic urge to smolt and migrate. For over 100 years, this genetic migratory trait has been passed down to each succeeding generation of steelhead in the Great Lakes.

The American Fisheries Society reclassified rainbow trout (including steelhead), previously known as *Salmo gairdneri,* to *Oncorhynchus mykiss,* indicating a distinct population split between Atlantic *(Salmo)* and Pacific *(Oncorhynchus)* salmon and trout. The distinction had been found in fossil records and was later confirmed through DNA testing. Rainbow trout were found to be more closely related to Pacific, than to Atlantic, salmon.

Fresh fall-run steelhead are at their peak of physical conditioning, beauty, and power.

Even though there are no physiological differences between rainbow trout and the many strains of steelhead, there are many visual and behavioral variations between the varieties of *Oncorhynchus mykiss*. Steelhead have been able to adapt to unique environmental habitats and find many niches for themselves within the various regions of the Great Lakes. For example, Lake Superior steelhead have different run timing, spawning schedules, and foraging behaviors than do Lake Erie steelhead.

Identifying characteristics of steelhead vary throughout their life cycle, but include two dorsal fins, one of which is an adipose fin, 10 to 12 rays in the anal fin, and a white mouth and gums. Small spots can extend across the length of the back, from the head to the entire tail. Steelhead change color as they migrate up a tributary, from a snow-white belly with a silver side on freshly run fish from the lake environment, to a light to dark olive back with lavender or rose-colored cheeks and sides on fish that have spent time in the tributary. Males turn dark olive with scarlet sides and cheeks when spawning. Their name is thought to be derived from the bluish-green to dark charcoal-gray back, body, and head of the fish, which looks much like forged steel.

The average size of Great Lakes steelhead depends on a variety of genetic and environmental factors, but most fish weigh from 4 to 10 pounds and measure up to 30 inches long. The Great Lakes that contain good alewife and smelt populations,

Male steelhead, called bucks, darken as spawning time approaches, developing hooked lower jaws called kypes and a nasty set of teeth. They can light up a stream bottom with their scarlet cheeks.

Female steelhead are called hens and have a shorter, blunter head than a buck's elongated snout and lower jaw.

such as Lake Michigan and Lake Ontario, tend to produce larger steelhead that can surpass 20 pounds. Genetic traits such as those found in the Skamania strain can produce larger fish that live and grow in the lake for an extra year before they migrate. The Great Lakes record is a staggering 31.19-pound fish caught in Lake Ontario in 2004.

By following the run timing of the various genetic pools of steelhead, it is possible to catch steelhead every month of the year, though each fishery definitely has its prime times. Wisconsin, for example, stocks three genetic strains of steelhead for its Lake Michigan program: Skamania (summer-run), Chambers Creek (fall- and winter-run), and Ganaraska (spring-run) strains.

Pennsylvania has created its own unique stock of steelhead from a mixture of domestic rainbow trout, previous Skamania steelhead stockings, and Washington State steelhead, resulting in a fishery that produces fantastic fall runs. Mild winters can create almost nonexistent spring runs because most of the spawning takes place from late November through early March. Many of the so-called "chromers" caught during a Pennsylvania spring are actually wintered-over dropback hens that have spawned out and attained a pale white cast over their normal coloring from living under the ice. When exposed again to light, these thin, spawned-out fish begin to regain a silver cast before dropping back to the lake. Holdover hens' bellies can be gray and scarred or have sores from lying on the flat shale bottom through the winter. Fresh, spring-run hens have snow-white bellies full of eggs.

I can sometimes extend the south shore Lake Erie spring steelhead season a full month by following the run in Ohio. Ohio stocks Little Manistee (also called Michigan-strain) steelhead with eggs obtained from the state of Michigan. Fresh runs of steelhead still enter Ohio tributaries during the spring, occasionally into early May. The eggs are taken from wild, naturalized steelhead on Michigan's Little Manistee River and raised to smolt-size before being stocked by the Ohio Department of Natural Resources (ODNR). Ohio's program produces beautiful fish that are larger and fight harder than the Pennsylvania "mutt" steelhead, which have a variety of genetic histories. Some of the biggest fish of the year come to the net late in the spring season because of longer feeding opportunities in the big lake and those Michigan Manistee genetics. These large, late-run steelhead may not travel far up a tributary system and usually spawn quickly as water temperatures increase.

The Washington Fish and Wildlife Commission first developed Skamania-strain steelhead at the Skamania Fish Hatchery on the Washougal River. A Skamania steelhead runs and spawns early and spends one extra year in the ocean. This "three-salt" genetic trait results in giant fish weighing from 12 to 23 pounds that are four years old when making their first spawning run. Most Skamania runs occur from June through August, when rain increases water levels and offshore winds cool the water on the lake shore and tributary mouths, though some fish still trickle in during the fall and spawn in the winter.

History of Great Lakes Steelhead

Michigan's Au Sable River, a tributary of Lake Huron, received the first Great Lakes planting of steelhead in 1876. All early Great Lakes stockings of steelhead came from eggs obtained from the McCloud River system in California. Unlike domesticated strains of rainbow trout, these original stocks of steelhead contained the genetic signals to smolt and migrate downstream to an open body of water. In 1878, Caledonia's Spring Creek and the Genesee River, both tributaries of Lake Ontario, received plantings from McCloud River broodstock, which fish culturist Seth Green raised at the Caledonia Hatchery in New York. These fish migrated downstream, and Lake Ontario became seeded with its first generation of steelhead.

In 1882, a new hatchery was established on the Muskegon River in Michigan, which also received McCloud River stocks. By the early 1900s, wild steelhead were ascending Michigan's Muskegon and Pere Marquette rivers. Because of its quality coldwater habitat and fisheries management programs, Michigan has since become the epicenter for wild steelhead production in the Great Lakes Basin. Runs of more than 10,000 naturally reproduced adults have been documented on the Little Manistee River, which is now the primary source of egg collection for Michigan's steelhead program.

This pure strain of McCloud River steelhead has proven to have better return and growth rates compared to other strains of steelhead. The strain has been so successful that other state fisheries agencies are now using it for stocking programs. Kevin Khale of the ODNR brought the Little Manistee strain of steelhead to the suburban Lake Erie shoreline of Ohio. Eggs come directly from wild fish captured by the Michigan Department of Natural Resources (MDNR). Because of egg collection from wild fish and less crowded hatchery conditions, these primarily spring-run steelhead

Steelhead and other salmonid species migrate back to their natal streams by using either their sense of smell or possibly the earth's magnetic field to guide them but stocked steelhead, salmon, and brown trout meander throughout the entire Great Lakes Basin, providing unstocked tributaries with runs of stray fish. Straying is enhanced by the fact that heavy rains can flush stocked smolts out of a tributary and into the lake after only a few days.

Naturalized steelhead that have spent their first year or two in one tributary are more likely to return to that same tributary because of stronger and longer imprinting on that particular stream. These natives also show a strong tendency to take fly patterns that imitate stonefly, mayfly, and caddis nymphs, reflecting the natural foods they feed on in the streams of their birth.

Life Cycle and Run Timing

Mature steelhead that have entered a tributary eventually seek suitable spawning habitat, characterized by pea-size gravel and cool flowing water with high levels of dissolved oxygen. These areas are generally found in pool tailouts and riffles in the upper tributary sections or feeder streams. Once she finds a suitable location, the female moves the gravel with vigorous tail sweeps until she forms a depression up to a foot deep in the stream bottom, called a redd. Plumes of sediment and the flashing of the spring-run hen's silver sides give away her location. Darker males, called bucks, jockey for position and spawning rights. Bucks caught during spawning time often have teeth slashes on their sides that are the result of fighting for dominance on the spawning gravel.

have beautiful pectoral and dorsal fins and a whale tail that gives these fish superior power.

Pennsylvania began its modern steelhead fishery in 1961 with fingerlings obtained from Washington State. Lake Erie tributaries already contained populations of lake-run domesticated rainbow trout, and during the 1960s and 1970s the Pennsylvania shoreline was fondly referred to as "Rainbow Row." Interbreeding and crowded hatchery conditions (over 1 million smolts are raised annually) have caused Pennsylvania steelhead to have abnormal, blunt, or missing fin structures on some returning fish.

In 1966, a local sportsmen's group called the 3-C-U Trout Association seined wild steelhead fry that were descendants from these initial stockings in several Walnut Creek tributaries. Raised to smolt size and stocked the following spring, the returning wild adults provided broodstock for Pennsylvania's modern steelhead management program. Skamania-strain steelhead stocked in the 1990s may have added early-run genetics. Erie, Pennsylvania, is now referred to as the epicenter of "Steelhead Alley," the tributary-laced shoreline running from Cleveland, Ohio, to Buffalo, New York.

New York State began releasing rainbow trout fingerlings and yearlings into the headwaters of Cattaraugus Creek, a Lake Erie tributary, in 1899. Wild progeny from this initial stocking were some of the first trout I ever caught on dry flies while fishing Clear Creek, an upper Cattaraugus tributary located near Arcade. New York now hatches eggs from returning Chambers Creek–strain steelhead and raises smolts for the state's stocking program in Lake Ontario's Salmon River hatchery in Pulaski. Wild fish, which have been documented in Lake Erie and Lake Ontario tributaries, supplement the state's steelhead fishery.

By the early 1900s, Canada started importing rainbow trout eggs from the United States for hatcheries on Lake Superior and Lake Huron. By the 1940s, naturalized populations of steelhead that could successfully reproduce swam throughout the Great Lakes.

Wild steelhead parr from Crooked Creek, Pennsylvania. In streams with limited habitat, parr may migrate to the lake before smolting.

Once a dominant buck has established hierarchy on the redd, the female deposits her eggs into the depression and the attending male quickly fertilizes them. With mouth agape and body shuddering, he releases his sperm (milt) onto the eggs. The female then covers the eggs with gravel, using more vigorous tail sweeps as she moves upstream to dig another redd, repeating the process if necessary until all her eggs have been laid. Spawning activity attracts more fish that form groups or pods, with the larger, dominant fish taking up the best spawning sites. Large alpha males hang around a spawning area, biting and chasing away smaller suitors (nature's way of ensuring genetic superiority), waiting to spawn again with new waves of fresh hens.

Buried underneath layers of gravel, the fertilized eggs develop into embryos that may take four to seven weeks to hatch, depending on water temperature. Stable water and oxygen levels are needed for successful natural recruitment and to ensure a young steelhead's growth. Newly hatched fry feed on plankton and other microscopic organisms under the protection of bankside cover.

After spending one to three years feeding on invertebrates and fish eggs while growing in tributaries, the young steelhead smolt and move downstream under cover of darkness. Most smolting of wild Great Lakes steelhead occurs at two years of age. Smolting is the name of the physiological changes during which the juvenile parr loses its oval markings, turns silver, and migrates to open

Steelhead feed on baitfish before entering the tributaries, making streamers a good early-season choice for fresh fish.

water in the spring. It is the single life cycle phase that separates a steelhead from a rainbow trout.

At around 7 or 8 inches long, the smolts are large enough to escape many Great Lakes predators, but they become delectable targets for adult salmon, steelhead, walleye, lake trout, bass, and birds. I've caught monster Lake Erie smallmouth bass in late April and early May that have coughed up steelhead smolts. Cormorants and gulls also take a heavy toll as the smolts migrate closer to shore.

Roaming schools of young steelhead soon develop aggressive feeding behaviors and seek ideal water temperatures in the upper 50s. Steelhead have been able to adapt and prosper despite the ecological and environmental changes constantly occurring within the Great Lakes. While Pacific salmon species prey predominantly upon the dwindling alewife populations, steelhead are much more versatile predators and feed upon a larger variety of foods, including baitfish species and invertebrates. ODNR analysis on the stomach contents of adult steelhead caught aboard charter boats from the central basin of Lake Erie showed that more than 90 percent of the consumed biomass was composed of baitfish species, such as emerald shiners and smelt. But even as adults, steelhead still have a larger invertebrate component in their diets than salmon, feeding upon Mysis shrimp, *Hexagenia* nymphs, windblown terrestrials, and spiny water fleas.

Most one-year-old stocked steelhead live in the lake for two years before making their first spawning run as three-year-old adults. Many wild, stream-born steelhead live in the tributaries for up to two years and return as four-year-old adults. Female steelhead require at least three years to become sexually mature and develop eggs. A "one-salt" Great Lakes steelhead that has lived in the open water for one year is called a "jack" and is not considered an adult, although these little males can spawn successfully. These juvenile steelhead enter Great Lakes tributaries during the fall to gorge on salmon eggs and during the spring to feed on steelhead eggs.

Steelhead can make multiple spawning runs. Most sexually mature females make their first run at three years of age.

As the days grow shorter, genetic imprinting and a remarkable olfactory system lead steelhead back to the stream or river in which they were previously stocked or born. Some scientists believe that salmon and steelhead may also use the earth's magnetic field for navigation. The age at which steelhead actually begin spawning is determined by run timing, species genetics, water temperatures, and water levels. I've seen steelhead spawning as early as mid-October on southern Lake Erie tributaries.

Some basic knowledge of the run timing of the different strains can help keep you on the fish. Ganaraska steelhead are a Canadian spring-run strain that run and spawn from March through May. Chambers Creek–strain steelhead, stocked by the state of New York, are a fall- and winter-run strain that spawn from November through March. Little Manistee–strain steelhead, also known as Michigan

Tiny nymphs work well in clear, cold water—perfect for winter fly fishing.

strain, run from late fall through early spring and spawn from February through April. Major runs of Skamania-strain steelhead can appear from June through September, with smaller runs through the fall and into early winter. Skamania-strain steelhead that run in the summer hold over in tributaries until spawning begins in midwinter.

As adults, steelhead can make as many as five successful spawning runs. Tributaries with quality habitat and cool, steady groundwater can support wild, naturalized steelhead. Though there are wild populations in the Great Lakes, many tributaries (especially those with poor habitat or that suffer from thermal warming problems) are stocked.

Fishing Characteristics

A steelhead's predatory personality allows anglers to use a wide variety of fly patterns and presentations. When the fish are in, on the bite, and the water conditions are good, steelhead can seem relatively easy to hook. Last year my guest and I hooked and broke off a fish. Later in the day, and farther upriver, the fish ate again on its upstream journey. We hooked it on the same fly pattern, and the other fly was still hooked deeply in the fish's mouth.

Even though steelhead seem easy to catch at times, you still need to change your techniques, the areas where you look for fish, and your fly selection to adapt to changing water conditions, water temperature, and the time of year. Swinging streamers works well for fresh-run fall fish and during the spring, when hungry, spawned-out steelhead head back to the lake. Bottom-bouncing and nymphing techniques become more important as water temperatures drop in late fall and winter and a steelhead's metabolism slows down. Holding positions constantly change. In higher water conditions with warmer water temperatures, fish hold in riffles, pocketwater, and inside current seams in relatively shallow water. As water levels recede, steelhead drop into deeper runs, depressions, and pools that offer more security and cover.

Fly selection can be just as perplexing as choosing when and where to fish. Warm, dirty, and high water may require large, bright or black streamers. Cold, dirty, and high water may call for large, bright egg patterns. A streamer can still work in low, clear, and warm water, but if the water is cold you may have to use a small egg or nymph pattern. Steelhead will also eat an egg or nymph pattern during the fall or spring, just as they still hit a streamer during the winter. Still, I'd rate being in the right spot at the right time with good technique and thoughtful presentation as being much more important than fly selection. Putting it all together is what makes fly fishing for steelhead so interesting and addictive.

Prominent Great Lakes Steelhead Fisheries

New York (Lake Ontario)

Primary tributaries: Niagara River, Oak Orchard Creek, Genesee River, Oswego River, Salmon River, North and South Sandy Creeks

Secondary streams: 18 Mile Creek, Sandy Creek, Irondequoit Creek, Maxwell Creek, Johnson Creek, Little Salmon River, Grindstone Creek, Stony Creek

New York (Lake Erie)
Primary tributaries: Cattaraugus Creek
Secondary streams: Buffalo Creek, 18 Mile Creek, Chautauqua Creek, Canadaway Creek

Pennsylvania (Lake Erie)
Primary tributaries: 20 Mile Creek, Walnut Creek, Elk Creek, Conneaut Creek
Secondary streams: 16 Mile Creek, 12 Mile Creek, 7 Mile Creek, Crooked Creek, Raccoon Creek

Ohio (Lake Erie)
Primary tributaries: Conneaut Creek, Grand River, Chagrin River, Rocky River, Vermillion River, Ashtabula River
Secondary streams: Cowles Creek, Wheeler Creek, Arcola Creek

Michigan (Lake Michigan)
Primary tributaries: St. Joseph River, Kalamazoo River, Grand River, Muskegon River, White River, Pere Marquette River, Big Manistee River, Little Manistee River, Betsie River, Platte River
Secondary streams: Dowagiac River, Rogue River, Pentwater River, Boardman River, Boyne River, Jordan River

Michigan (Lake Huron)
Primary tributaries: Ocqueoc River, Au Sable River, Rifle River, Black River, East Branch Au Gres

Michigan (Upper Peninsula, Lake Superior)
Primary tributaries: St. Mary's River, Two Hearted River, Carp River, Chocolay River, Big Huron River, Ontonagon River
Secondary streams: Tahquamenon River, Sucker River, Mosquito River, Miner River, Hurricane River, Whitefish River, Falls River, Gratiot River

Michigan (Lake Erie)
Primary tributary: Huron River

Indiana (Lake Michigan)
Primary tributaries: Little Calumet River, Trail Creek, Salt Creek

Wisconsin (Lake Michigan)
Primary tributaries: Root River, Milwaukee River, Sheboygan River, Manitowoc River, West Twin River, East Twin River, Kewaunee River, Oconto River, Peshtigo River
Secondary streams: Menominee River, Oak Creek, Pike River, Sauk Creek, Pigeon River, Branch River, Ahnapee River

Wisconsin (Lake Superior)
Primary tributary: Bois Brule River

Minnesota (Lake Superior)
Primary tributaries: Knife River, Baptism River, Temperance River, Devil Track River
Secondary streams: Nemadji River, Blackhoof River, Split Rock Creek, Cross River, Palisade Creek, Poplar River, Cascade River

Ontario (Lake Superior)
Primary tributaries: Jackpine River, Cypress River, Steel River, Michipicoten River, St. Mary's River
Secondary streams: Mackenzie River, Wolf River, Black Sturgeon River, Coldwater River

Ontario (Lake Huron)
Primary tributaries: Nottawasaga River, Beaver River, Bighead River, Saugeen River, Maitland River
Secondary streams: Sauble River, Nine Mile River, Bayfield River

Ontario (Lake Erie)
Primary tributaries: Grand River, Big Creek
Secondary streams: Potter's Creek, Normandy Creek, Fishers Creek, Young's Creek, Nith River, Whiteman's Creek, Big Otter Creek

Ontario (Lake Ontario)
Primary tributaries: Niagara River, Bronte River, Credit River, Rogue River, Humber River, Wilmot Creek, Ganaraska River
Secondary streams: Bowmanville Creek, Soper Creek, Highland Creek, Don River, Duffins Creek

Chinook Salmon

Hooking into a Chinook salmon (also called king salmon, because of their large size) with a fly rod is like dangling your fly off a bridge and hooking the back end of an eighteen-wheeler doing 65 mph down the highway. Few Great Lakes gamefish have the sheer size and strength of a fresh-run king salmon, or inflict such big-fish madness. A fresh-run Chinook is a prized trophy that truly tests your tackle and stamina.

Native to the Pacific, Chinook salmon *(Oncorhynchus tshawytscha)* were first stocked in Lakes Michigan, Huron, Erie, and Ontario in 1873. At first, naturally reproducing populations were unsuccessful, and by the 1960s and 1970s millions of Chinook salmon were being stocked in the Great Lakes—more than 6 million per year in Lake

Chromer kings test every component of your tackle. ALAN CARTER PHOTO

Michigan alone. The monumental runs of huge fish that resulted from these stocking efforts soon had fishery managers resorting to legitimizing snagging to harvest the fish before they died. To accomplish this, heavily weighted treble hooks, called Michigan stingers, and plugs with large trebles were cast and ripped through pools with heavy, surf-size spinning tackle. Snagging has since been banned.

These large initial stockings provided an alewife predator and also supported a rapidly growing offshore sport fishery. But such overstocking of salmon led to a depletion of prey species that caused poor feeding conditions and correspondingly increased mortality levels among stressed populations. An outbreak of bacterial kidney disease (BKD; also known as salmon disease) in the late 1980s caused a severe decline in the Chinook population of Lake Michigan, and management agencies began to question previous stocking policies. BKD is an internal infection in salmonid species that was in the eggs first obtained from Pacific salmon and is thought to occur when fish don't get enough to eat. In 1999, Lake Michigan management agencies reduced lakewide stocking of Chinook salmon to 4,400,000 fish in an effort to better balance these predator and prey populations. Lake Ontario management agencies have also reduced their Chinook stockings for the same reasons.

Several Great Lakes states, including Ohio and Pennsylvania, have eliminated all salmon stocking in favor of better returns yielded by liberal steelhead stockings. States such as Michigan have significantly reduced Pacific salmon stockings to better balance the predator and prey populations in Lake Michigan, where the average weight of salmon has decreased.

Zebra mussels, which filter-feed on minute zooplankton, and the Clean Water Act of 1977, which reduced phosphate discharges into the Great Lakes, have since "cleaned" the Great Lakes, reducing the zooplankton base that alewives feed upon. Since the Chinook salmon thrived on the abundant schools of alewives, there is a direct correlation between the decline of Great Lakes alewife populations and the decrease in business for the Great Lakes charter fleet that primarily targets coho and Chinook salmon.

However, better tributary water quality during the 1970s and 1980s, beginning with the Clean Water Act and combined with the protection of spawning and rearing habitat, started to produce excellent natural recruitment of Chinook salmon throughout the Great Lakes. A New York Sea Grant (NYSG) project, conducted by the State University of New York College of Environmental Sciences and Forestry and completed in 2006, showed natural, juvenile Chinook populations numbering in the millions in the Salmon River the previous year. Stabilized, year-round flows instituted by power companies since the late 1990s have enhanced the spawning success of Chinooks. The magnitude of wild recruitment is far higher today than during initial studies, which were conducted thirty years ago. As many as five million Chinook salmon per year are now naturally reproduced in the river system. As NYSG Fisheries Specialist David MacNeill said, "The good news now is that the Salmon River obviously has good habitat for natural spawning, but this number of naturally produced salmon may create additional pressure on prey fish populations."

Fisheries managers in Michigan have also seen a high survival rate of wild salmon in their fisheries. Over 50 percent of returning runs in Michigan now consist of wild, naturally produced Chinooks. Increasing the ability of Great Lakes tributaries to produce wild recruitment is becoming a focal point for fisheries managers working to improve and maintain the fantastic sport fisheries in the Great Lakes. More research is needed to better understand how many of the wild fish are surviving to fishable size.

Identifying characteristics of the Chinook salmon include two dorsal fins (of which one is an adipose fin located near the tail), small spots on the upper back and tail, 15 to 17 rays on the anal fin, and a black mouth with black gums. Spawning Chinooks generally have rose-red flanks and dark olive backs. Warranting the title of "king," Great Lakes Chinook salmon average around 20 pounds, with a 30-pounder considered a large specimen. A 47-pound, 13-ounce Great Lakes record king salmon was caught in New York's Salmon River in 1991.

Life Cycle and Run Timing

Chinooks are the earliest-running salmon species, often entering tributaries by late August, if tributary, tributary mouth, and lakeshore temperatures align in the mid-60s and water levels allow upstream migration. The sight of king salmon swimming up a tributary is awe-inspiring. Whitewater explodes in riffles as the huge fish move upriver, dropping into bottom depressions and holding in deep runs between heavy riffles.

Pacific salmon have notably different life cycles and behaviors from steelhead and brown trout. Both Chinook and coho salmon perish within several weeks after spawning. The life cycle of a Chinook salmon begins as the female lays her eggs in a bed of gravel, with the male guarding the redd and then fertilizing the eggs. Each hen may make several redds in the course of spawning, covering them with gravel after they are fertilized.

The eggs hatch in three or four months. The following spring, 3- to 4-inch-long Chinook salmon fingerlings migrate downstream and head into the lakes. They feed on an abundant nearshore zooplankton base, seeking sheltered areas away from predators before becoming large enough to feed on baitfish.

After two to three years of feeding in open water environments of the Great Lakes, king salmon begin to stage near river mouths as daylight photoperiods (length of daylight vs. darkness) begin to shorten, in late summer and early fall. Run activity for all salmonid species is determined by length of daylight, stream temperature, lake temperature, lake water levels, tributary water levels, precipitation, and dam or canal releases that raise river flows and encourage runs.

Changing photoperiods can trigger various salmonid species, including king salmon, to run. Fall- and winter-run fish are imprinted on decreasing length of daylight, while spring- and summer-run fish are imprinted on an increase in length of daylight. Imprinting is related to when broodstock or eggs are collected by fisheries agencies. If, for example, eggs are collected from salmon early in the run, during late August or September, the offspring have imprinted on longer photoperiods than those making their spawning runs in mid-

Chinooks can enter tributaries as early as August. ALAN CARTER PHOTO

October. If broodstock for summer-run steelhead are captured in June and July, this early-running trait is passed to the next generation, which then continue to migrate during these longer daylight photoperiods. Some states, including Pennsylvania, try to collect eggs from steelhead at various seasons and stages of the run to spread the run out over a longer time period.

Despite genetic urges, low, warmwater tributary conditions and warm lakeshore and tributary mouth temperatures can prevent the fish from migrating upstream. They may stack up at the tributary mouth or in the lower portions of a tributary. Rain—as well as dam or canal releases that raise water levels and cool tributary temperatures down to the mid-60s—can trigger the run.

Optimal conditions may only occur for a short period of time, and a run can stall out as fish move up the tributary when water levels drop or water temperatures rise. We had poor timing on the Salmon River one season, during which 95 percent of the river was completely devoid of fish. Several days before our arrival, a low-pressure system dropped a good amount of rain, but we only saw one or two kings moving up through the Douglaston Run on the lower river. A run came through all right, but most of the fish ran the 13-mile river relatively quickly and were already stacked up in the large pools upstream from the town of Altmar, where the fish felt secure.

With all these variables, it can be hard to predict run timing, even on a regional basis. Dropping nighttime air temperatures coinciding with precipitation can elicit king salmon runs as early as August. Peak numbers of fresh kings are usually found in tributaries during September and early October, though I've also seen low and clear tributaries come alive with fresh runs of salmon when you'd least expect them to. This is more likely to happen when tributary and lake mouth temperatures align. Fish move the most in low-light conditions, but I've also seen them travel in the middle of the day.

By mid-October or early November, king salmon begin moving into deep, swift-moving gravel runs, riffles, and pool tailouts to spawn. Males darken and grow hooked protrusions on the end of the lower jaw, called kypes. The mouth of an adult buck king salmon can be downright nasty and becomes a formidable tool for displaying the fish's dominance on the spawning gravel. Hens develop obese bellies, full of maturing eggs.

Because of their size, king salmon spawn in main river channels, riffles, and tailouts, where depth and current velocity would inhibit other coldwater species from spawning. The female moves gravel and small rocks with vigorous tail sweeps to build redds on the stream bottom. Males establish dominance by chasing away smaller suitors. The female deposits her eggs into the depression, and the attending male fertilizes them quickly.

Fishing Characteristics

For years people thought that Pacific salmon would never hit a bait, lure, or fly when making spawning runs. Because of this, many fishery agencies endorsed snagging both king and coho salmon, but this has since been banned. While the digestive tract shuts down as the salmon get close to spawning time, their instinctive predatory and territorial responses still cause them to strike at and take a fly.

The best time to get chromer kings to eat a fly is early in the run, on the lower sections of tributaries. I've watched king salmon swim over 4 feet to inhale an Estaz Egg, and they aggressively chase and hit large streamer patterns soon after entering tributaries. As they approach spawning time and sexual maturity, king salmon may refuse to eat and become harder to catch. Since fish are in different stages of the spawn, and therefore in different "moods" regarding whether they take a fly, you need to cover a lot of fish to find any willing takers.

Tributary sections contain taking water, where a presentation is likely to result in a hookup, and dead water, where fish might be present but less likely to take the fly. Taking water can be a depression in a pool tailout, a foam line entering a pool, the soft water in a boulder-strewn riffle, or a deep slot along the far bank. Dead-drifted flies work best where Chinooks are found lying along deep ledges.

Even though a king salmon will take a dead-drifted nymph or egg pattern, nothing is quite as exciting as watching one chase and trash a streamer. Watching a 15- to 20-pound fish charging out of a logjam to chase a fly will give any angler heart palpitations. Michigan outfitter and guide Ray Schmidt has designed a streamer called Ray's Salmon Snake that closely mimics the action of a wobbling plug. The Magic Head on the front of the fly is like the acrylic bill of a plug and induces the wobble. Ray fishes this fly with a 10-weight rod and a Scientific Anglers Streamer Express 350- to 400-grain line.

Salmon are less likely to feed once they start spawning, but males instinctively slash and snap at any flies invading their space. By this point, the salmon have weakened significantly from the rigors of the run and from defending their spawning sites. They are now dying, and no longer worth fishing for.

Prominent Great Lakes Chinook Salmon Fisheries

New York (Lake Ontario)
North and South Sandy Creek, Salmon River, Oswego River, Genesee River, Oak Orchard Creek, 18 Mile Creek, Niagara River

Michigan (Lake Michigan)
St. Joseph River, Grand River, Muskegon River, White River, Pere Marquette River, Little Manistee River, Big Manistee River, Betsie River, Carp River

Michigan (Upper Peninsula/Lake Superior)
St. Mary's River, Two Hearted River, Chocolay River, Big Huron River, Ontonagon River

Michigan (Lake Huron)
Ocqueoc River, Au Sable River, Rifle River

Wisconsin (Lake Michigan)
Root River, Milwaukee River, Sheboygan River, Kewaunee River, Oconto River, Peshtigo River

Wisconsin (Lake Superior)
Bois Brule River

Minnesota (Lake Superior)
Knife River, Temperance River

Ontario (Lake Superior)
Steel River, Michipicoten River, Nipigon River, St. Mary's River

Ontario (Lake Huron)
Nottawasaga River, Bighead River, Saugeen River, Maitland River

Ontario (Lake Ontario)
Credit River, Wilmot Creek, Ganaraska River

Coho Salmon

If the Chinook salmon is the veritable king of the salmon world, the coho salmon is the smaller, equally regal queen. Called "silvers" on the Pacific Coast, coho salmon are known for their rampaging acrobatics when hooked. Cohos were the first of the Pacific salmon species to be stocked, and the revival of Great Lakes sport fisheries rode on the sleek and muscular steel-blue backs of coho salmon.

In 1933, Ohio released coho salmon *Oncorhynchus kisutch* into Lake Erie. These native West Coast salmonids survived, but they did not establish naturally reproducing populations. Stockings of coho and Chinook greatly increased in the mid- to late 1960s, chiefly to provide a predator species that would reduce the Great Lakes alewife explosion. This invasive marine fish species spread throughout the Great Lakes via the Welland Canal, which bypasses Niagara Falls and connects Lake Erie to Lake Ontario and the St. Lawrence Seaway, which then empties into the Atlantic Ocean. By the 1950s, populations of this plankton-feeding member of the herring family had spread throughout the Great Lakes, resulting in massive winter kills that littered shorelines.

It wasn't until 1966 that plantings by the state of Michigan established a wild coho population within the Great Lakes. Coho are now spawning successfully in most Lake Superior tributaries, and in eastern and western Lake Michigan tributaries, and have developed some limited naturalized populations in other Great Lakes regions. Most popu-

Coho salmon, also called silver salmon, are known for their raging acrobatics when hooked.

lations within the Great Lakes must still be sustained by stocking hatchery fish, however.

Cohos are distinguished from king salmon by their smaller average size, spots found only on the upper half of the tail, and gray or white gums between the teeth. Burnt rose flanks and dark olive backs are the coho's spawning dress. Where forage fish like alewives and smelt are more abundant, cohos can attain an average weight of 7 to 10 pounds. Where forage species are less abundant, such as in Lake Superior, average weights may only reach 5 pounds. The Great Lakes record is a 33-pound, 7-ounce fish taken from Lake Ontario in 1998.

Unfortunately, coho salmon have become an increasingly minor component in Great Lakes coldwater fisheries and are no longer stocked by states like Ohio and Pennsylvania. The Root River in Wisconsin might see runs of 9,000 to 10,000 Chinooks, but only 1,000 to 2,000 coho salmon. Biologist think that the larger Chinook salmon are displacing cohos during spawning time.

Life Cycle and Run Timing

Cohos usually run after king salmon, but run times vary by region and can span as long as four months. Some Great Lakes tributaries, like the St. Joseph River, have early runs in August, while peak catches on New York's Salmon River occur in September. Other tributaries, like the St. Mary's on the Michigan-Ontario border, have later runs that occur during the month of November and extend into the Christmas season.

Naturalized populations of coho salmon spawn in the same environments as Chinook salmon but prefer lower stream velocities and shallower water with smaller gravel. Females may lay as many as 10,000 eggs, which are then born in three to four months. After hatching, the young salmon (called alevin) is about one-and-a-half inches long. These young salmon are also called sac fry because they still retain the egg sac, which is used as food for early growth. After finishing the egg sac, they look like very small salmon and are called fry. High dissolved oxygen levels and adequate stream cover are important for fry survival. Mortality is especially high during the tributary life stages, and death is often the result of poor forest, agricultural, and development practices that contribute to poor water quality during runoff. Coho salmon remain in their natal stream for over a year, feeding on zooplankton, aquatic insects, and small fish before migrating to the lake as silvery smolts.

Once they reach the lake, their distribution and feeding behavior is similar to Chinook salmon. During spring, they move inshore to feed on smelt and alewives, but as summer approaches, they move progressively offshore. Sexually mature fish congregate around tributary mouths in late summer and early fall before making spawning runs.

Fishing Characteristics

Coho salmon love to chase things and generally take a fly better and for a longer period of time than Chinook salmon, which spawn earlier and quickly reach sexual maturity once they have entered a tributary. Early-run fish will hit brightly colored pink, purple, orange, or white streamers with rod-jolting strikes when swung down and across through pools and runs. Black, olive, and purple Woolly Buggers are deadly when stripped in front of fish holding in pool flats.

Staging coho often prefer the deeper side channels and the slower-moving, shallow pool flats away from the larger kings. In the slower-moving water, a good technique is to use a longer 10- to 12-foot leader and a floating line to strip weighted black or olive flies containing a minimal amount of flash. Brighter, flashier patterns seem to work better in faster water, where a fish has less time to think about striking.

Coho salmon become harder to hook as they begin spawning. Bottom-bouncing nymphs and egg patterns are effective at this time, although streamers can still induce takes from aggressive fish protecting their beds.

Coho salmon take a variety of orange and pink egg patterns. They can be distinguished from Chinook salmon by the white gums between their teeth.

Prominent Great Lakes Coho Salmon Fisheries

New York (Lake Ontario)
Salmon River, Oswego River, Genesee River, Oak Orchard Creek, Black River

Michigan (Lake Michigan)
St. Joseph River, Grand River, Muskegon River, White River, Pere Marquette River, Little Manistee River, Big Manistee River, Betsie River, Platte River

Michigan (Upper Peninsula/Lake Superior)
St. Mary's River, Two Hearted River, Chocolay River, Ontonagon River

Wisconsin (Lake Michigan)
Root River, Milwaukee River, Sheboygan River, Kewaunee River, Oconto River, Peshtigo River

Wisconsin (Lake Superior)
Bois Brule River

Minnesota (Lake Superior)
Knife River, Baptism River, Temperance River, Devil Track River

Ontario (Lake Superior)
Nipigon River, Jackpine River, Cypress River, Steel River, Michipicoten River

Ontario (Lake Huron)
Nottawasaga River, Maitland River

Ontario (Lake Ontario)
Credit River

Atlantic Salmon

In the early 1800s, Lake Ontario sustained one of the most plentiful freshwater Atlantic salmon populations in the world. The famous Salmon River in New York was named for its population of Atlantic, not Pacific, salmon. The fish were so abundant that they were easily speared, clubbed, or captured in pound nets and weirs. Native Americans and early settlers relied on the species for sustenance. Even though Britain's Magna Carta theoretically granted the Atlantic salmon rights of protection, they were wiped out by the late 1800s in their historical Lake Ontario habitat due to a wide range of changing environmental factors and other human disturbances, including dams, deforestation, general habitat destruction, and pollution. Approximately forty of Lake Ontario's tributaries once supported runs of Atlantic salmon that were upstream migrators, with Niagara Falls serving as a natural barrier to the rest of the Great Lakes.

Research has suggested that another biological factor—the introduction of alewives, in the late 1800s—may have played a role in the disappearance, and may be hindering modern restoration efforts. Alewives contain an enzyme that breaks down thiamine. Thiamine deficiencies have been shown to be a major source of mortality in egg and fry survival of salmon, and as Atlantic salmon ate large quantities of the exotic alewife, there was a higher mortality rate among their young. Coincidently, the Great Lakes sport-fishery tradition began with Pacific salmon stockings, intended to reduce these alewife populations.

After more than 100 years, Canada and the United States have not yet established any self-propagating populations of Atlantic salmon in the

Great Lakes. In the 1970s and 1980s, Michigan and Wisconsin stocked strains of ocean-run Atlantic salmon obtained from Quebec and a landlocked strain from Sweden into Lake Michigan and Lake Superior. These mostly unsuccessful attempts to reestablish and restore self-sustaining populations in the Great Lakes have been researched by Dr. Robert Scott at the University of Guelph's Axelrod Institute of Ichthyology, in the province of Ontario. Scott says that it was clear that Chinook salmon set up social hierarchies and would physically and aggressively displace Atlantic salmon in a variety of tributary and open-lake habitats.

Atlantic salmon have also been reintroduced into the Salmon River in New York with landlocked strains from the state of Maine. After initial plantings of 50,000 Atlantic salmon smolts in 1983 on three high-quality Lake Ontario tributaries, adults returned to all three tributaries and spawned successfully, but the number of naturally produced fish was not high enough to continue the program after 1987. In a 1996 program change to reestablish native salmonid species and provide more fishing opportunities, the Salmon River was stocked with 30,000 Atlantic salmon smolts in the hope that stabilized water releases could provide quality habitat in the river's main stem. The Black River and Oak Orchard Creek also received plantings of Atlantics. In 1998, fly anglers began catching these returning fish that had spent two years feeding in Lake Ontario.

The chance for restoration of Atlantic salmon in Lake Ontario and the Salmon River may depend on the strain of Atlantic salmon being used for reintroduction, since return and survival rates have been found to vary by strain. Grand Lake–strain

Atlantic salmon were plentiful in Lake Ontario when Europeans settled North America. They disappeared from these waters due to habitat degradation, dam and mill building, deforestation, and pollution. Restoration programs in Canada and the United States are working toward restoring self-sustaining populations of this native species. SUPINSKI PHOTOGRAPHY

Atlantics, currently being used by the New York State Department of Environmental Conservation (NYSDEC), come from the state of Maine and are outlet-spawning landlocked salmon that may be lost to migration through the St. Lawrence Seaway, which empties into the Atlantic Ocean. Outlet-spawning salmon make their spawning run downstream into lake outlets, not upstream and into lake inlets or streams that feed the lake. The agency plans to stock Sebago Lake–strain Atlantics from Maine that are upstream (or inlet) spawners and could yield better returns. These salmon should have a better genetic urge to run upstream into Lake Ontario tributaries, not downstream and into the St. Lawrence Seaway. Great Lakes fisheries agencies continue to develop experimental strains of Atlantics intended to have the genetic makeup to survive and reproduce in Great Lakes.

The sprawling St. Mary's River that connects Lake Superior to Lake Huron is probably the most successful and well-known Great Lakes Atlantic salmon fishery at this time. The fishery has had higher than normal return rates of stocked Atlantics (around 5 percent), and natural reproduction has also been documented. The program began in 1987 when the first Atlantic salmon were raised and released from eggs obtained from the state of Maine. An aquatic research laboratory was founded in the massive hydroelectric plant that spans the river in a cooperative effort between Lake Superior State University and Edison Sault Electric Company, where the salmon were hatched and raised before being stocked. These Grand Lake–strain Atlantics first returned in 1989, with continual stockings of around 50,000 fish occurring on a yearly basis. With good returns, a viable fishery has been established.

The Ontario Ministry of Natural Resources (OMNR) and its research partners are currently implementing a recovery strategy to restore Atlantic salmon in Lake Ontario. The goal is to have self-sustaining populations within 10 to 15 years. Objectives for the first five years include: stocking of fry, fingerlings, and yearlings into three tributaries; creating spawning runs to establish a self-sustaining population; and developing and maintaining broodstock from at least three different strains of Atlantic salmon.

Identifying characteristics of the Atlantic salmon are two dorsal fins, including one adipose fin, a narrow pointed tongue with four to six small teeth, large pectoral fins, a forked tail, and nine rays in the anal fin. Average sizes of 18 to 24 inches and 2 to 6 pounds were probably typical in the historical populations of Atlantic salmon in Lake Ontario, although according to old records, fish over 40 pounds were occasionally caught. Modern Great Lakes Atlantic salmon have an average weight of 6 to 15 pounds. Caught in 1981, a 32.62-pound, 41-inch-long Atlantic salmon taken from Lake Michigan stands as the Great Lakes record.

Life Cycle and Run Timing

Most Atlantic salmon spawn in fresh water and spend most of their lives in the ocean. Those in the Great Lakes are often referred to as landlocked salmon. Unlike their Pacific cousins, Atlantic salmon do not die after spawning; they make multiple spawning runs, sometimes reaching six or seven years of age. Lake-run adults can enter tributaries anywhere from May through November. During spring, warmer water and abundant food sources attract salmon closer to shore and into the lower ends of tributaries. When lake water temperatures reach the mid-50s, Atlantic salmon begin to move offshore and feed on their preferred food source, rainbow smelt. Sexually mature fish move back toward the lakes' shorelines during the fall, seeking their natal stream or the location where they were stocked.

Atlantic salmon are fall spawners. The female chooses a gravel bottom riffle upstream or downstream from a pool to dig a nest (or redd). The male simultaneously releases his sperm as the female releases her eggs into this depression. Adults hold and rest in the river before returning to the lake, and males may remain in the tributary all winter. These "kelts" can provide good fishing in early spring as they migrate back to the lake.

Eggs hatch the following spring, with the newly hatched young growing for two or three years in the stream's riffles and pools until they are about 6 or 7 inches long. They grow rapidly after migrating to the lake and can weigh from 3 to 6 pounds after one year. Some return to their spawning streams after a year in the lake, while others may wait another year and grow to a weight of about 6 to 15 pounds. The cycle repeats itself as fall approaches and salmon again come shoreward.

Fishing Characteristics

The highly regarded royalty of Great Lakes cold-water fisheries, Atlantic salmon are spectacular fighters noted for their aerial displays, hence their Latin name *Salmo salar,* the leaper. When in a fly-taking mood, Atlantic salmon are known to be more aggressive than steelhead and to respond well to surface or near-surface presentations. They readily smash a fly on the swing or come to the top for a waking Bomber when they first come into the river. For subsurface presentations, Muddlers, sculpins, and smelt imitations tied with rabbit strips that undulate in the water are good choices.

Atlantics hanging in low and clear tributaries, where they feel exposed, may respond better to dead-drifted scud, mayfly, and Mysis shrimp patterns. As spawning approaches and they become more aggressive, try fishing Egg-Sucking Leeches and orange, pink, or chartreuse egg patterns.

Prominent Great Lakes Atlantic Salmon Fisheries

New York (Lake Ontario)
Salmon River, Oak Orchard Creek, North and South Sandy Creeks, Black River

Michigan (Upper Peninsula, Lake Superior/ Lake Huron)
St. Mary's River

Ontario (Lake Superior/Lake Huron)
St. Mary's River

Ontario (Lake Ontario)
Credit River, Wilmot Creek

Brown Trout

Most Great Lakes fly anglers only dream of catching giant brown trout that weigh in the double-digits—a fish so big, your heart jumps into your throat when it slowly sloshes to the surface, thrashing its head back and forth. With better-managed brown trout fisheries, there has never been a better time for a Great Lakes fly fisher to land a lunker brown trout than right now.

Brown trout, a relative of the Atlantic salmon and of European origin, were first established in the Great Lakes in 1883, when the state of Michigan released them into the Pere Marquette River, a tributary of Lake Michigan. The province of Ontario began stocking its waters with brown trout around 1913. Many of these early plantings did not survive, and small numbers of brown trout were subsequently stocked into the Great Lakes. These stocking policies changed in the mid-1960s when, as part of the rehabilitation efforts conducted in the Great Lakes, browns were once again liberally stocked throughout the Great Lakes. The state of Wisconsin, for example, currently stocks approximately one million brown trout into Lake Michigan each year.

Several different strains of brown trout are stocked, though all brown trout in North America have European origins. Seeforellen brown trout are a European strain that live longer, grow larger, run later, and are more disease-resistant than domesticated strains such as the Wild Rose and the St. Croix. All three strains are stocked by the state of Wisconsin. After a ten-year layoff, New York once again began stocking brown trout into Lake Erie and its tributaries in 2002 with a Randolph strain of trout that has been showing good returns.

Lake-run brown trout are an important component in many Great Lakes coldwater fisheries. This full-bodied hen ate a Three Loop Pink Lady on Elk Creek in December. ERIC SCHLABACH PHOTO

Domesticated strains are named for the state hatchery where they were raised.

Good base flows are needed before browns migrate into the tributaries. Water releases from the Erie Canal sometimes stimulate runs of trout into New York's Oak Orchard Creek, Sandy Creek, and the Oswego River if precipitation amounts are low. Dam releases can trigger runs on tributaries like New York's Salmon River. After each high-water cycle, lake-run browns can be found in locations similar to those that hold resident trout. They stay out of heavy current by using current breaks and depressions where they can rest and ambush or intercept forage fish and aquatic insects. In-stream structure such as fallen trees, logjams, and large boulders or rocky areas attract holding and resting browns.

Brown trout go through several color phases after spending time in a tributary, but those that have recently migrated from the lake retain a silvery cast. The dark-brown and red body spots characteristic of their stream-dwelling cousins are often absent on lake-dwelling browns. Browns right out of the lake can be hard to spot when they're holding among schools of steelhead or salmon, but when they start to change color and take on a yellow cast, they are easier to spot even if holding in front of or behind schools of steelhead and salmon.

As spawning approaches and the fish have spent time in a tributary, male brown trout begin to have dark bellies, fins, and backs, turning almost black—much like a salmon near the end of its life. Females often retain a lighter color. Browns have light-colored pectoral fins, a squared off tail, nine to ten rays on the anal fin, and a large tooth-filled mouth.

Life Cycle and Run Timing

Brown trout show up in Great Lakes tributaries anytime between early fall and early summer. Pennsylvania's state record was caught at the mouth of Walnut Creek in July, and every year we land a small number of lake-run browns during the spring steelhead season that are not winter holdover fish, but fresh spring-runners. Brown trout sometimes run before salmon, often showing up in the lower ends of tributaries by early September. They can sometimes be found within groups of spawning salmon or migrating steelhead, with peak runs normally occurring from October through December. According to Wisconsin Fisheries Biologist Steve Hogler, Seeforellen trout tend to run later in the fall than the Wild Rose strain.

Interestingly enough though, data from the NYSDEC on non-Salmon River tributaries showed that 58 percent of the total catch of brown trout was made in November while data from the Salmon River showed that only 21 percent of the estimated brown trout catch occurred during that month. Large catches were also made in September, December, and April on New York's Salmon River. Brown trout are late-fall spawners, with most fish spawning after salmon have completed their life cycle, usually in mid- to late November, but we've caught fat, fresh hens full of eggs right into February. Genetic factors appear to have a primary influence on the predisposition of brown trout to migrate, and it seems that migratory populations rarely develop from strictly resident ones.

After ascending the tributary, trout choose shallow, rocky, and gravelly substrates in headwater areas for spawning. The female creates a shallow depression (redd) into which she deposits her eggs. Much like salmon, smaller males jockey for spawning rights, though I've never seen brown trout form large pods of spawning fish the way I have with salmon or steelhead, maybe because of the smaller numbers of brown trout found in Lake

Buck brown trout develop kypes and tooth-filled mouths just like salmon or steelhead when spawning time approaches. LANDON MAYER PHOTO

Lake-run brown trout can also be caught from Great Lakes tributaries during winter and spring. This one was caught at ice-out by photographer Jack Hanrahan.

Erie. The dominant male fertilizes the hen's eggs, which will hatch in five to eight weeks.

Lake-dwelling browns prefer water temperatures from the upper 50s to the mid-60s and feed on insect larvae, crustaceans, mollusks, and other fish. The average lake-run adult brown trout weighs from 6 to 8 pounds, although they can grow to be much larger because of their longer life spans of up to 12 years.

Fishing Characteristics

Pre-spawn brown trout are aggressive and readily take streamer patterns. Brown and olive rabbit-strip leech patterns and tan and white Double Bunnies swung through deep runs and pools can draw aggressive strikes from early-run fish. Because runs of brown trout overlap with salmon runs, brown trout become accustomed to seeing and eating drifting salmon eggs and can often be located downstream from actively spawning salmon.

Larger size 10 to 12 egg patterns work better earlier in the fall when salmon are spawning, and smaller egg patterns in size 14 or 16 are a better choice later on as water temperatures drop and trout eggs become available from spawning brown trout and steelhead. My favorite egg pattern for lake-run brown trout is a Three-Loop Pink Lady that these fish often take on the first pass through a pool, even if the pool contains steelhead or salmon. Orange Otter eggs—a translucent, soft rubber egg—are super-realistic and super-effective. Chartreuse eggs are also effective in stained water.

Deep, dark runs and depressions downstream from gravel attract feeding brown trout and steelhead that gorge on salmon eggs. Running-line and bottom-bouncing techniques are needed when using egg and nymph patterns in these water types. Actively spawning salmon that are moving gravel also release caddis and stonefly nymphs into the drift, which are then taken by feeding trout that hit the gravel soon after the salmon.

Brown trout preoccupied with spawning may not give a fly a second look, but brown trout that are done spawning drop back into runs and pools ranging from 3 to 6 feet deep, looking to intercept baitfish, drifting eggs, or invertebrates. After spawning, lake-run browns hold over in a tributary through the winter. A slight increase in afternoon water temperatures can put fish on the bite at this time of year.

Nymph patterns become even more effective as water temperatures drop and browns take up winter residence. High-sticking small stonefly, caddis, and mayfly nymphs along undercut banks and the slow inside edge of current seams and indicator nymphing deep, slow pools are the most effective techniques when browns will not move far to eat a fly. In cold water, you've got to get the fly in front of the fish if you want to get the bite. Repeated drifts are often needed to induce takes.

Brown trout also provide spring dropback fisheries on many Great Lakes tributaries, most notably in New York, Michigan, and Wisconsin. As water temperatures reach the mid-40s to low 50s during early spring thaws, holdover browns that have spent the winter in the tributary start to migrate back to the lake. Having rested from the fall spawning runs, the fish are now aggressive and hungry, frequently moving several feet to hit streamers tied with marabou and rabbit strips. Dropback browns take holding and feeding positions along current seams and slow backeddies containing structure. Migration back to the lake can take several weeks.

Lake-roaming browns that didn't make a fall spawning run sometimes enter the lower ends of tributaries in the spring to feed on the massive schools of baitfish that start to gather just after ice-

No need to travel to the bottom of South America for giant brown trout. Trophy trout expert Landon Mayer holds an enormous fish taken during early fall on a Lake Ontario tributary. LANDON MAYER PHOTO

out. During spring runoff, large numbers of emerald shiners, smelt, and alewives migrate to tributary mouths to feed and spawn. The increase in flow also attracts fresh, spring-run brown trout that normally don't move far upstream and usually stay near baitfish schools located closer to tributary entrances. Brown trout dropping back to the lake will also linger in the lower ends of tributaries, taking advantage of the abundant feeding opportunities provided by smelt and emerald shiners that gather there in early spring.

Prominent Great Lakes Brown Trout Fisheries

New York (Lake Ontario)

Primary tributaries: Salmon River, Black River, Oswego River, Genesee River, Sandy Creek, Oak Orchard Creek, Eighteen Mile Creek, Niagara River

Secondary streams: North Sandy Creek, South Sandy Creek, Grindstone Creek, Marsh Creek, Johnson Creek

New York (Lake Erie)

Primary tributary: Cattaraugus Creek

Secondary streams: 18 Mile Creek, Chautauqua Creek

Pennsylvania (Lake Erie)

Primary tributaries: 20 Mile Creek, Walnut Creek, Elk Creek (mostly strays from New York stockings or planted catchables that migrate to the lake)

Michigan (Lake Michigan, Lake Huron, Lake Superior)

Most of Michigan's tributaries receive seasonal runs of brown trout

Wisconsin

Most of Wisconsin's tributaries receive seasonal runs of brown trout

Ontario (Lake Ontario, Lake Huron)

Most of Ontario's Lake Huron and Lake Ontario tributaries receive seasonal runs of brown trout

The Ontario Ministry of Natural Resources (OMNR) and many of the state agencies stock brown trout along the lake shorelines to create shoreline fisheries where no tributary exists and because strains being stocked do not migrate downstream after stocking. This shoreline stocking results in much straying, and streams which are not actively stocked often receive runs of these stray fish.

CHAPTER TWO

Seasons

Fishing through the changing seasons of the Great Lakes lets you watch the true ebb and flow of life. The life cycles of other species become woven inescapably into your own, and you become tied to the water and the land that surrounds it. The water, weather, and landscape are constantly changing, and to be a successful angler, you must adapt to these changes.

We never really know what a salmon or steelhead is thinking, so we thrust upon it virtues of our own making. Gallant, beautiful, smart, and cunning all describe these fish in the human mind. I think we do this so that we can feel closer to something so wild, something that can never truly be contained. Fishing through the different seasons helps you come just a little closer to this wildness and gives you a better understanding of the pulse, the natural heartbeat, of a stream.

Above: Floating down Great Lakes tributaries during the fall is a great way to enjoy the sights and sounds of a rushing river—and solitude.

Fall

Late August and early September low-pressure systems, with accompanying precipitation and a drop in air and water temperatures, can trigger early runs of Chinooks, coho salmon, and a smattering of Skamania-strain steelhead and brown trout.

Early fall fish are the hottest of the year. The kings, steelhead, cohos, and browns are at their peak of physical beauty and power. The fish still retain a fast metabolism and predatory feeding instincts soon after running up a tributary, ensuring aggressive fish and spectacular battles until spawning time approaches. Anglers refer to salmon and steelhead that have recently entered a tributary as "chromers" because the fish still have their open-water colorations: a bright silver, reflecting side, snow-white belly, and slate-gray back. Fresh-run brown trout will also be silvery until time spent in the tributary brings back some of their characteristic spotting and coloration.

The strong schooling tendencies of salmon and steelhead can send large groups of fish upriver at the same time. Optimum conditions for migration upstream into tributaries from the lake occur when low-pressure systems create precipitation, a rise in water levels, and accompanying cooler water temperatures. Migrating salmonid species

When tributary levels and flow increase during fall months, lake-run species begin their annual migration.

This early-run steelhead was hooked on an egg pattern as it traveled upstream. KARL WEIXLMANN PHOTO

occasionally porpoise, splash, and roll at the surface as they travel upstream.

These fish are scattered and moving, and are not normally interested in feeding or striking a fly until water levels recede and they drop into holding positions. However, a good presentation can sometimes take these moving fish, and I remember a particular steelhead that photographer Jack Hanrahan hooked on Elk Creek that we spotted moving up through the riffle and into the flat at the tail end of a pool. I told Jack that there was no possibility that the fish would eat; it was moving too fast. Jack moved quickly upstream of the fish, made a perfect cast and mend of the line, and I watched in amazement as the fish swam over to inhale the pink Sucker Spawn.

One of the best ways to target fresh-run cohos and kings is to position yourself up- and across stream from a depression that the fish drop into as they move up the river. They'll rest there briefly before continuing upstream, allowing for several fly presentations. Depressions can be found in tailouts, riffles, behind boulders, or in steep chutes between pools. A pool tailout can load up with fish as they move up through the downstream riffle. The slower current of a tailout allows fish to rest for a longer period of time and becomes a primary holding lie for fall-run steelhead.

Early fall steelhead can also be targeted with near-surface, dry-line swinging techniques in the large surface window that a tailout provides, and water temperatures from the low 50s to low 60s

Steelhead often suspend in the water during early fall, making this one of the best times to take a steelhead on top with a dry fly.

are prime for these types of presentations. In these temperatures, there is also the possibility of catching steelhead by waking, skating, or dead-drifting dry flies.

Because of the exceptional numbers of steelhead stocked along Steelhead Alley, they will occasionally rise and eat your indicator. Perhaps they remember the surface-feeding opportunities they had in the hatchery when food pellets splatted on the surface, although a bright orange or red-and-white artificial indicator looks nothing like hatchery food. If this occurs, try fishing a dry fly to take advantage of the fish's willingness to rise. Having one on hand that looks like the indicator doesn't hurt, and this fly can double as an indicator when using a dropper rig.

Fall-run steelhead are aggressive and will strike plug-size streamers that are 6 inches long. Swinging and stripping streamers through the heads of pools, in front of logjams, and through pool tailouts can induce rod-ripping grabs that are vastly different from the dainty winter takes. Tailouts provide one of the best areas for targeting salmon and trout with downstream swinging presentations. Depending on water depth and current speed, you may need a sinking-tip line to get your fly to the fish.

Peak fall runs of steelhead and brown trout normally occur during or after salmon have spawned. At this time, abundant food drifts in the river, mostly in the form of salmon eggs. Steelhead and brown trout stage downstream from spawning salmon and gorge on drifting eggs and invertebrates that are kicked up by spawning salmon in a last-chance feeding binge before hitting the gravel themselves or dropping into winter holding patterns. Now is the time to dead-drift egg patterns in the riffles, runs, depressions, and deep slots downstream from spawning salmon.

Brown trout hit the gravel soon after the salmon, in mid- to late November or early December, and some Great Lakes steelhead populations also commence spawning during late fall and early winter. As water temperatures drop in late fall, nymph patterns and nymphing techniques become more effective because there is less forage available and fish metabolism is lower, causing them to slow down and not move far to take a fly.

In early fall, steelhead and other lake-run species can be found where cool, well-oxygenated riffles dump in at the head of pools. Surface current textures decrease light penetration and provide overhead cover, making the fish feel secure and not exposed.

Winter

Winter is my favorite season. The crowds have mostly dispersed, and I can once again visit my favorite old haunts. While the kings are gone, some coho salmon might still be found into early December and runs of steelhead and brown trout can occur in December, January, and February. Brown trout can also hold over in some of the tributaries throughout the winter months. These browns seek deep, slow-moving pools and live under the ice until the spring thaw.

As tributary temperatures drop below 42 degrees, steelhead start to drop back from the heads of pools and stronger currents into deeper and slower pools. As a steelhead's metabolism slows down and water temperatures drop, it seeks out the slowest-moving water available that still offers

A couple of diehard winter steelheaders are rewarded for braving the elements. Photographer Jack Hanrahan and the author pose briefly before letting this winter-run hen go.

depth or cover. Whereas you might have found fall fish in fast runs, chutes, and pocketwater, they now prefer backeddies, pool guts, pool flats, slow-moving tailouts, moderate flowing runs, and the slow water behind current breaks or ledges.

The metabolic rate of steelhead can differ between individual fish during winter months. Fresh-run winter steelhead recently migrated from the big lake still have high metabolism rates and may remain in a semi-migrating mode. Some fish have been in the river for months and have slowed down their metabolic rates, dropping back into tailout flats and taking holding positions where they do not have to expend a lot of energy.

The one great aspect of winter steelheading, the one great glory that comes from braving the elements, is that steelhead will still eat a fly in subfreezing weather. I've had good fishing even with stream temperatures reading 33 degrees and chunks of ice and slush in the stream. They may not be the big-number days of the fall, but the fish are there, and they can be caught—even under the most adverse conditions.

Tailwater rivers such as 18 Mile below Burt Dam (NY), Salmon River (NY), or Manistee River below Tippy Dam (MI) are good winter steelhead fisheries because they can remain free of ice and slush when other tributaries are frozen or clogged with ice for months at a time. Dams that halt migration and warmwater discharges into tributaries and along lakeshores also congregate lake-run species during the winter.

Air temperatures that hover in the lower twenties the previous night usually produce surface slush in the flow at first light, so hitting the water at this time is usually a waste of time. I like to wait until about midmorning before venturing out on bright, sunny days during the colder winter months. Ice buildup in rod guides will also be less severe. The sun has been up for a couple of hours, raising air and water temperatures by several degrees, becoming more favorable to the fish and the angler. The best winter fly-fishing conditions normally occur in the early afternoon, after slush and ice have had time to melt and a couple of degrees rise in water temperature stirs the fish into feeding. Look for dark-colored bottoms, which absorb the winter sun, giving warmth and life to the stream.

Steelhead continue to feed during winter, mostly on smaller food items such as midge larvae, tiny black stoneflies, caddis pupae, and salmon and steelhead eggs, much like a stream-resident rainbow trout. Good winter techniques include short-line indicator nymphing in slow-moving pools and bottom-bouncing in deep, slow runs. Thin,

Steelhead can be caught during the worst possible winter conditions and readily take a fly in water temperatures of only 33 or 34 degrees. Heavy shot may be needed to penetrate surface slush, but the fish will still bite.

level running lines build up less ice on the line and rod guides and shoot better in harsh conditions. Slinky rigs or heavy shot are sometimes needed to penetrate slush and ice flows.

Winter steelheading is a game of finesse, where tiny flies, minuscule tippets, and repeated drifts are needed to entice lethargic fish. In addition to nymphing with 4X or 5X tippets and size 16 to 20 black stonefly, green caddis, black or red midge larvae imitations, and small egg patterns, I've also had good success drifting small soft-hackles under an indicator. The soft, webby partridge hackle moves enticingly in subtle currents and can trigger lethargic fish in cold water.

Winter steelhead all have different metabolic rates. Fish that entered the tributary during the fall have resided in the stream for a longer period of time, and as the water temperature drops, so does the steelhead's metabolic rate. Steelhead that have recently entered a tributary still have the predatory impulse to chase and eat baitfish. Every winter, we catch steelhead on streamers in water temperatures from the low to mid-30s; temperatures that I used to think were too cold for steelhead to eat streamers.

In late winter, drift flies upstream or downstream from large gravel areas that soon attract spawning fish. Large alpha bucks stage near spawning areas in deep, slow tailouts and pool guts upstream or downstream from large spawning riffles. During milder winter weather, they can drop back and hit the gravel all winter long.

Sunny days in late winter can raise water temperatures and trigger massive hatches of early

A good selection of small nymph patterns is essential for success in the winter.

Indicator nymphing is an effective technique during coldwater periods when fish won't move far for a fly. Repeated drifts through small strike zones are often needed to trigger takes.

stoneflies that clamber all over the snowbanks along the stream's edge and in turn trigger feeding fish. After swatting a few of these stoneflies off the back of your neck, you realize that spring is finally awakening life from the earth. As stream temperatures rise above 40 degrees, the steelhead's metabolism increases, daylight photoperiods lengthen, and the spring spawn commences.

Winter Gear

To stay warm, comfortable, and dry during the winter, you need a layering system of clothes made of synthetic fibers (no cotton). Layering allows you to remove or add clothing items, depending on the weather conditions.

The first layer should consist of a lightweight synthetic material that wicks moisture from the skin, such as treated polyester. This first layer absorbs, dissipates, and evaporates any perspiration. Patagonia is one of the originators of layering systems and produces a material called Capilene that makes an excellent first layer for the upper and lower body.

A second layer of heavier Polarfleece pants and pullovers provides insulation underneath a windbreaking outer shell. Your outer shell should be completely waterproof and breathable. A heavy fleece jacket can be worn under any lightweight wading jacket that is waterproof and breathable, or choose an insulated Gore-Tex parka.

Nymph patterns should include stonefly, mayfly, and caddis imitations.

Layering with polyester, fleece, a windbreaker, and a warm hat helps fly fishers endure the elements during the winter months. KARL WEIXLMANN PHOTO

To keep feet warm, polyester foot liners should be worn underneath heavy wool socks. Make sure your feet have room to move and that you can still wiggle your toes when putting wading shoes on over the neoprene booty used in breathable waders. Constricted feet lose circulation and quickly become cold. Breathable waders are good for warm- and cool-weather wading, but I wouldn't want to be without a pair of 3mm to 5mm neoprene boot-foot waders for winter fishing.

The same layering system can also apply to anglers who wear neoprene waders, but less layering is required. Neoprene wetsuits, developed for use by scuba divers in subfreezing weather, create an insulating pocket of warm air between the material and your skin. The insulation and waterproofing qualities of neoprene make it the perfect material for wading in cold water. On the other hand, breathable waders with wading shoes worn over a neoprene booty stuffed with layers of socks can cut off circulation, making your feet very cold. Boot-foot neoprene waders let you move your feet and give them breathing room, allowing warm air to circulate.

Snow sticks to wet, felt-bottom wading shoes, making walking and wading hazardous.

When air temperatures drop below 32 degrees, rod guides and fly lines ice up. Lubing the guides with ChapStick may help briefly, but Loon Outdoors Stanley's Ice-Off Paste lasts longer when generously applied before fishing. Several applications are normally required throughout a day's fishing. In brutal conditions there's not much you can do to prevent ice from accumulating on the line and leader other than to melt or even (carefully) bite off the ice chunks and get the line back on the water quickly before it freezes again.

I usually do not wear gloves while fishing in cold weather, preferring precise line control over the clumsy fumbling that typically happens when wearing them. If I am wearing gloves, I use thin fleece and not rag wool. Those shake-and-bake heat packs and butane handwarmers, stuffed inside the chest, pockets, or socks can help keep your body core and your feet warm. Take breaks when needed and dry hands thoroughly whenever they get wet.

Wading staffs can help prevent spills and provide stability when crossing streams. So do studded or felt wading shoes, but snow builds up on felt and quickly becomes dangerous when walking or wading. Rubber bottom carbide-studded boots are the best choice for all-purpose fishing. Korkers convert felt bottoms into a good anchoring system for your feet, giving extra traction on the stream bottom.

Spring

A rush of new life permeates the air along a swollen spring stream as steelhead splash and spawn in the riffles before returning to the open

Springtime is streamer time! Hungry dropback and fresh-run spring steelhead will hammer large streamers swung through pools and runs.

During the spring, steelhead are often found upstream and downstream from gravel-bottomed tailouts and riffles.

water of an inland sea. My first steelhead on the fly came to hand under the dark skies of a cold, overcast, and drizzly March evening—perfect spring steelhead weather. Through a rain-spotted lens, my brother David took pictures of the long, classic chrome hen that glistened silver in the pop of the flash. A swollen Little Sandy Creek, a New York Lake Ontario tributary, provided the perfect background.

In the spring, bucks and hens hit shallow gravel-filled tailouts and riffles. It's an awe-inspiring sight to watch the spawning life cycle, as fresh-run silver hens push plumes of sediment into the current as they dig their redds and big buck steelhead dominate gravel riffles, chasing and slashing at the smaller males. Dead-drift or swing your flies downstream from actively spawning fish. As with kings, some will take your fly, others will ignore it. Spawning fish that are spooked will drop downstream from gravel, pre-spawn steelhead will hold downstream from gravel, and the smaller steelhead that the big ones are beating up on will drop downstream from gravel.

Casting to fish spawning on gravel may be frowned upon where there are wild, river-born populations, but it's generally accepted where fisheries must be sustained by stocking and natural recruitment is limited. I'll freely admit that I love swinging a streamer in front of a deep-holding alpha buck during the spring spawn and watching him chase and eat it. It's where they are, you can see them, and you can sometimes catch them. Some Great Lakes tributaries are protected during the spring spawn, though most of these are in Canada. Make sure to check local regulations.

My heart still skips when I spot a trophy fish on the gravel. When targeting spring spawners, I like to hunt up a big buck terrorizing a tailout in water deep enough that it enables a good dead-drift or a good downstream swing of the fly. I'll sometimes walk right by fish after observing their behavior and determining that I can't get a good drift on them. Instead I'll look for fly-friendly fish, those in water deep enough to allow fish to feel secure and water with enough movement or current that enables a good drift or swing of the fly. Fly-friendly steelhead are also those that exhibit aggressive behaviors, such as a big buck biting and chasing away other smaller males. This aggressiveness can induce hits on streamer patterns, although I've fished over aggressive fish that wouldn't bite, probably due to angling pressure.

Fish typically won't take your fly if they are digging redds or laying eggs. These steelhead seem interested only in procreation, and even the best presentation won't be given a second look. If the fish won't take a good presentation, I move and find fish that will. The fish's reaction to the fly lets me know whether it can be caught. A steelhead that moves away from the fly has probably been fished over and will be hard to entice. I also pass by fish that are spawning in water so shallow that their backs are out of the water.

Because your first presentations to spawning steelhead are the most important, stealth is needed for up- and across-stream positioning from spotted fish. I'll even wear my turkey hunting camo for concealment, crawling into position and fishing while kneeling. Spooked fish don't bite, and spring fly fishing for steelhead is like hunting big game with a fly rod. The bottom line is that lake-run species that are used to the open expanses of a Great Lakes environment are out of their element when they enter the tributaries. They are now in a confined space, exposed, and feel threatened and vulnerable. Approaching spotted fish in the same way you would approach a big-game animal while hunting will lead to more success.

When dead-drifting flies in front of bottom-hugging spawning fish, you should adjust your terminal tackle based on stream velocity and depth. Once you cast up- and across stream, mend your line upstream so that the fly sinks faster and floats drag-free, right in front of the fish.

Jim Whitaker, the former proprietor of Whitaker's Sports Shop and Motel on the Salmon River in Pulaski, New York, always advised my brother and me to fish big streamers during the spring season—and he was right. Spawning bucks can aggressively chase streamers; hungry, spawned-out dropback steelhead love the meal a streamer represents; and fresh-run hens are prime candidates for a swung streamer.

When swinging streamers to spawners, a soft swing is needed in front of the fish, and not through the fish. You may need to move farther out into the current or farther upstream. Doing this reduces the angle at which the fly swings and also slows the swing because there is less fly line on the water for the current to push. A harsh swing can either foul-hook the fish or push it off the redd. Cast far enough upstream to give the fly enough time to get to the bottom. You may need to make several upstream mends to adjust the speed of your swing. As the fly starts to swing below you and nears the fish, drop the rod tip and tighten the line.

The strike from a fresh-run spring hen can be aggressive, while a buck may only slash at the fly. Tracking the fly during the drift or the swing allows you to set the hook by sight. In many instances, I've actually seen a fish turn its head, open

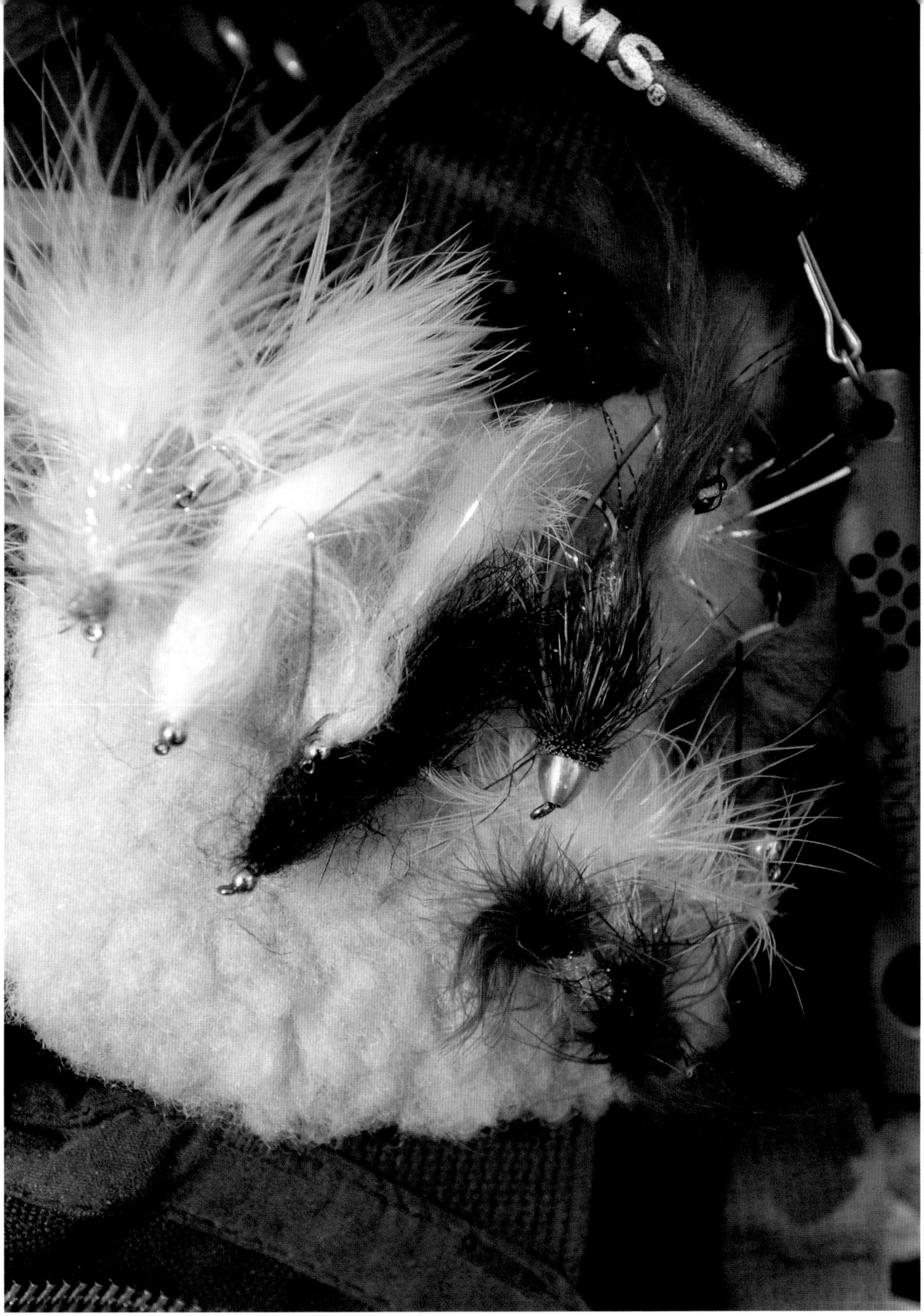

A good selection of streamers should include light and dark patterns in a variety of sizes.

its white mouth, and eat the fly. By watching your fly, you can also adjust your mends and tell whether you need to adjust your terminal tackle. For instance, if the fly passes over the fish's back or tail and not in front of its head, you should shorten your cast and either add more weight or mend the line more (or both), to get the fly down in front of the fish's face where it can see the fly and react.

I don't often use indicators when fishing over spawners, since I can normally see the fish and watch its reaction to my presentation. These fish are holding very tight to the bottom in relatively shallow water with good current. Dead-drift bottom-bouncing techniques are the most effective, and swinging techniques work well on deeper holding fish. Indicators just get pushed out of the strike zone too quickly by the current, and the fly can frequently hang bottom, resulting in false dunks and foul-hooked fish. I also don't like to use tandem fly rigs when presenting to spawning fish that I can see. Pods of spawning steelhead often form tightly compacted groups, and fishing two flies increases the potential for foul-hooking fish.

White streamers are easy to track in the water, and fresh-run spring hens certainly take a liking to them. Buck steelhead on the gravel seem to prefer a darker streamer pattern, one that looks like the brethren that they are chasing, such as a big olive Zonker with some red marabou mixed in. Egg-Sucking Leeches work well in stained water and either sex will take a properly drifted egg pattern.

Dropback steelhead, fish that have spawned out and are heading back to the lake, can offer good fly fishing into May. Two factors determine how quickly the fish drop back—water conditions and food availability. High water can push them out to the lake quickly, but moderate flow causes them to take holding positions on their way downstream. If there is plenty of food, steelhead stay in the stream longer, feeding and replenishing themselves from the rigors of the spawn.

Late spring brings dry-fly opportunities when fish look up at hatching insects. Lower water levels at this time are conducive to dry-fly presentations to fish that are dropping back to the lake. While hatches may not be common in all the tributaries, steelhead are known to rise to Hendrickson duns on Ontario's Grand River and gray drake hatches on Michigan's Muskegon River. Lake Erie guide Royce Terrell uses Bivisible patterns successfully during the spring, even if nothing is hatching, by fishing the fly dead-drift on an up- and across-stream cast and letting the fly skate across the surface as it drifts downstream.

Populations of browns that have wintered over in the tributary are now dropping back to the lake and can be caught with a variety of techniques. As they prepare to spawn in early spring, baitfish schools congregate around the entrances and the lower ends of tributaries, attracting feeding browns from the lake. Each spring, I see freshly migrated brown trout entering tributaries to feed on these abundant baitfish populations, steelhead eggs, and the eggs from spawning spring-run suckers. These browns are there for a short period of time and normally do not move far upstream.

Summer

Most summer steelhead fisheries in the Great Lakes rely on Skamania-strain steelhead stockings. This unique strain of steelhead originated from the Skamania Fish Hatchery on Washington's Washougal River and have been genetically bred to produce large, early-run fish. The Great Lakes Skamania fishery first gained national prominence in 1971 when Washington State Skamania-strain steelhead were stocked into Indiana's Lake Michigan tributaries. By 1982, this strain of steelhead had become extremely popular with fisheries managers and anglers alike, and "Skamania mania" was here to stay. Indiana is now the premier producer of Skamania-strain steelhead, providing eggs to many states for production and planting.

Skamania steelhead spend more time feeding in open-water environments. This "three-salt" ge-

Skamania-strain steelhead run some Great Lakes tributaries during the summer when conditions are right. Tom Harris released this one in August on the St. Joseph River in Michigan. TOM HARRIS PHOTO

netic trait means that the steelhead has lived in an open-water environment for three years before making its first spawning run as a four-year-old adult. It enables a Skamania steelhead to reach 30 inches or more and from 12 to 24 pounds by this stage in life. Skamanias have been deemed "genetic Frankensteins" and have been bred to ensure these early-running and spawning traits. Fishery managers harvest eggs and milt from early-running fish to keep the genetic migrating signal intact. If egg taking does not occur until late summer, early-running traits may become diluted, pushing future runs into a later photoperiod and creating fall-run fish. Fresh runs of summer steelhead in October and November have been documented, possibly due to unfavorable conditions for migration in the summer.

Quality summer steelhead fishing normally requires increased flows on watersheds that sustain cool aquifers during the heat of a Great Lakes summer. The Dowagiac, a St. Joseph River tributary, has limestone influences that keep summer water temperatures below 60 degrees. On the Salmon River in New York, water releases from the reservoir for whitewater rafting races trigger runs. One of the most important factors for migration is the correlation between lake and tributary water temperatures. Consistent offshore winds that blow warm shoreline water out into the lake create an undercurrent of cold water that brings Skamanias into nearshore waters during summer months.

This event coinciding with precipitation and an increase in tributary flow results in ideal conditions for migration. Runs of Skamania steelhead quickly swim up and spread out in a tributary system, moving as many as nine or ten miles in a 24-hour period. Once they take up residence in a tributary, summer steelhead are subjected to the negative effects of warm water and low summer flows, seeking tributary sections where shoreline debris provides overhead cover and current provides cool water and oxygen. Fish concentrate where smaller and cooler tributaries enter larger and warmer rivers or wherever spring seeps and limestone springs lower water temperatures.

More time spent feeding out in the lake deeply ingrains the Skamanias' predatory disposition and fly-taking qualities. When they migrate upstream in mid- to late winter or early spring, with spawning months away, Skamania take a wide variety of fly patterns and presentations. Fresh-run Skamanias are aggressive and will hit large marabou and bunny-strip streamers in hot pink, hot orange, flame red, chartreuse, and black combined with Flashabou or Krystal Flash. Matt Supinski, the godfather of Great Lakes coldwater-species fly fishing, found Skamania-strain steelhead feeding on windblown terrestrial insects in offshore scum lines. Successful patterns were developed for summer steelhead using banding of yellow and black or chartreuse and black that imitates bees, hornets, and other terrestrials found there.

Certain Wisconsin, Michigan, Indiana, and New York tributaries receive runs of summer steelhead when good conditions allow fish migration from May through September. Wisconsin alone stocks twelve rivers with Skamania-strain

Caddis patterns are effective for all Great Lakes steelhead.

steelhead. One of the most notable tributaries receiving summer runs of steelhead is Indiana and Michigan's shared St. Joseph River system where 280,000 to 350,000 Skamanias are stocked annually. Matt Supinski recommends hitting the river from mid-July through mid-August for the largest numbers of fish.

Other tributaries of note include Michigan's Big Manistee; Wisconsin's Root and Sheboygan Rivers; Indiana's Little Calumet River, Trail and Salt Creeks; and New York's Salmon River. The province of Ontario has some wild summer runs on the Steel River, a Lake Superior Thunder Bay tributary, and on several of the Lake Huron Georgian Bay tributaries. Lake Erie's Grand River and the Credit River on Lake Ontario's north shore also see limited runs. Stray Skamania steelhead end up running tributaries where they are not planted, and some tributaries in Michigan, including the Pere Marquette, Boardman, and Betsie, have very small, remnant wild runs from previous plantings.

Atlantic salmon are also available to the adventurous Great Lakes fly fisher during the summer, with run timing similar to that of Skamania-strain steelhead. Flowing between Lake Superior and Lake Huron, the St. Mary's River is perhaps the premier summer playground for fly fishers seeking to do battle with *Salmo salar,* but opportunities are expanding in Lake Ontario tributaries in New York and the province of Ontario. In 2006, the OMNR doubled its Atlantic salmon fry production to 400,000 fish. Funding is being allocated to upgrade and increase the capacity of OMNR facilities and develop broodstock to produce yearling Atlantic salmon. Unique management programs are being put into place, including in-stream and streamside incubators for raising eggs and fingerling salmon with the intention of imprinting the fish to prime spawning and nursery habitats.

Cool and wet summers that keep tributary temperatures below 70 degrees can trigger migrations of Atlantics from May through early fall into New York's famous Salmon River, where 30,000 Atlantic salmon smolts are stocked annually. Fran Verdoliva, program coordinator for the Salmon River corridor in New York, notes that runs of Atlantic salmon and summer steelhead have been increasing over the last several years and that this past season saw more returns than ever before.

Both species can be caught at the same time, with runs peaking on the Salmon River from early June through the first week of July and picking up again from September through October. Don't expect instant success—you're going to have to work for your fish—but Verdoliva has landed as many as seven Atlantic salmon in a single evening, with his top fish measuring 38½ inches, and weighing 22 pounds. The average size of Atlantics on the Salmon River is from 10 to 12 pounds.

Atlantics move upstream at a slower pace than Skamania steelhead, taking holding positions at the heads of pools and in boulder-strewn pocketwater that have well-oxygenated water. Atlantic salmon have large pectoral fins that help anchor the fish to the bottom in such turbulence. Summer-run salmon are sometimes found in front of boulders and in fast, deep runs or riffles and pool tailouts that have measurable flow. Verdoliva has watched fish rocket from the bottom of 8-foot-deep pools to take a fly and targets fish with a floating line and surface or near-surface swinging techniques using either traditional patterns or hairwing dry flies.

As summer wanes into early fall, the prayer for rain is sometimes fulfilled, bringing with it a new season of probability, hope, and bent fly rods. I can usually tell if a run of steelhead came in without even heading to the river by how much water is leaking into the basement.

Summer Steelhead Fisheries

New York (Lake Ontario)
Salmon River, Black River, Oak Orchard Creek

Indiana (Lake Michigan)
Little Calumet River, Salt Creek, Trail Creek

Early morning can provide the best fly fishing along Great Lakes beaches in the early fall before the sun and warming water temperatures drive fish into deeper water.

Michigan (Lake Michigan)
St. Joseph River, Big Manistee River
Wisconsin (Lake Michigan)
Root River, Sheboygan River, Milwaukee River, Oconto River, Kewaunee River
Ontario (Lake Superior)
Michipicoton River, Steel River, Nipigon River
Ontario (Lake Huron)
Saugeen River
Ontario (Lake Erie)
Grand River, late summer

Great Lakes Shoreline and Beach Fly Fishing

You've just spent six hours driving to your favorite Great Lakes tributary. Internet reports have indicated a fresh run of fish, and you've got the itch really bad. But between the time you read the report a day or two ago and the time you reach your destination the water conditions have completely changed—and you're now facing a low, clear, and warm tributary holding coldwater species. Not a good recipe for success. Sure, the fish are there, and the report was correct. There they are, stacked up in some of the large, slow-moving pools close to the lake. But the fish are getting beat up, have become exposed, and are now skittish and spooked. After a couple of casts you realize your efforts here will be futile. What are you going to do? In these situations, I hit the beach.

Landing a steelhead, brown, or salmon off the beach is a big challenge and great way for the tributary fly fisher to find some solitude and plenty of room to cast. One or two fish off the beach on a glorious early fall morning with a tangerine sunrise in the background more than makes up for several hours of constant casting and time spent without a hookup. You've got to put some time in to consistently catch coldwater species from the lakeshore, but I would still rather catch a couple of steelhead off a lonely beach than a dozen in a crowded Great Lakes tributary.

Out here the only boundary is the land behind you. The hit can be electrifying; the fish are at peak physical condition, and with a lot more room to run and leap, the fight is absolutely exhilarating. If perchance you've yet to see your backing while fly fishing the tribs, this is where you're finally going to find out what color it is. In the early light, no fish are visible. You have a huge expanse of water in front of you, but your hopes for a hookup are based on experience and a previous scout of the water. A roll in the surf or a splash on the surface lets you know that the fish are there, and a hit could come on any cast.

In tributary fly fishing, you know what you've got. The fish are in a contained space. You look at the current water conditions, assess where the fish are going to be, and form a game plan. The unknown element is what makes beach fly fishing so exciting. On one cast you can hook a rampaging steelhead, on the next a silver coho. I know a few Lake Ontario and Lake Michigan guides who land monster browns every year and even take lake trout from the surf.

Because trout and salmon migrate around the lake looking for food and preferred water temperatures, they can be caught from piers, breakwalls, jetties, harbors, and beaches when conditions are right and cold water is near shore. Fall, winter, and spring are when the beach fly fisher is most likely

When tributary conditions are poor, target steelhead, salmon, and brown trout along Great Lakes shorelines. Pure chrome is the reward for those willing to take the time to explore the beach.

to encounter steelhead, salmon, or trout in near-shore environments. Offshore winds that create undercurrents where cold water is brought near shore during summer months can also give a fly fisher a chance to catch coldwater species when least expected. In winter, warmwater discharges from power plants attract baitfish species such as shad, smelt, alewives, and emerald shiners, which in turn attract predatory species. In the spring, these baitfish congregate in and around tributary mouths and nearby beaches. Fly fishers should not discount shoreline fishing as a way to catch fish when they are not in tributaries or when tributary conditions are not favorable. The big water can be intimidating at first, but an honest effort is all that's needed to ride the cutting edge of Great Lakes fly fishing.

Tributary mouths and adjacent beach fronts are good places to start searching for feeding and traveling fish in late summer or early fall. If a tributary mouth has an accompanying jetty, breakwall, or pier, so much the better because these structures can ease access and funnel the fish. Tributary mouth harbors sometimes contain these manmade structures that attract migrating coldwater species. Feeding activity can be heavy and intense along Great Lakes beaches as fish go on a last-chance feeding binge before making spawning runs. A blitz of feeding fish and diving gulls, where baitfish schools are chased, scattered, and fed upon, is normally associated with saltwater fly fishing but also occurs in fresh water and adds an exciting element for fly fishers along Great Lakes shorelines. Blitz activity normally occurs when the light is low.

On the south shore of Lake Erie, start looking for steelhead schools cruising beach fronts near tributary mouths in late August and early September when lake water temperatures drop into the mid- to upper 60s. Any tributary pumping cooler water into the lake can attract fish. Wind-created currents can push this colder water along the shoreline, creating a funnel for fish travel. During these early weeks of the season, the best fly fishing normally occurs in low-light and overcast conditions, although we've also caught fish with a high sun during the middle of the day. First light is prime time, yielding the coolest water temperatures of the day. Roving schools of fish will hang in shallower water before the sun drives them away from shore and into deeper, cooler water.

Gear anglers making long casts with spoons, spinners, and plugs catch a lot of fish from Great Lakes shorelines, and in most situations the fly fisher should try to emulate their success. Saltwater-style fly-fishing techniques and equipment excel on the big water. Distance can be a factor, and a fast rod that can handle large flies and throw some line with a double haul is a better tool for this kind of fishing. That extra 10 feet could help you reach those blitzing steelhead crashing into schools of emerald shiners. When wading, a 9½- to 10-foot rod helps to keep the line off the water and the shoreline behind you. Longer two-handed rods can reach extreme distances when cast overhead style with shooting heads and running lines.

Sink-tip lines, like the Jim Teeny series, can be effective where conditions warrant their use in deeper water. On beaches with shallow slopes that drop into 6 feet of water or less, intermediate and bullethead-style weight-forward floating lines work well. For versatility, I always carry an extra spool rigged with 100 feet of running line, a thin level floating fly line that I can loop sinking, floating, and intermediate head sections to. This running line can also be used for bottom bouncing, slinky rigging, or even indicator nymphing.

Stripping baskets are helpful and can increase distance by keeping the surface tension of the water off the line, though they are useless when wading in deeper water. I use a homemade version, which is a large Tupperware storage container about 10 inches deep, with holes drilled into the bottom to drain the water. Zip Ties inserted through smaller holes drilled in the bottom and pulled tight up into the basket at a 90-degree angle help keep the fly line from tangling when

Pontoon boats give fly fishers a stealthy approach to visible schools of steelhead cruising along Great Lakes shorelines.

Emerald shiner and smelt imitations both make good choices for fly selection when fly fishing the big water.

stripped into and shooting out of the basket. A bungee cord, hooked through holes drilled into the side corner of the basket closest to the waistline, will keep the basket securely in place and allow you to swivel it around your waist and into a comfortable stripping position.

The schools of steelhead that I've observed along Lake Erie beaches are normally in a constant state of motion, cruising parallel to the lakeshore in areas of deeper water. The fish can be anywhere in the water column, from cruising just under the surface to cruising right along the bottom, searching for tributary outflows or schools of bait. I've also watched them take holding positions close to shore, underneath and along current seams created by tributary outflows. Scout the shoreline you wish to fish when the water is clear and the sun is high instead of using a chuck-and-chance-it technique. Just like a tributary, a section of beach or shoreline contains dead water without any fish-holding characteristics.

Dark water has just as much appeal off a beach as it does in a tributary, and it is normally an indication of depths that are used as travel routes. Depressions in the lake bottom, troughs, bowls, and drop-offs where the tributary enters the lake are all visible in well-lighted conditions and are good spots to fish. Underwater structure, such as weedbeds, boulders, and remnant rock piles from shoreline stabilization or construction, attract baitfish and the predators that feed upon them. Obvious feeding activity, splashes, and rolls can also help pinpoint targets.

If you can reach them, cast to the far edges of deeper troughs and depressions, because the fly will sink and fall toward you. After the cast, allow the fly to sink as you count—one, one-thousand-one; one, one-thousand-two; one, one-thousand-three; and so on—until you find the fish. This method also works where sinking lines are used for penetrating deeper water around jetties, breakwalls, and piers.

You need a saltwater-style retrieve to attract roving fish and get them to chase your fly. Your retrieve should imitate the mad fleeing of a baitfish hell-bent on escaping a chasing predator, and I firmly believe that you cannot outstrip a steelhead that is intent on eating your fly. Slowing a fly down or stopping its movement will more than likely turn the fish away from your fly.

The two-handed retrieve popular in the salt works well. Tuck the grip of your rod in your armpit and retrieve the line hand over hand into the stripping basket. Another productive retrieve is to use your noncasting hand to strip line in short, sharp spurts that mimic a wounded or dying baitfish while keeping your fly line tight to the rod cork between strips with the middle finger of your casting hand. You need heavy tippet for large, hard-hitting salmonid species on the beach. The hit can also come on the strip. I've been snapped off when using 3X (8-pound test) and recommend nothing lighter than 1X or 2X fluorocarbon when stripping large streamers.

Pattern selection for the beach should start with streamer patterns that imitate the size and color of the baitfish present along the beach or shoreline you are fishing. This can change depend-

As the sun beats down on the water, searching the deeper troughs found farther offshore with a streamer pattern can be productive.

ing on water temperatures and the season. Look for the schools of baitfish that are present to determine the species. Emerald shiners are more predominant in late summer and early fall, before cooler water brings in gizzard shad, alewives, and then smelt. Fly patterns with lots of flash get more attention and catch more fish off the beach.

One of my favorite fly patterns for the beach is a marabou-tailed Clouser Minnow in all white or olive over white with a lot of silver, pearl, or Mirage Flashabou added as an underwing and left longer than the bucktail. The marabou, Flashabou, and bucktail combination creates an amazing amount of movement in the water, and the weighted eyes give the fly a great up-and-down action. This fly is also deadly in the tributaries. Standard Clouser Minnows, Emerald Candies, Tubular Smelt, and Angel Hair Alewife patterns also work well.

The proliferation of salmon eggs during the fall sometimes makes egg patterns the flies of choice in tributary outflows. Specialized equipment and distance casting are not always imperative for catching fish. Indicator nymphing techniques with

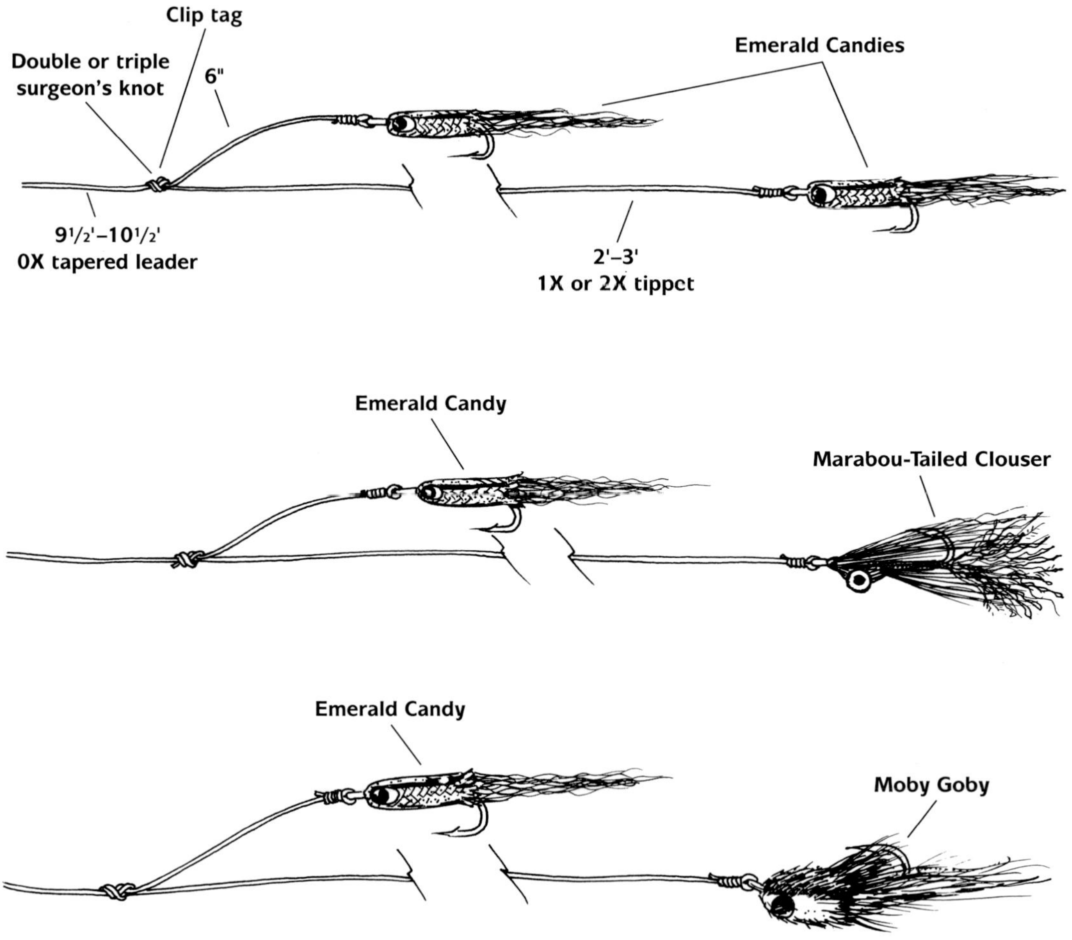

Fly rigs for the beach

With a tangerine haze burning on the eastern horizon, the author casts for steelhead along a secluded beach.

long leaders can also hook fish in deep, nearshore lake channels, river mouth entrances, and power plant outflows when the water is cold.

Rigging for the Beach

Sure, casting just one fly off the beach works, but sometimes fishing with two flies in tandem really helps get a roving fish's attention. As stated previously, I really pay attention to how spinning, center-pinning, and gear anglers catch fish and try to incorporate or refine those techniques where they can be used for fly fishing. I was watching *In-Fisherman Television* one Sunday morning when Doug Stange, *In-Fisherman* editor, was explaining a new smallmouth technique in which two plastic swimbaits fished in tandem on jigheads were really slamming the fish. The technique and style of rigging authentically triggers the chase and feeding responses in predatory fish and works wonders on gamefish that have never seen this type of presentation.

Many fly fishers are familiar with tandem rigs for steelhead tributary fishing, such as a nymph fished below an egg or a deadly double-egg setup, but rarely do they consider two streamers, either for tributary fishing or casting flies from the beach. The rigging is simple and rarely tangles when tied correctly. It also allows for the streamers to swim together on the strip so that they look like one fish chasing another or a school of escaping baitfish.

At the end of a standard stiff-butt, 10- to 12-foot tapered leader that will turn over larger flies and two-fly setups (remember, you're lengthening the leader but approximately 6 inches of the leader becomes the dropper), splice in a 24-inch piece of tippet material using a double or triple surgeon's knot. A blood knot would put the dropper at a 90-degree angle to the leader and doesn't make the flies swim properly. I like a longer 12- to 14-foot (total length) leader when using floating fly lines. Use shorter leaders with clear-tip intermediate fly lines and sink-tip or sinking lines.

When splicing in the tippet material with a surgeon's knot, leave about 6 inches at the end of the leader below the knot. This becomes the dropper for your top fly. Trim the top tag end of the knot and tie in your anchor fly to the bottom of the tippet section. This puts the flies about 18 inches apart. The tippet material should be at least as strong as the end of your leader, and I recommend using 0X or 1X fluorocarbon in most situations for steelhead.

Good tandem fly selections for this rig include double Emerald Candies or Tubular Smelt; a rabbit strip streamer, such as an Emerald Bunny chasing a nymph; or a larger and heavier marabou-tailed Clouser Minnow fished below an Emerald Candy. Tandem flies can also be used on larger tributaries where fish are spread out and not confined in tight spaces.

CHAPTER THREE

Reading the Water

The ability to see fish is more than just having acute vision; it's the ability to look closely where fish are supposed to be. You do that by reading the water, and yes, I've had clients cast at logs, rocks, and plastic bags wavering in the current before I realized it wasn't a fish. But hey, I'd rather be safe than spook a potential hookup.

The ability to decipher the location of a fish in the stream is at the essence of Great Lakes fly fishing. Reading the water is a skill learned through many years spent drifting and swinging flies through various water types. You catch a steelhead drifting a nymph along the inside edge of a current seam and continue to fish likely looking spots, hooking fish in similar areas of bottom composition and water hydrology. You hook a big brown on the far side of a boulder or next to a log with an undercut bank. A salmon charges out from a dark green tailout and hits your streamer. With time, you'll gain the ability to walk a piece of

Above: Pools downstream from natural or artificial barriers can concentrate lake-run species.

Steelhead will use a variety of water types as they migrate upstream.

water and tell yourself, "I should be able to catch a fish here, here, and over there." Experience tells you where the most likely spot is to hook up. Positioning in the stream for fly delivery becomes an important component to consider to get a hookup. You could be just inches off on the drift and not get the bite.

Reading the water comes from observation, looking into the heart of the water and through layers of water, seeing how it moves, and how it behaves around different structure types. Looking at how it flows here, observing how it flows there, you develop an intuitive feel for the water. You become immersed in the movement of current and mesh with the flow. You eventually start to think like a fish, although this may not rate your intelligence level very high in some circles. "Now, if I were a steelhead, I'd be sitting right there!" you might say to yourself. And sure enough, you present the fly, and there he is. I've guided on many Great Lakes tributary sections that I had not yet fished, but by reading the water, I was able to have a successful trip.

Reading the water also entails interpreting its subtle color changes that give clues where fish could be or let you see the fish. The first characteristic of water color is that it is either light or dark. Defining the shades of water color within these light and dark spectrums is the key to really understanding what is happening beneath the surface.

Dark water is normally associated with deep water and light-colored water is normally associated with shallow water. Dark green water attracts my attention the most because it can indicate depth, a depression, a trough, algae-covered rocks, weeds, logs, undercuts, or a school of fish. Dark water also offers concealment to lake-run species that have slate gray, dark olive, and dark charcoal-colored backs. My number one rule on the relatively shallow south shore Lake Erie tributaries is that if you cannot see the bottom, fish through the water like you know a fish is there.

Once you've determined that dark water also has depth, don't wade any closer for a better look. Most fly fishermen, including myself, have made the mistake of stepping in for a closer look only to spook holding fish. Fish can sometimes be seen holding in dark water and can appear as lighter or darker torpedoes within these confines. Fresh-run fish can be hard to spot but give themselves away as light green torpedoes, wavering slightly in the current. A steelhead will adapt to its environment, taking on the color of its surroundings. I use the term "yellow backs" to describe fresh-run steelhead that change color, adapting to lighter-colored, shale-bottomed streams.

Keep the sun at your back when reading the water and looking for fish so that glare and reflection are aimed away from you and the sun is not right in your eyes. Fish can also be spotted by looking through flat spots on the water's surface. These windows will open and close in rippled or turbulent water. Looking through these areas as they travel downstream allows you observe the stream bottom for a longer length of time.

Lighter-colored water, often a light brown gravel bar, yellow sand bar, or light green shale shelf, can indicate shallow, fishless water and should more often than not be eliminated as po-

Great Lakes steelhead camouflage themselves in the tributaries. This Lake Erie steelhead retains a yellowish olive back to blend better into the shale-bottomed tributary from which it was caught.

tential holding water. Look for anything darker than the surrounding water that could possibly indicate fish or fish-holding structure. Dark areas in rocky or gravelly shallows can hide fish and should be thoroughly inspected or fished from a distance to determine whether fish are present.

Great Lakes tributaries can have many variations in water color that are determined by drainage type. Agricultural drainages often retain a muddy cast, with limited visibility even after high water has receded. Tributaries of the upper Great Lakes and streams that drain hemlock and cedar forests often have a tannin (or tea-colored) stain to the water. Tributaries draining shale-bottomed plateaus along the southern Great Lakes shores take on a green cast caused by suspended clay particles. Emerald-green water that has receded from a high-water period signals prime fishing conditions. The fish have stopped moving up the tributary and are now in holding and taking positions.

Breaking down a tributary into sections and water types can make reading the water easier. Long sections of some tributaries are sometimes featureless, without fish-holding characteristics, currents, or structures. Eliminating these areas can narrow your search, but with lake-run migratory species, one day they're there, and the next day they're not. I'll start off by breaking tributaries

Keep the sun behind you while maintaining a low profile and look for fish close to the bank before presenting a fly to the deeper and darker depressions found farther from shoreline.

down into sections before looking at individual characteristics and water types that can hold fish.

Tributary Sections

The mouths or lower sections of tributaries are the first places to see runs of migratory fish and are often slower moving, wider, and deeper than the middle and upper portions. During low water, migratory species stack up in the lower section before higher water sends them upstream. In the lower section of a tributary, salmonid species will be hot, chrome, and fully conditioned to enter your backing.

Bank baitfishers and gear throwers can clean up on the lower ends of tribs. Crowding is a concern for fly anglers looking for casting room, but these lower sections often contain the only fish-holding water, especially early in the season. Look for areas of current to attract the fish. Even subtle current is potential holding water. Fish can be caught in these "frog water" sections by casting and retrieving flies or by indicator nymphing with fly patterns that have lots of movement. The first good gradients found upstream from slow tributary mouth sections quickly attract lake-run species and are a prime target area for anglers as runs begin. Here, populations of lake-run species that have not yet been pressured fall for a variety of techniques and presentations, depending upon water conditions. Tributary current—whether easily visible or barely discernable—attracts fish, creates feeding opportunities, and provides oxygen. Look for current in the lower sections of tributaries near man-made structure like bridges, piers, concrete walls, and rock riprap used for bank stabilization. River bends, channel constrictions, and bottom rises can also create current and concentrate fish.

The amount of rain is a major factor in run timing on most Great Lakes tributaries, but some produce runs with dam and canal releases that raise their water levels. I was on tiny 4 Mile Creek in Erie, Pennsylvania, one early fall day when the golf course upstream pulled the plug on its retention pond, resulting in a nice run of steelhead and some good fishing until the water became too dirty to fish any longer.

Fishing down low in a tributary is a good early season approach, but constant waves of lake-run species enter these sections, allowing for outstanding fly fishing throughout the entire season. The lower ends of tributaries often have the best holding water for winter steelhead, and this tributary section is also good in mid- to late spring, when fish won't migrate far from the lake because of warming temperatures. Some of the largest steelhead, salmon, and trout are caught in these lower sections of tributaries. They may not push farther up into a tributary because of their sheer size, and the lake provides a sanctuary close by when water levels drop.

The traditional tactic of staying in contact with fresh-run fish is to follow a run upstream into the middle section of a tributary. Here, salmonid species stage before making the final push into headwater sections for spawning. Middle sections of tributaries are often composed of classic riffles, pools, and pocketwater in succession. The size of this tributary section depends on the length of the drainage.

How quickly migratory species move through the tributary depends on many variables like water levels, water temperatures, and tributary length. Some tributaries have short lengths because of impassable barriers and can fill up with fish quickly. High water levels on larger tributaries allow fish to move many miles upstream. Lake-run species can also run a portion of tributary and then return back to the lake, waiting for more suitable conditions before making an earnest run.

Middle sections of tributaries often start to branch and split into smaller streams. Lake-run species can often be found just downstream from these branches, waiting for another push of water before traveling into spawning areas. The Salmon River in upstate New York, for example, provides

When tributary conditions are not conducive to migrating, fish may drop back to the lake and wait for conditions to improve. ALAN CARTER PHOTO

good king salmon spawning habitat throughout its middle and upper sections, while the best steelhead spawning habitat is in its tributaries, such as Orwell Brook and Trout Run.

The upper regions and feeder streams of most Great Lakes tributaries are the smaller capillaries feeding the larger arteries, giving lifeblood to the entire watershed. Though diminutive in size, the headwater sections on many Great Lakes tributaries can give the fly fisher solitude, provided that he's willing to walk for his fish and that this tributary section is open to fishing. This is where many lake-run species actually spawn, and on many tributaries this is where the best spawning habitat is found.

Well-oxygenated riffles and pool tailouts containing pea-size gravel attract spawning fish where their life cycle will be completed. Steelhead and brown trout also enter these areas when salmon are spawning, feasting on their eggs. Steelhead and

When water levels are up, small tributaries and headwater sections can provide good fly fishing for migratory species. KARL WEIXLMANN PHOTO

As water temperature drops during early winter, steelhead move into slow-moving runs and deep pool tailouts where they can escape heavy currents.

browns spawn in headwater sections, normally after the salmon have seeded the next generation.

The best tributaries for wild steelhead and salmon have cool groundwater supplies and springs in their headwaters, sustaining the newly hatched juveniles through the warm summer months. However, many Great Lakes tributaries suffer from thermal warming even in headwater regions, and the spawn is unsuccessful.

Good water levels are a must for fish to reach headwater regions, and a good time to fish them is when the lower sections are too high and muddy to fish. By following a tributary upstream into headwater sections during blowout conditions, you can find clearer water and catch fish where you'd least expect them. Small streams that you could formerly jump across now have enough water to hold fish.

The best times to explore headwater regions are late fall through early spring. The timing of this final push into spawning areas also depends on species, species genetics, water levels, and water temperatures. The actual spawn times of lake-run species are staggered to a great degree throughout the Great Lakes region.

Runs of salmonid species on small tributaries are often subject to the whims of Mother Nature, but chances are that if they have a good flow of water feeding into the lake, a salmonid species can enter them at one time or another. Smaller tributaries may require a big push of water just to allow fish passage and to blow out sand bars or accumulated gravel at stream mouths. Optimum conditions exist for only a short window of time, as these streams drop quickly, usually within 24 to 48 hours.

Fish Location and Tributary Hot Spots

The length, shape, and form of water types found within a tributary section can vary greatly. Some tributaries contain pools that are hundreds of yards in length or longer, while others have pools that are only ten yards long. Most Great Lakes tributaries are in a constant state of change. Environmental influences such as floods, droughts, or development can alter a river's course and change the river bottom by moving gravel bars, boulders, rocks, or wooded debris into new areas. This in turn creates new concentrations of fish on a seasonal or yearly basis.

Riffles and pocketwater make good spots for fly presentation during periods of high water and when fish are on the move.

Riffles and Pocketwater

Many tributary fly fishers walk right by pocketwater and riffles in a hurry to get to the next pool. Where stream or river gradients increase and constrictions occur, rapids, riffles, and pocketwater are created. Riffles with boulders, depressions, and broken bottoms provide numerous holding positions for lake-run species as they move up through a tributary. Boulders create current deflections and ideal resting and feeding opportunities for fish. Unpressured fish often lie in the soft water up- and downstream of obstructions, in the slower water between current seams, and along shoreline creases where the current is weakest.

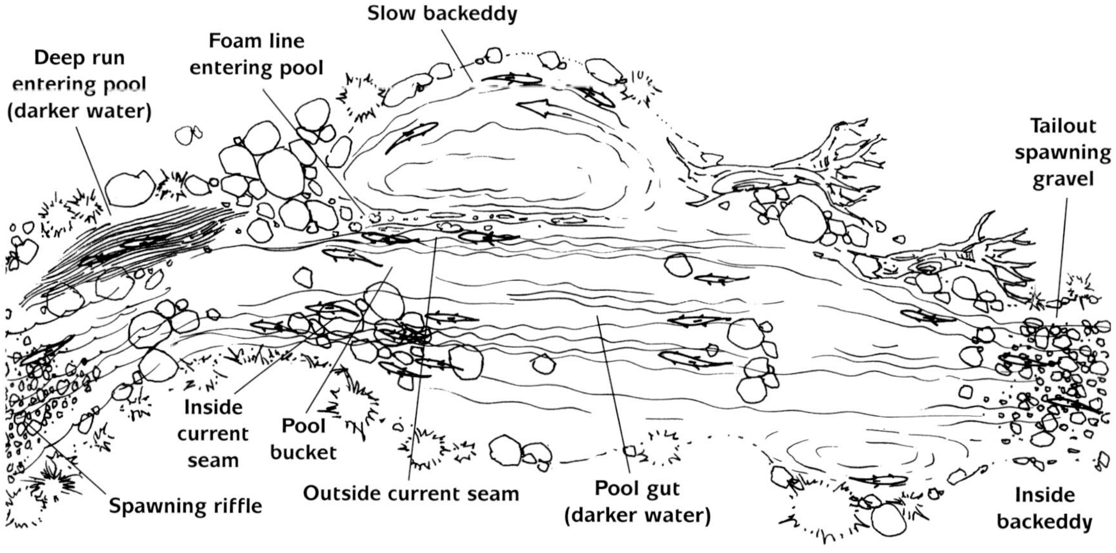

Seasonal holding positions

Whitewater plumes from current forced upward by bottom structure create downstream holding positions and unseen fish. Surface turbulence that prevents light penetration also provides overhead cover. This water type is also cooled by the current and is well-oxygenated, attracting coldwater species during warm weather.

For a fish to see and take a fly in pocketwater and riffles containing fast currents, you must present your fly so that it sinks immediately. A tuck cast incorporated with high-stick nymphing techniques gets the fly down fast and in front of fish in tight holding positions.

Current Seams

Migrating fish follow the path of least resistance, slipping in and out of current seams as they travel and finding the soft edge of the path while swimming upstream. Current seams are areas where fast and slow water meet, creating ripples. Current seams allow lake-run species to feed, travel, and rest along the slow water edge before darting out into the current for drifting forage, such as crippled shiners or nymphs.

Stream structure such as boulders or fallen trees, directional changes like river bends, or river bottom drop-offs and contour changes all create

During periods of high water, lake-run species swim through the riffles.

Fallen trees make excellent hiding and holding areas for lake-run species as they migrate upstream. A good current seam is formed off the end of the tree trunk in this photo.

Lake-run species use the soft water behind boulders to rest while migrating upstream. Here, a steelhead lies behind a boulder.

current seams. Boulders can create an inside and an outside current seam, with an area of slow water in the middle. Fish could lie on either side of these boulder-created seams or in the soft water behind the boulder. The deepest edge is where the fish will be, and large, long riffles can contain hundreds of these minor seams. Look for seams that contain the deepest, darkest water and concentrate on fishing these spots.

River bends create fantastic inside current seams that concentrate migrating fish. Logs and fallen trees create good seams where the structure meets the water. Current seams can form and dissipate as water levels rise and fall within a tributary system. An inside seam that is traveled extensively by migrating fish during periods of high water may not be there the next day. A drop in water levels will push a seam farther out from the bank. Current seams located farther away from the bank and associated with deep water are used by fish in lower water conditions, while outside seams—those closest to the bank—hold fish in higher water conditions.

Current seams created by heavy riffles that dump in at the heads of pools can sometimes provide the best fishable seam in the system. Here, fish have access to deep, well-oxygenated water and a steady supply of food. Working the inside edge of this seam is often the ticket to instant hookups on pools that have yet to receive angling pressure.

Depressions

While pools tend to concentrate anglers and fish, a lot of fly fishers walk right by small depressions in the stream bottom without giving them a close look. Depressions are most often seen as darker water surrounded by lighter-colored water and are simply dips in a stream or river bottom that offer deeper water and a sense of security to migrating, lake-run species.

A depression that offers only six to twelve extra inches of depth may hold fish. Take the time to work these areas thoroughly before rushing off to the next pool. A good fly fisher can catch fish out of depressions all day when the pools are locked up and the deep runs are crowded.

There is a certain depression on Cattaraugus Creek in southwestern New York at the back end of a long run that feeds a bend pool. While the best water for holding fish is found upstream in the deep, boulder-strewn run, this spot is often taken by anglers who arrive early. I've learned that hooked fish upstream often spook other fish downstream and into the depression, where I wait for them to settle down before presenting a fly. This depression is also the first good piece of holding water for any fish moving upstream out of the bend pool. They shoot through the heavy riffle that feeds the bend pool, drop into the depression, and hold.

Depressions are one of the most desirable spots to target during periods of migration. Watching a king salmon blow up through a riffle, drop into a depression, hold, and eat your fly is one of the greatest experiences in tributary fly fishing. During times of peak migration, depressions in the middle of a long section of riffles can provide nu-

The first good presentation along the inside edge of the current seam entering a pool often results in a hookup.

Depressions found in riffles are good spots to target migratory species as they move up the tributary.

merous targets throughout the day. Traveling fish are much less likely to eat than fish in a holding position. These depressions allow fish to hold and rest. What was once a fish hell-bent on getting up the river becomes a "happy" fish that will eat your fly. Depressions can also be found where riffles dump into banks, within the riffle itself, in the run leading into a pool, and within the pool.

Runs

Deep depressions containing good current are often referred to as runs. These areas can stack up with lake-run species, especially when accompanied by structure. The best runs contain bottom structure that includes rocks, boulders, gravel, fallen trees, logs, shale cuts, or ledges. A nice, long, deep run is attractive to lake-run species because the deep currents give fish a sense of security. The current speed in the upper column of a run is often faster than the current speed near the bottom, where fish can hold with little effort while picking off any drifting food.

Pools

Pools contain the largest mass, volume, and depth of water within a tributary, therefore concentrating lake-run species as water levels recede. Because of this, they often receive the most fishing pressure. A classic pool starts with pocketwater and heavy riffles that dump current into a deep trough at the front portion of a pool, called a pool gut or bucket. This is one of the primary holding and taking lies for all lake-run species in a pool. Pool flats form where the pool widens and the current slows down and bottom depth is usually even from bank to bank.

Where fish hold in a pool is mostly determined by water levels. High water pushes fish toward the bank where less energy is needed to hold. Bankside structures and inside current seams are good areas for fly presentation under these conditions. As water levels recede and pool mass and volume decrease, lake-run species will move into deeper pool sections.

Every pool has an area where the fish will take a fly the best. Professional bass anglers refer to a "spot within the spot" on a piece of structure that concentrates fish. One reason some fly fishers seem to catch more fish than others is because they pay attention to where these sweet spots are and identify them by reading the water or watching other people catch fish from them. Only one or two areas of a pool might contain these sweet spots, and if you are the first angler to fish through a pool, you'll likely be rewarded with a hookup.

Likely areas include the inside current seam at the edge of bucket, drop-offs that create current breaks, a rise in the pool bottom, a depression on a pool's flat, or the pool tailout. These features concentrate fish. Here, lake-run species feel secure, the current allows the fish to easily breathe, surface

The top end of this corner pool makes a great spot for swinging a streamer.

Lake-run species congregate in pools located downstream from tributary junctions.

During warm weather, edge pools create whitewater hiding places and well-oxygenated water. Current seams are easily visible in the photo, and they make great places for fly presentation.

currents provide overhead cover, and feeding opportunities abound.

A pool contains subtle depth changes throughout its length that can also concentrate fish. A rise in a pool bottom creates visible surface current textures, current seams, and downstream depressions. Structure within a pool, such as boulders, rocks, gravel, or fallen trees, increases fish-holding potential. It's a given that when other structure types are limited any substantial form of wood structure attracts cover-loving lake-run species. Swinging or stripping streamers in front of pool logjams can induce jaw-dropping chases and strikes.

The pool tailout is classic taking water. Tailouts provide a decrease in flow and current that allows fish to rest as they migrate upstream. The constriction of currents creates deeper water along the outside bend. Large boulders and wooden debris that are frequently found in tailout sections make ideal holding positions and provide current deflection for lake-run species. Tailouts also provide a large window for surface or near-surface dry-line presentations. The end of the tailout also begins another series of riffles and pocketwater, where the river constricts or gradients increase.

Surface Structure

Surface current, also called surface texture, is broken or rippled water that allows fish to hide from predators and avoid penetrating light. Large fish can be hooked in relatively shallow water containing a lot of surface disturbance. Spooked fish will move into these areas, knowing that they cannot be easily spotted.

Areas of whitewater where currents converge or plunge create thousands of bubbles that hide a fish and provide well-oxygenated, cool water. In warm weather, lake-run species use these areas of swiftly moving water. Most anglers will not see fish in these places and walk right by, but they should be fished with bottom-bouncing techniques even if fish are not obvious. When you actually spot big fish in these locations, they'll look like a Labrador retriever trying to hide its head in a bush with its tail hanging out and wagging.

Foam lines are another form of surface structure where lake-run species can congregate. Foam is home, wherever it is created—where fast water

High-stick nymphing techniques using small amounts of weight will work where riffles slow down over bottom depressions containing holding fish. A good foam line is formed where a backeddy cuts against the far bank, creating good holding positions in deeper water. JAY NICHOLS PHOTO

meets slow water, the foam line entering a pool, or the heap of foam in front of or behind a logjam. Surface texture lets the fly fisher know where underwater current breaks occur, reducing flow and attracting lake-run species. A rise in the streambed pushes and deflects current to the surface in the form of broken and rippled water.

Ice is a form of surface structure that steelhead and lake-run brown trout use during winter. Many times, I have walked out along edge ice and kicked out a steelhead. They are here because they know that they cannot be seen and because ice only forms in the slowest water, which is exactly what steelhead seek in the coldest water temperatures. Winter steelheaders who recognize this ply the edges of the ice or drift flies underneath the ice.

Adjusting to Water Condition Changes

The key to catching steelhead and other lake-run species throughout an entire season is the ability to adjust to daily water condition changes with tackle, presentation, and fly selection. My answer to the frequently asked questions of "Where are we are going to fish?" or "What fly pattern is working?" is usually "I won't know until I wake up in the morning and look at the water." Trying to predict where, when, and how lake-run species can be caught on any given day is usually an exercise in futility. Anything and everything can happen on a Great Lakes tributary, so it's best to be prepared for any circumstance.

Adjusting to changing water conditions is a complex issue for a guide who deals with water conditions and temperatures that can change hourly. Great Lakes weather—air temperature, water temperatures, and precipitation—are fluctuating constantly. Tuning in to these changes, by choosing which watershed or water type to fish or by adjusting technique to the situation at hand, is what keeps the rods bent on a continual basis.

Water condition changes can be minute: for instance, an inch or two increase or decrease in water levels or clarity or a couple of degrees rise or fall in water temperature. They can also be dramatic, as in a full-blown flood. Water height, speed, and turbidity all increase with precipitation, snowmelt, or dam and canal releases. They all decrease as water levels recede. Subtle changes in water height, speed, and clarity can have a direct impact on that particular day's fishing, and some tributaries can take weeks or months to flush annual sediment buildup. As with any destination fishery, fly fishers planning trips to fish the Great Lakes region should make an extra effort to get in more than just one day of fishing. What a difference a day can make. Getting more time on the water can result in a mother lode of fish.

All Great Lake tributaries, and the Great Lakes themselves, are in a constant flux of rising or falling water, either manmade or weather-related. Dams can stabilize flows on some watersheds, but even these tributaries have changing conditions that are dictated by Mother Nature. Great Lakes weather patterns are often localized. Though both are in the same county, I've seen 20 Mile Creek blown out and Elk Creek running low and clear, all in the same day. Sometimes you just have to just go look before making a change in plans. Many Great Lakes tributaries have gauges that can give anglers an idea of current water conditions, with tributary height and flow in cubic feet per second given over the Internet.

Amount of rainfall, length of rainfall, type and length of tributary, and development surrounding that tributary all affect current fishing conditions. Large agricultural drainages can take weeks to clear and become fishable while small, forested freestone or shale-bottom type tributaries might clear within hours after rain. Runoff from urban and suburban areas can quickly raise water levels to flood stage. A day or two after a blowout might produce great fishing on many of the small- to medium-size tributaries.

Lake-run species like to hold in the bucket where the current dumps into a slow-moving pool. JAY NICHOLS PHOTO

Several simple rules of thumb can help keep you on fish and good water conditions. If the small to medium tributaries are running low and clear, get on the largest tributaries available. If the big tributaries are blown out, get on the smaller ones. It's that simple. If I'm on a large tributary that blows out, I look at the feeder streams instead, determining the season or stage of the run before making a watershed change. High-water cycles that raise water levels allow fish to spread out through a tributary system, with each cycle allowing lake-run species to reach areas previously devoid of fish.

In each Great Lakes region, a wide variety of tributaries are available to choose from, and many tributary sizes exist within one watershed. Larger ones can have drainages that expand for hundreds of miles and take a week or longer to clear and attain fishable conditions. My job as a guide is to get you on the best water conditions found within my region to find fish that will bite. Notice I said fish that will bite. It can be easy getting on fish in Pennsylvania, but low, clear-water steelhead are some of the toughest fish in the world to catch, especially if they receive any amount of fishing pressure. Why waste time here, when I can jump over to a larger tributary like the Grand River in Ohio or Cattaraugus Creek in New York, and find more water volume, greater depth, and usually less clarity, which equates into fish that will bite.

Lake-run species are out of their element once they enter the tributaries. They've spent their entire adult life in the deep, open waters of the Great Lakes and feel exposed and vulnerable in tributaries as water levels drop, light levels rise, and clarity increases. In low water they become keenly aware of fishing pressure. They become what European salmon anglers call "stale" and are harder to catch.

Ideally, the best conditions are on tributaries that have begun to recede after high water. I look for 12 to 18 inches of visibility on larger tributaries or 6 to 12 inches on the smaller tributaries. As water levels recede, a number of tributaries attain such optimal conditions for a period of time, until the water becomes too low and clear for me to want to fish it. With limited visibility, I'd rather be fishing on a smaller tributary than a larger one. Fish that are concentrated into smaller holding positions are more likely to see your fly in high-water conditions. Although 4 to 6 inches of visibility is still considered fishable, the fish will be more spread out on a larger tributary during high-water conditions and less likely to see your fly.

I have a tributary checklist to follow when guiding. If a certain tributary is blown out, another nearby will usually have just the right conditions. By following falling water throughout the season and from tributary to tributary, I can stay on top of optimal conditions throughout the region after each period of high water. One tributary is going

Small tributaries are sometimes a challenge to fish but can save the day during high-water and runoff conditions.

Room to fish can often be found on the first pool up from the lake during harsh conditions. STEVE MAY PHOTO

to fish well and have optimal conditions within 24 hours after a blowout, while another is going to have optimal conditions within 48 hours, and so on down the line. I start with the smaller tributaries and work my way back to the larger watersheds, repeating the process as time progresses and high-water episodes occur.

High-Water Strategies

While fishing smaller tributaries is an effective high-water strategy, you can still catch fish in the larger tributaries with as little as 4 to 6 inches of visibility. With high water and an increase in current velocity, the fish get pushed shallow and toward the bank, where more visibility is afforded and less current enables the fish to hold. Large current breaks in the form of ledges, logs, and large boulders also let lake-run species avoid heavy current and debris. Continual drifts through holding areas give fish a chance to see the fly and eat it. As little as 12 to 24 inches of depth can make fish feel secure when the water is dirty.

Areas previously devoid of fish will now have fish moving and holding in them. Riffles, pocketwater, and shallow depressions are good places for high-sticking techniques during these high-water periods. Running lines and slinky rigs can save the day and become more applicable as water levels and current velocities increase. Indicator techniques work from the bank out to the first good

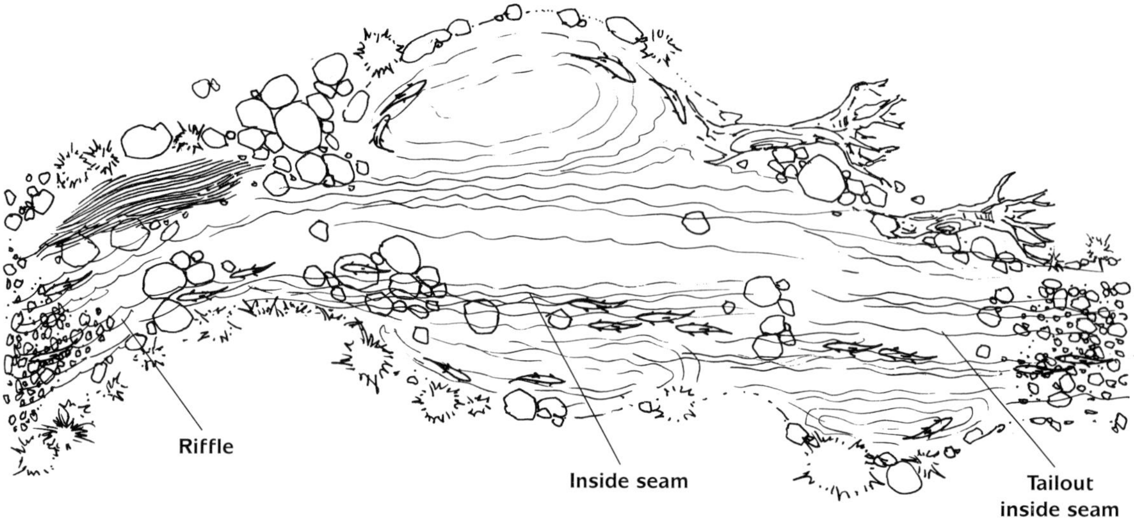

High-water fish location

They might be wet, but the fishing was wild. Fly fishing for lake-run species during rising or falling high-water episodes can lead to a mother lode of fresh-run fish.

current seam. The slower and shallower water next to the bank also holds resting and traveling fish. Fish move deeper as water clarity increases and current speed and velocity decrease. For a fish to be able to eat your fly, it has to see it. Go-to patterns for me in high water are bright eggs patterns or large streamers such as big, black Woolly Buggers or purple Egg-Sucking Leeches with accents of flash and bright, fluorescent colors like chartreuse and flame orange.

Low-Water Strategies

In low water, try to find the largest tributaries in the region. As water levels recede, lake-run species drop back into the deepest, darkest water and stack up in large pools. Fish also move into areas of surprisingly shallow water where surface current provides overhead whitewater structure.

The most important thing to avoid in low water is spooking the fish. Carefully observe the water in front of you before approaching it, looking closely at anything dark that indicates the presence of fish or gives away their location. Any

Randy St. John gets down and dirty with an Ashtabula River steelhead during high-water conditions. High water levels can lead to good fishing, either before or after a tributary becomes blown out.

section of stream that is darker than the surrounding water might be deeper and possibly hold fish.

Approach any fish you spot or any likely-looking lie as if you were stalking a big-game animal. On many occasions it might be necessary to stay out of the water and maintain a low profile, or crawl on your hands and knees into a casting position. Stay as far away from potential holding water as possible and fish it like you know the fish are there. Getting any closer and taking a peek may ruin your opportunity. The fish may not give you more than a half-dozen shots before becoming skittish or spooked.

When fly fishing on low and clear Great Lakes tributaries, you generally have to downsize and use long, 14- to 18-foot leaders. I start with size 14 or 16 flies on 4X tippet and drop down to 5X and smaller patterns if that's not working, but I can usually get fish to eat a size 14 on 4X or 5X fluorocarbon. Fluorocarbon leaders and tippet material simply outfish nylon in low water. I also use smaller indicators, if I use an indicator at all, and less shot.

Lake-run species become keenly aware of their environment when the water is low. I've seen many a school of steelhead part like the Red Sea for Moses when a bright orange indicator came floating over them. To address this problem, I started using a black Sharpie permanent marker to color the bottom two-thirds of the indicator. It doesn't spook the fish as much and I have had great results. The bottom of a Thill pencil float painted black makes a great indicator for tough fishing condi-

Maintain a low profile when approaching a tributary during low- and clear-water conditions. Keep any vegetation between you and the fish to help mask your approach. Make your first shot count, and cast from a kneeling position where appropriate. The fish may only give you several presentations before spooking or shutting down.

tions in low, clear water. Another option is to use white indicators that blend in with bubbles and foam lines, though these can be harder to see on a clear day with sun on the water.

A neat trick I learned from Barry Beck, intended for nymphing low-water steelhead and trout, is to use a small piece of white Glo-Bug yarn treated with floatant as an indicator. Attach the yarn with a slipknot in the leader. This makes hardly any noise or splash when it hits the water. Foam and polystyrene indicators have weight and make noise and displace water when landing, which is an important consideration when fish give you only a couple of casts and you've got to make them count.

Low, clear water is common in the early part of the season. The other way to trigger these early-run, low-water fish is to strip or swing a streamer

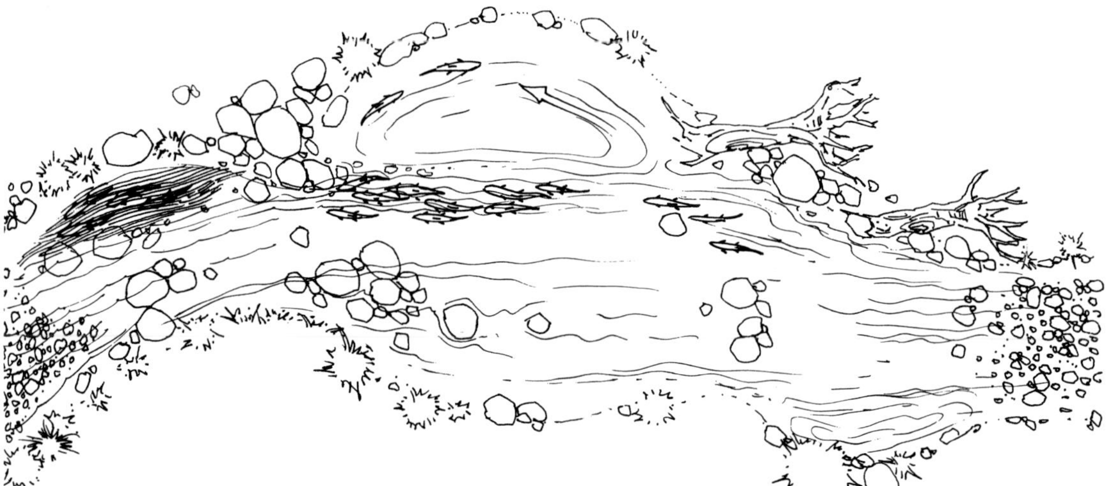

Low-water fish location

in front of them. Even though the water is low and clear, the predatory instinct may still be intact and the fish are still accustomed to feeding on baitfish. Make long, down- and across-stream casts while keeping a low profile. Your first series of presentations is the most important and should be spot-on. After a couple of hits and chases, the fish are likely to shut down, but the visual thrills keep you coming back for more.

Floating Great Lakes Tributaries

Floating the larger Great Lakes tributaries offers many advantages that shore-bound fly fishers cannot enjoy. Jet boats, drift boats, and pontoon boats can put you on fish other anglers can't reach and help you get away from the crowds that gather at easy access points. Floating also gives you the ability to cover large distances in search of fresh-run fish. Migratory species are sometimes found in certain tributary sections, while other expanses of the tributary are completely devoid of fish.

Many guides and outfitters offer float trips with jet and drift boats on some outstanding fisheries in the Great Lakes region. Jet boats (also referred to as jet sleds) have impeller-driven outboard motors that enable the operator to run across shallow riffles and rapids merely 3 inches deep, where prop-driven outboards would be hazardous to operate or bottom out. Steelhead guru Matt Supinski operates a 20-foot jet sled on various Michigan tributaries. You can easily cover 30 to 35 miles of river in a single day using one of these boats.

McKenzie-style drift boats give anglers a quieter, more leisurely way to explore a river system and thoroughly work the water. These rugged vessels are now manufactured with a combination of fiberglass, Kevlar, and steel. On Michigan's Muskegon River, guide Kevin Feenstra runs what he describes as an 18-foot hybrid drift and flat-bottomed boat, manufactured by Rogue Marine. Kevin uses an outboard to motor up the river—and experienced oarsmanship—to set up a 7- to 8-mile drift. Drops are made using an electric anchoring system. Ken Collins of Grand River Troutfitters in Fergus, Ontario, emphasized that his guides fish directly from the boats and don't use their 15-foot Clackacraft drift boats merely as taxis to fishing spots that can be reached on foot. A good oarsman, Ken explained, can hang in the current, giving fly fishers numerous presentations to holding water along current seams other anglers just can't reach. Fly fishing from a hard boat during the winter is a much more enjoyable experience than standing in limb-numbing water all day long. Furnished with propane heaters and propane cook stoves, they make the harsh elements much easier to take.

One- and two-man pontoon boats are increasing in popularity on medium- to large-size tributaries and on many of the larger walk-and-wade streams when water levels are suitable for floating. You might also consider a canoe for these waters, but a pontoon boat is a much more stable craft with more maneuverability. Pontoon boats have widely separated air bladders with thick vinyl covers, giving these vessels the ability to navigate and float tributaries where a hard-bottomed watercraft would be hazardous or even impossible to operate. The soft bottom of a pontoon boat allows it to glide over and bounce off most underwater obstructions. With their shallow drafts, pontoon boats have a distinct advantage on tributaries containing large numbers or expanses of shallow riffles and boulders. They can help put you on water that would be otherwise hard to get at, and put you on fish that don't get pounded on a daily basis.

Small, single-person pontoon boats are easy to transport and easy to set up or break down on your own. I strap mine, already fully assembled, right to the roof of my vehicle. Recommended one-man pontoon boats have 48-inch-wide aluminum frames with elevated seats. Floatation is provided by vinyl-covered air bladders from 8½- to 9½ feet long strapped to the curved sides of the outer frame. Oarlocks are mounted to the top

Dry-Fly Tactics and Techniques

It took me twelve years of guiding to figure out where, when, and how to catch steelhead on a dry fly in the Great Lakes tributaries. In fact, in low, clear water when fish are suspended, the dry fly—or a dry fly fished with a nymph dropper—is absolutely the best presentation. You'll find these conditions during early fall and late spring, but we've caught steelhead on dry flies as late as the second week of November.

Early fall steelhead will run a tributary after it rains, but the water levels in these tributaries can drop like a rock because water tables are low this time of year, leaving the fish stuck in slow-moving pools, pool tailouts with little current, or at the head of the pool where the current dumps in. This is the only part of their shrunken environment where they feel comfortable. In this deeper water, the fish often suspend, hovering in layers near the surface, sometimes with their dorsal fins or tails breaking the water's surface. Spring fishing with a dry fly is mostly for spawned-out fish moving back to the lake that take the same holding lies as early fall-run steelhead in low and clear water.

In these water conditions, a dry fly is the least obtrusive presentation you can make to fish that are exposed and out of their element. The fish are already looking up because they are suspended, not hunkered down near the bottom in cold water where normal presentations will work. An indicator and split shot will splash and send them scurrying for cover or swimming around in spooked circles. You could use a piece of white Glo-Bug yarn looped on the leader as an indicator to reduce splash, but why miss the opportunity to fish a dry fly? You might get a few chasers or hits on the streamer during the first couple of casts, but after that the fish will normally shut down.

A dry fly fished on a long leader alights softly on the water without any surface disturbance, which is especially important in slow-moving pools and tailouts. If the fly, leader, or line doesn't fall over the fish, you can make repeated presentations. A waking or moving dry fly seems to draw the most attention and the most strikes in these conditions, while a dead-drift works best in areas with steady current, like the heads of pools.

To cast to suspended fish in a tailout or slow-moving pool, crouch and move slowly up- and across-stream. Stay low while you get into position and deliver the fly with slow arm movements and casting strokes to avoid spooking the fish. If they spook, hold still: the pod usually reforms, although they may reform upstream or downstream from where they originally were. Cast down- and across-stream at a 45-degree angle, much like you would a streamer. Check the forward cast to let the fly land softly. You want the fly to drop upstream of the fish and swing down in front of them. You may need to mend upstream in areas with current. As the fly swings in front of the fish, begin to wake the fly.

Where the current is extremely slow, wake the fly by lifting the rod back toward you. In tailouts with enough current, you can wake the fly naturally against the resistance of the current, pushing the belly of the fly line and leader by dropping the rod tip and pointing it at the fly.

You can usually tell by a steelhead's behavior whether it is interested in a dry fly. In low, clear water, the first couple of casts will be the most important. An interested fish will break from the pack and chase the fly. I've missed fish that came out of nowhere, and I've watched steelhead charge over the backs of other fish to attack a dry and hit it like a bass blowing up on a topwater plug. Survey the entire stream and concentrate presentations to those fish that seem interested. Sometimes repeated presentations are needed to drum up the fish, especially when steelhead are suspended underneath areas of good current.

I like to use a 12- to 14-foot monofilament nylon leader tapered to 3X for presenting dry flies. My go-to pattern this season has been a size 10 or 12 yellow Stimulator. The wings and tails of Stimulators contain a lot of hackle and hollow deer or elk

Orange Bomber (Karl Weixlmann)

Hook:	**#6-8 Mustad Signature Dry**
Thread:	**Orange 6/0**
Tail:	**White calf tail**
Body:	**Orange deer body hair, spun and clipped**
Wings:	**White calf tail, split**
Hackle:	**Rooster, dyed orange**

Erie-sistable (Karl Weixlmann)

Hook:	**#8-10 Mustad Signature Dry**
Thread:	**To match body color**
Tail:	**Bucktail tips or calf tail**
Body:	**Spun deer body hair, clipped in a teardrop shape**
Wings:	**Bucktail or calf tail tips, split**
Hackle:	**Dry-fly hackle, to match body color**

Note: Effective colors include chartreuse and orange, red and white, or all orange. The fly can be fished by itself, or add a nymph dropper to the bend of the hook, using the high-riding dry as an indicator.

hair, which makes them extremely buoyant and good candidates for fishing droppers underneath them. Steelhead might react to this fly because of their imprinted feeding behaviors: feeding on Hexagenia mayflies that hatch profusely throughout the Great Lakes. Yellow Stimulators make good matches for that mayfly species. Other dry-fly patterns that have worked for me are the Erie-sistable, the Bomber, and classic Bivisibles in brown and tan or orange. Kirk Klingensmith, an avid fly fisherman from New York state, took two steelhead on top one day last fall, using a western-style yellow foam body stonefly.

If the fish show no interest in the dry, I'll put on a nymph dropper with a piece of 4X or 5X flourocarbon tied to the bend of the dry fly. Droppers under dry flies are absolutely deadly on low-water steelhead. The length of the dropper depends on where you see the fish. For steelhead hovering near the surface, a short 6- to 12-inch dropper works. You may need a dropper up to 3 feet long for deeper fish or for fish in a heavy current. I generally use a size 16 or 18 beadhead nymph as the dropper and have successfully used Crooked Creek Caddis, Pheasant Tails, Copper Johns, Princes, and soft hackles. Copper Johns work well on a deeper drop, maintaining a tight line to the dry fly for strike detection. You can use tiny micro-shot between the dry and dropper if needed.

Try experimenting with other types of patterns as well. One day on Elk Creek, Jeff Brausch from Cleveland asked me to try a small egg, which worked great with a longer dropper and a tiny micro-shot between the dry and the egg. We watched the egg drift down and set the hook by sight when we saw a fish slide over and engulf the egg. A San Juan Worm was just the ticket another day on 20 Mile Creek.

When a steelhead takes the dropper, the dry fly might give a good dunk or it might hesitate on the drift. But I've also watched steelhead slide underneath the dry and eat the dropper without the dry moving at all. In clear water, it's sometimes best to watch what is going on *underneath* the dry, rather than watching the drifting dry fly itself. Look for fish movement and a white mouth opening up, or a head shaking back and forth, and set the hook.

Last fall, we had a fish hooked up on the dropper. It was thumping its head back and forth when the dry skittered across the surface. Another steelhead came up and trashed the dry fly. For the briefest moment, that was the one and only double hookup on steelhead with one fisherman that I've ever seen. The bottom fish immediately snapped off on the lighter dropper, but we eventually landed the fish that ate the dry, making it the third steelhead of the day landed on a dry fly.

of the frame on both sides of the seat. It's easy to maneuver the craft with a pair of oars while drifting downstream; however, you have to row through any long or level sections with little current, which slows down and lengthens the duration of a float. Two-person pontoon boats are available in the 11- to 12-foot range and have retractable casting platforms for the angler in the front of the boat.

Safety should be the first concern when floating any Great Lakes tributary, especially when operating a personal watercraft. Always conduct floats with another party in another vessel in case of emergencies, and make sure someone at home is aware of where the float trip is planned. Scout rapids and obstructions in advance to determine the best route, and take precautions to ensure that the float ends before darkness settles in.

A few years back, we were late getting a pontoon float started on New York's Cattaraugus Creek. As it turned pitch black, I had a hard time seeing and navigating between the whitewater plumes created by the current rushing into underwater boulders, while we were still several bends upstream from the takeout. I eventually hit one of these boulders, and the force of the current behind me lifted the entire boat, dropping me into the drink. I found myself thrashing around in the water like a spawning salmon while my pontoon boat continued its drift downstream, unattended. This experience underscored the need to wear a personal floatation device (PFD) in any craft. Luckily, photographer Jack Hanrahan was able to grab the boat before it drifted downstream from the takeout or it may have made it all the way to Lake Erie with my gear.

Floating the larger Great Lakes tributaries with drift boats is a classic way to keep anglers on the fish. SUPINSKI PHOTOGRAPHY

Inflatable pontoon boats help the fly fisher escape from crowded access points.

When using pontoon boats to float tributaries, point your feet at obstacles and row away from them.

The first piece of operational advice I can give (and this comes from a guy whose nicknames have included "Flipper" and "Crash") is to always point your feet at any obstruction and row away from it. Work the oars upstream to slow the speed of your drift. Go through rapids and riffles feet first, and don't be scared of a little whitewater as long as it's fairly deep. You'll bounce right through it—hooting all the way.

If you get sideways to the current, make an immediate adjustment with the oars to straighten your line. Going through rapids backwards will only put you at the mercy of the current and push you into unseen obstacles. By facing downstream and keeping your feet pointed downstream, and with proper oar manipulation, you can control the craft and its drift. On some models, locking oars allow you to spin the vessel around and walk it through shallow water.

Accessories provided with pontoon boat packages typically include several rectangular zippered storage containers strapped to the frame sides and fold-down seats with snap attachments. A mesh or metal plate is strapped or pinned in place to the frame behind the seat where you can add storage, keep coolers tied in place with a bungee cord, or mount a marine battery. Some models have brackets welded to the frame for mounting electric trolling motors. Additional accessories can be purchased to further enhance the fishability of a pontoon boat, such as waterproof storage containers, marker buoys, rod holders, and anchors.

When water levels are up, you can successfully float tributaries 100 feet wide or less with pontoon boats. On these medium-size tributaries, probably the best approach is to use the boat as transportation to predetermined fishing spots—if you've floated the tributary previously and know where the fish are holding. If it's a first-time float, the excitement is in the exploration and in learning the nuances of that particular stream.

You should get out of the boat and fish through productive water before floating through it. On larger tributaries with wading hazards and deep sections, you can fish slower-moving current directly from the pontoon boat, by anchoring slightly upstream and to the side of the holding water for a down- and across-stream presentation of the fly.

The length of a float with a personal watercraft depends on the season, the amount of daylight, tributary type, and water levels. Tributaries with steep terrain and a lot of current or water volume will float quicker than those with long stretches of slow-moving frog water that you need to row through. On local waters, we learn this through trial and error, but most floats with pontoon boats should range from 5 to 6 miles long, if you want to get in a decent amount of fishing without a lot of rowing.

Float-Fishing Opportunities by State and Province

This list is meant to point anglers in the right direction when considering a float trip down one of the many suitable Great Lakes tributaries. While you may be able to run a pontoon or hard-bottomed craft down a tributary, some tributaries or tributary sections are not good candidates because of dams, angler pressure, or insufficient flows during low water. I've tried to omit these from the list. Look at the upper sections of the tributary and roadless sections when considering a float trip with a personal watercraft. We use a DeLorme Atlas &

Flies tied with marabou, soft hackles, and rabbit strips catch fish in slower moving currents. The slightest amount of current can impart movement to these materials.

Gazetteer to find roads that cross tributaries for convenient put-in and takeout spots, and if necessary, seek permission for launching or taking out on private property. Access points and guides offering float trips can also be found in the numerous web site listings in the Access section in Chapter 7. Local laws may prohibit anglers from getting out of vessels and wading or walking the shoreline, so be sure to check local regulations before floating any tributary. I'd like to thank Kevin Feenstra, Ken Collins, Chicago Fly Fishing Outfitters, and Matt Supinski for helping compile this information.

New York
Salmon River: Primarily a drift-boat fishery
Oswego River: Power and drift-boat fishery
Cattaraugus Creek: Pontoon boats when water conditions are good
Niagara River: Power boats

Ohio
Conneaut Creek: Pontoon boats when water conditions are good
Ashtabula River: Pontoon boats when water conditions are good
Grand River: Pontoon and drift boats

Michigan
St. Joseph River: Hard-boat fishery
Dowagiac River: Pontoons
Kalamazoo River: Hard boats
Grand River: Hard boats
Muskegon River: Hard-boat fishery, large pontoons
Pere Marquette River: Hard boats and pontoons
Big Manistee: Hard boats
Little Manistee: Pontoons
Rifle River: Pontoons

Michigan-Upper Peninsula
Big Huron River: Pontoons
Chocolay River: Pontoons
Ontonagon River: Pontoons
St. Mary's River: Power boat fishery

Wisconsin
East Twin River: Power boats
West Twin River: Power boats
Manitowoc River: Pontoon boats
Branch River: Pontoon boats
Kewaunee River: Pontoons and drift boats
Oconto River: Pontoons and drift boats
Bois Brule: Drift boats and pontoons

Ontario
Grand River: Pontoon and drift boats
Big Creek: Pontoon boats
Maitland River: Pontoon and drift boats when water levels are good
Saugeen River: Pontoon and drift boats
Bighead River: Pontoon boats
Beaver River: Pontoon boats
Nottawasaga River: Drift and pontoon boats

CHAPTER FOUR

Essential Flies and Foods

With heavily pressured fish and clearer water because of zebra mussels, today's trend in Great Lakes fly patterns is to go smaller and sparser. Small, sparsely dressed, natural-toned flies for low, clear water, and larger, brighter patterns in murky water is the general rule of thumb most days on the river—except when your buddy is slamming them on hot pink and purple, in low, clear water. There are many exceptions to the rules in all fishing, the first of which is that if you're not catching any fish, try something else!

I've learned that a blue Sucker Spawn will catch salmon or steelhead in clear water, and that a blue Glo-Bug with a red dot will catch them in stained

Above: Fall-run steelhead will take a variety of fly patterns and presentations, and these should be fine-tuned according to the current water conditions.

water. Findings reported in the *Journal of the Fisheries Research Board of Canada* show that rainbow trout have a distinct preference for blue eggs. Steelhead and salmon take a liking to pink, in all water conditions. And while chartreuse alone or combined with another color is deadly in water conditions with limited visibility, it still catches fish in clear water, though mostly in smaller sizes.

If I had only two choices of color in fly selection for Great Lakes salmonid species (although I'm glad that's not the case!), it would have to be all white or all black and I believe that statement holds true for almost all species of gamefish, in fresh or salt water, with any fly or lure. Erie fly fisherman Mark Wyman says that the only fly needed for Great Lakes tributaries is a white Woolly Bugger, and he could be right. White and black have universal appeal to all lake-run species, too. White is a primary baitfish and fish egg color, easily imitated by a white Zonker or a white Sucker Spawn. White excels in a variety of water conditions, as does black. Black Hare's Ear Nymphs and black rabbit strip streamers are impressionistic imitations of a variety of prey species, from stoneflies to leeches. Both colors work in high and dirty or low and clear water. These basic colors, by themselves or with accents of another color, account for many fish brought to my net each season. Blue and red are good colors to incorporate with white or black. Pink, purple, and olive are good colors to incorporate with white, though I'm certainly glad that somebody invented chartreuse.

Woolly Buggers are versatile fly patterns for all lake-run species.

If you want to simplify pattern selection even further, I'd say that only three fly patterns are needed for Great Lakes tributary fly fishing: a streamer, an egg, and a nymph. For my purposes, I'll take a white rabbit strip streamer, a Three-Loop Pink Lady egg, and a black Axxel Flash Hare's Ear—all in assorted sizes. With these three fly patterns, I can catch any Great Lakes coldwater species on any tributary at any time of the year. Also, people just learning the art of fly tying can easily and effectively tie these three patterns—a great reason to start hitting the vise. They work just as well as more complicated fly patterns.

Even though I think presentation is more important than fly selection, study the food forms available in your region and note their colors, sizes, shapes, silhouettes, and movements. For instance, some Great Lakes tributaries hold large populations of *Hexagenia* mayflies, while others do not. By knowing what foods are available, fly fishers can at least make educated guesses in fly selection.

Tying your own imitations based on observation increases success and is rewarding. Remember

Golden stoneflies are among the largest invertebrates found in Great Lakes tributaries. ALAN CARTER PHOTO

that exact imitation is not needed in a representative fly pattern. Traditional wet flies, attractor dry flies, Spey flies, and tube flies all catch lake-run species. Classic wet-fly patterns for trout, such as The Professor and soft-hackles, also work on steelhead that reject the standard flies.

I enjoy tying complex patterns, but when guiding I want a relatively simple pattern that is quick to tie and catches a lot of fish. A pattern that spares both steps and materials saves me time at the vise as well as money. I don't want a fly that took me 15 minutes to tie ending up in a tree branch on the first cast. I also need a pattern I have confidence in, one that I know will catch fish when I tie it on the end of the leader. A white rabbit strip streamer, a Three-Loop Pink Lady egg, and a black Axxel Flash Hare's Ear all fit these requirements.

Fly patterns that catch Great Lakes salmonids imitate a wide variety of foods, and can be broken down into three basic categories: streamer, nymph, and egg patterns.

Streamers

Gizzard shad, smelt, emerald shiners, alewives, spottail shiners, silver shiners, chubs, dace, sculpins, gobies, and darter species are all important prey to Great Lakes fish. They have different body shapes, sizes, and colors that are important to consider when tying imitations, but there are some general color and shape themes to keep in mind that can simplify your tying.

White, gray, tan, and olive are the predominant colors in many Great Lakes baitfish. I think that light-reflecting and translucent synthetics closely imitate the variety of hues found in different baitfish species. Tied with flash material and color accents of blue, green, purple, and pink that represent the iridescence found in the fine scaling of baitfish, streamers will attract and catch lake-run species in almost all water conditions and are often overlooked by the fly fisher enamored with dead-drifting egg and nymph patterns.

Rainbow smelt dominate forage fish assessments throughout the Great Lakes and are a favorite food of all coldwater gamefish. Smelt have tubular body shapes that reflect a variety of colors from lavender to rose. Emerald shiners are abundant, and imitations of them are starting to dominate Great Lakes streamer boxes. Alewives have wider and thinner bodies with large white bellies, silvery sides, and a blue-green metallic luster along the back. Flies tied to imitate alewives and smelt should be from 4 to 6 inches long. Smaller, young-of-the-year emerald shiners are available in the spring at $1^1/_2$ to $2^1/_2$ inches long and become larger by the fall, up to 3 to 4 inches long.

Some streamer patterns such as Woolly Buggers may not imitate any specific food item but can still elicit strikes through aggression, territorial response, or impulse. Streamers tied with materials like rabbit strips and marabou that move enticingly through the water give the fly a lifelike wiggle in the slightest currents. Traditional bucktail streamers still catch fish, but many modern Great Lakes fly

White, black, and olive are good colors for basic streamer selection. Include bright and dark patterns that the fish can see in off-color water.

fishers overlook them. Consider all these patterns when fishing over lake-run species.

Fresh runs of Great Lakes salmonids coming in from the lake still retain the predatory instinct to chase and consume baitfish. There is no greater thrill than watching a fresh-run king, coho, steelhead, or brown trout chase down a streamer and trash it in front of your face. Streamer patterns excel in the early season, when dropback fish gorge on minnows on the way back to the lake. The streamer bite was so good this past fall that I didn't tie an egg pattern onto the end of a leader until almost November.

Coldwater species are just not supposed to hit streamers when the water temperatures drop much below 40 degrees, but this is simply not true and has been proven to me otherwise, more than once. Alan Carter continues to swing streamers with success on Ohio's Grand River below Harpersfield Dam in January and February, when all other area tributaries are locked up in ice and rendered unfishable. I've watched Jeff Brausch, a streamer specialist from Cleveland, whack steelhead on white Zonkers cast between floating icebergs in 33-degree water. I've caught coho salmon in December on pink marabou streamers. Even during a good egg or nymph bite, a streamer will often hook your biggest fish of the day. Big fish still eat little fish, even in the coldest water.

Streamers are great for spring and fall steelheading and account for some of the biggest fish that I see caught each year. Don't be afraid to

Many Great Lakes steelheaders are turning to tube flies for swinging presentations.

throw Rapala-size streamers, up to 6 inches long. Water conditions should dictate the color and size of the streamer you fish. Low, clear water may call for a smaller, sparser, tan or olive streamer without a lot of flash. Large, flashy streamers with hot fluorescent color schemes that the fish can see more easily can work better in off-color and high water, but I remember a day on Elk Creek when low-water steelhead chased and smashed size 6 purple and pink Popsicles. Black seems to have universal appeal in many water conditions, and many a day has been saved by a big black Bugger in water with little more than 6 inches of visibility.

Large can be as big as a 1/0 alewife imitation double-hauled from a lakefront jetty, and small can be as tiny as size 14 Woolly Bugger dead-drifted under an indicator in a tributary pool. My streamer boxes are dominated by size 8s and 6s, with a few 4s, and 2s, or 1/0s, for fishing over giants, and size 10s or 12s for fishing low and clear water.

Weight is an important consideration. Heavily weighted streamers are needed for depth penetra-

Egg, nymph, and streamer patterns are staples of Great Lakes tributary fly fishing.

Lake-run browns like olive rabbit strip streamers. LANDON MAYER PHOTO

tion in deep, fast runs and the top end of deep pools. Keep moderately weighted streamers shallow with a faster retrieve or allow them to sink before starting a slower retrieve. Fishing in shallow and slow water may not require weighting the streamer at all.

Different methods of weighting influence the fly's movement and the action of the fly when retrieved. Weighting the fly near the hook eye with dumbbell eyes gives it an up-and-down, hopping, and darting action that looks like an injured baitfish. The famous Clouser Minnow is really just a fly fisher's bucktail jig and will catch all the Great Lakes gamefish species from smallmouth bass to steelhead.

This jigging action can also be achieved in a simple beadhead marabou streamer by jamming wraps of lead wire into the bead before tying. All the weight at the front of the fly lets it plunge through the water headfirst, like an escaping minnow seeking the shelter of the stream bottom. This fly fisher's marabou jig is deadly on all lake-run species when tied in various colors.

A good way to weight streamers with marabou and rabbit strip wings is to wrap lead along the length of the hook shank, giving streamers good depth penetration with a uniform sink. Adjusting and varying the way a fly is weighted allows you to fish various water conditions and depths. One of the best ways for tributary fly anglers to find out what size, color, and presentation is working best on that particular day is to watch the other people who are catching fish. Duplicating a tried-and-true coho catcher, like a blue and silver spoon, is as simple as stripping a blue and silver Flashabou streamer through a tributary pool. Duplicating the deadly jig and bobber technique is as simple as fishing a beadhead marabou streamer underneath an indicator. Observing what spinning, center-pinning, and bait anglers are doing may lead you to new methods of presentation and help you catch more fish.

Senyo Sculpin (Greg Senyo)

Hook:	**#4-8 upturned eye salmon hook**
Thread:	**Olive 6/0 Uni-Thread**
Tail:	**Reverse-tied olive rabbit strip, olive Krystal Flash, and rainbow Flashabou**
Body:	**Peacock Ice Dub**
Gills:	**Barred olive marabou**
Head:	**Ice Dub**

Note: The head is tied with 1/8-inch clumps of Ice Dub, starting on top, then side to side, and then back to the top again to the eye of the hook. The whole head is then brushed with a wire brush and trimmed to form a wide and flat head. Good colors are peacock, purple, and flesh. I developed this pattern to imitate our native sculpins and the round gobies that have invaded Lake Erie, providing a new food source for steelhead. This pattern is best swung deep through pools and around submerged structures that steelhead tend to use as cover.

Grand River Special (Jerry Darkes)

Hook: #4 Daiichi 2220 or 200R

Thread: White or black flat waxed nylon

Tail: Marabou

Body: Hackle Flash

Back: Rabbit strip tied Zonker style

Hackle: Schlappen

Head: Small cone

Note: This pattern can be tied as a baitfish imitator or as an attractor. It has proven effective in high, off-color water conditions. Color combinations are endless, but I usually do a light version with a white back and a dark version with a black back.

Hackle Flash Zonker (Jerry Darkes)

Hook: #4 Daiichi 2220 or Tiemco 200R

Thread: White 3/0

Back: White or grizzly rabbit strip, tied Zonker style

Body: Silver, blue, or chartreuse Hackle Flash

Hackle: Schlappen

Note: This is a great fly for steelhead keying on bright, flashy baitfish and has great action on the swing.

Moby Goby (Karl Weixlmann)

Hook: #4-8 streamer

Thread: Brown flat waxed nylon

Tail: Gray rabbit fibers

Eyes: Red or yellow dumbbell eyes, sized to hook

Body: Dubbed gray and cream rabbit, mixed

Pectoral fins: Hungarian partridge

Wing: Underwing of six strands of copper Krystal Flash and pine squirrel strip; overwing of golden brown marabou

Head: Spun brown and gray wool, or similar synthetic

Note: Push pine squirrel strip through hook point before attaching. Invasive gobies now provide a huge forage base for all Great Lakes predatory species.

Angel Hair Alewife (Ron McGraw)

Hook: #4-6 Tiemco 5263

Thread: White 3/0 Gudebrod

Body: Pearl Ice Dub, wrapped around hook shank with a dubbing loop

Wing: Rainbow Angel Hair top, Pearl Angel Hair bottom

Eyes: Yellow dome, 5/32, epoxied

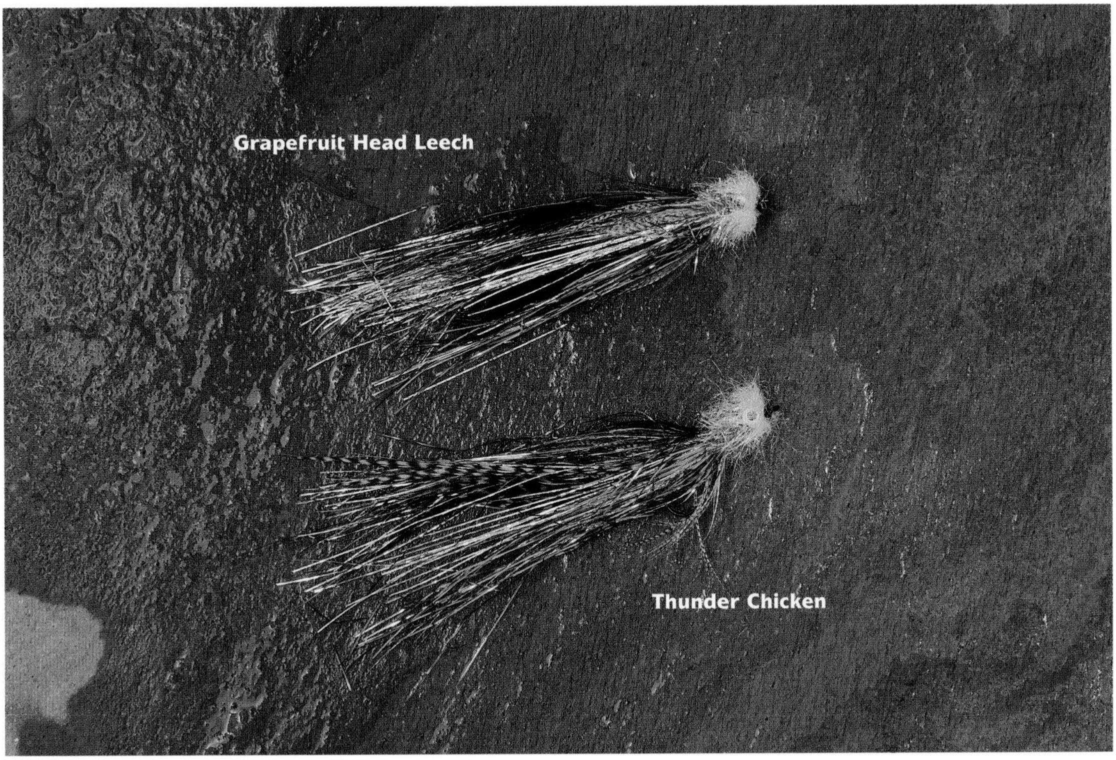

Grapefruit Head Leech (Kevin Feenstra)

Hook:	#2/0-4 Daiichi 2461 or equivalent 3XL streamer hook
Thread:	Color to match body
Tail:	Black marabou with sparse red flash
Hackle:	Medium to large blue-eared pheasant or dark olive schlappen
Body:	Dark Ice Dub or Leech Yarn
Collar (optional):	Large mallard flank
Flash:	Green, silver, pink, and blue holographic Flashabou
Head:	Fuchsia Cactus Chenille (large), followed by a veil of chartreuse Ice Dub. Lead eyes are optional.

Note: This is a great leech pattern for steelhead that works well in the fall but really shines in the winter and early spring. I often tie the silver and pink Flashabou as a tail and top the fly with blue Flashabou.

Thunder Chicken (Kevin Feenstra)

Hook:	#2/0-4 Daiichi 2461 or equivalent 3XL streamer hook
Thread:	Color to match body
Tail:	Two cree, grizzly, or blue barred hackle feathers topped with pearl Lateral Scale
Hackle:	A large mallard flank or pheasant feather, palmered through the body
Body:	Black peacock or peacock Ice Dub
Flash:	Pink, fuchsia, and silver holographic Flashabou surrounded by blue Flashabou
Head:	Fuchsia Cactus Chenille (large) or hot pink Ice Dub followed by a veil of chartreuse Ice Dub
Eyes:	Dumbbell eyes

Note: This is another colorful, narrow fly that sinks well and fishes particularly well during the winter for steelhead.

Grease Stain (Kevin Feenstra)

Hook: #1 Daiichi 2220 or #2/0-2 Daiichi 2461
Thread: Color to match body
Tail: Black marabou
Tail flash: A few strands of red Flashabou
Hackle: Olive/copper Polar Chenille or purple Hula Wrap
Body: Black or peacock Crystal Chenille. Dark Ice Dub can also be used and works even better if palmered with a schlappen feather
Collar: Large mallard flank followed by a couple wraps of purple Hula Wrap
Overwing: Copper Flashabou topped with holographic black Flashabou or bronze Flashabou
Eyes: Four to six small copper bead chain eyes on a strand, lashed under the eye of the hook
Head: Peacock, olive, or silver Ice Dub

Note: The Grease Stain is a good fly for angering steelhead when they just aren't on the bite. As a bonus it works very well when stripped for steelhead and brown trout. This aggravating fly has taken some large fish in the last couple of years.

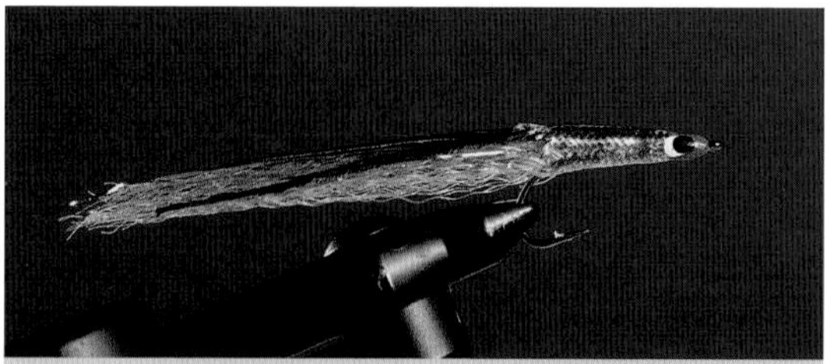

Emerald Candy (Karl Weixlmann)

Hook: #6-10 Mustad #9672
Thread: Fluorescent red 3/0 Danville
Belly: White Fishair or similar synthetic
Back: Mixture of silver, blue, pearl, and purple Krystal Flash or Flashabou; olive Fishair or similar synthetic; and a peacock herl topping all tied in at the eye
Body: Pearl Mylar tube, epoxied
Eyes: Hand-painted

Note: This is a good pattern to use near tributary mouths, beaches, and bays, where steelhead, salmon, and trout aggressively chase schools of emerald shiners in early fall and spring. Also works in tributaries as a swing fly or fished dead-drift under an indicator.

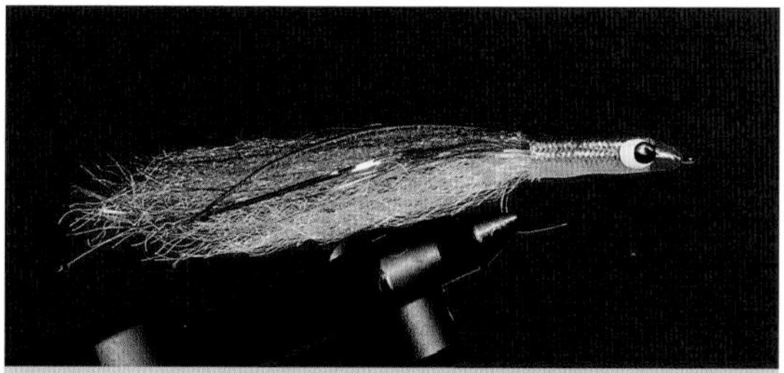

Tubular Smelt (Karl Weixlmann)

Hook: #2-8 Mustad Signature Stinger
Thread: Fluorescent red 3/0 Danville
Body and tail: Pearl /white Metz Deadly Dazzle, pink Deadly Dazzle, mix of pink Mirage Flashabou, silver Flashabou, Blue Krystal Flash, Purple Krystal Flash, topped with gray Deadly Dazzle and peacock herl
Eyes: Hand-painted

Note: When combined with a Magic Head, a cuplike plastic device, this fly becomes the fly fisher's Rapala, with a plug-like swimming action.

Marabou-Tailed Clouser Minnow (Karl Weixlmann)

Hook:	#4-8 Mustad Signature Streamer
Thread:	White flat waxed
Eyes:	Silver dumbbell
Tail:	White marabou with Mirage Flashabou accents
Body:	Dubbed pearl Lite Brite or similar synthetic
Wing:	Underwing of white bucktail tips; overwing of Flashabou and bucktail; substitute calf tail on smaller sizes

Note: A top producer on the beach, this fly can be tied in many color combinations. It also works for tributary fishing in slower-moving water.

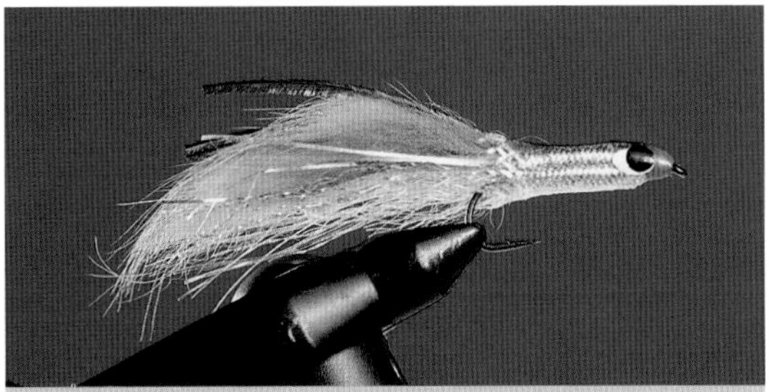

Emerald Bunny (Karl Weixlmann)

Hook:	#4-8 Mustad Signature Streamer
Thread:	Flourescent orange flat waxed
Belly:	White Unique Hair, Fishair, or similar synthetic
Back:	A mixture of pearl/pink or silver Flashabou with purple and blue Krystal Flash, tied to top of hook shank along with the rabbit strip and three or four strands of peacock herl
Body:	Pear Mylar tube, pushed over material and epoxied
Eyes:	Hand-painted

Note: This modified version of the Emerald Candy uses a rabbit strip to provide more movement. The stiffer synthetic underbelly prevents the rabbit strip from fouling around the hook bend.

Salmon Fry (Jerry Darkes)

Hook:	#6 Daiichi 1710 or Tiemco 200R
Thread:	Cream 3/0
Tail:	Grizzly marabou
Body:	Front part of feather, tied in at tail and wrapped forward
Yolk sac:	Pink/orange/yellow synthetic dubbing
Eyes:	Small plastic bead chain
Back:	Pearl Krystal Flash tied in front, then back behind eyes

Note: This is a simplified version of a pattern from Michigan guide and tier Kevin Feenstra.

HF Sculpin (Jerry Darkes)

Hook:	#2-4 Daiichi 2220
Thread:	White, olive, or brown flat waxed nylon
Tail:	Grizzly marabou
Body:	Hackle Flash
Back:	Mallard flank
Head:	Ram's wool
Eyes:	Red bead chain

Note: Tie in darker shades of black, olive, brown. Large head pushes water well for off-color water.

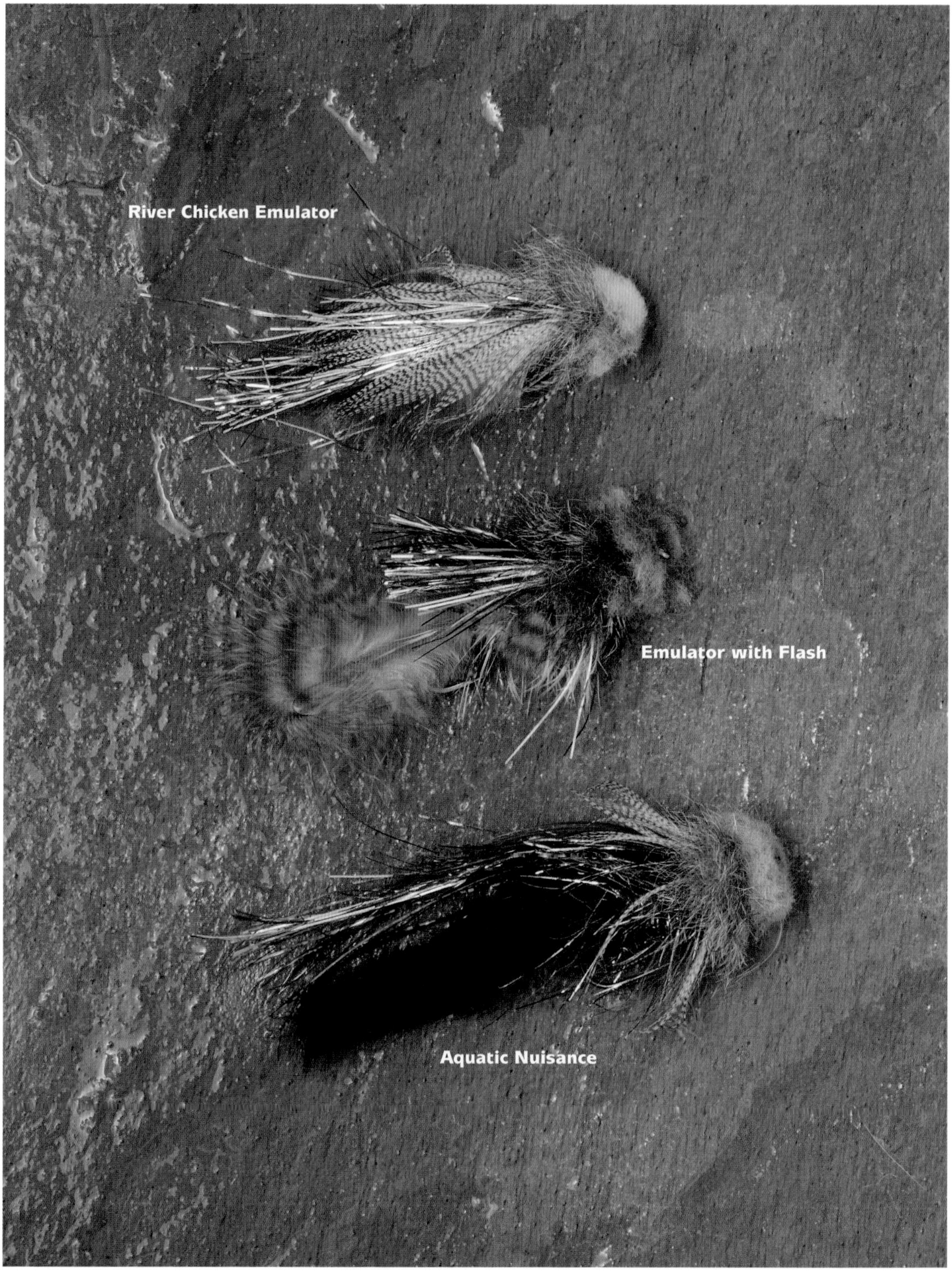
River Chicken Emulator
Emulator with Flash
Aquatic Nuisance

Emulator with Flash (Kevin Feentsra)

Hook: #1/0-4 3XL-6XL streamer hook
Tail: Grizzly marabou dyed tan or olive
Hackle: Tan or olive schlappen
Body: Two natural or olive emu feathers wound tightly forward
Collar: Large natural mallard or wood duck flank
Pectoral fins (optional): One grizzly marabou feather splayed on each side of hook
Flash: A thick clump of multicolored Flashabou, tied about half the length of the hook shank on either side
Head: A thick clump of Australian possum or olive ram's wool, tied around the front of the hook

Note: Emulators don't always take a lot of fish, but they are consistent at catching fish when other flies won't. Fish them deep and slow. Works well for steelhead and lake-run browns.

Aquatic Nuisance (Kevin Feenstra)

Hook: #1/0 or 1 Daiichi 2461 or equivalent 3XL-6XL streamer hook
Thread: Color to match body
Tail: Dark brown or dark olive rabbit strip, tied in as a tail at the shank of the hook and pulled forward over two thirds of the hook length
Body: Remnant of rabbit strip
Hackle: Copper Hackle Flash, wound through the rabbit strip (olive schlappen or black emu are good substitutes)
Collar: Large mallard flank
Wing: Copper Flashabou topped with a good amount of holographic green or bullfrog Flashabou
Head: Dark olive wool, Australian possum, or dark olive Ice Dub

Note: This slow-water fly is especially effective around boulders.

River Chicken Emulator (Kevin Feenstra)

Hook: #1/0-4 3XL-6XL streamer hook
Thread: Color to match body
Tail: Grizzly marabou dyed tan or olive
Hackle: Olive or tan schlappen
Body: Two natural or olive emu feathers wound tightly forward
Collar: Large natural mallard or wood duck flank
Pectoral fins (optional): One grizzly marabou feather, splayed on each side of hook
Head: A thick clump of Australian possum or olive ram's wool, tied around the front of the hook

Note: Works well for steelhead and lake-run browns.

Chaos Maker (Kevin Feenstra)

Hook: #1/0-2 Daiichi 2461
Thread: Color to match body
Tail: Bright yellow or orange barred saddle hackle, topped with pearl saltwater Flashabou
Overwing: Orange or fuchsia bucktail above and below the body
Body: Clump of yellow deer hair
Overwing: Several strands of pearl saltwater Flashabou or silver Mirror Flash
Head: Front half of hook covered with a thin layer of medium fuchsia Ice Chenille
Eyes: Four small or medium pink, gold, or silver bead chain eyes

Note: This colorful fly is fairly simple to tie and works well for king salmon.

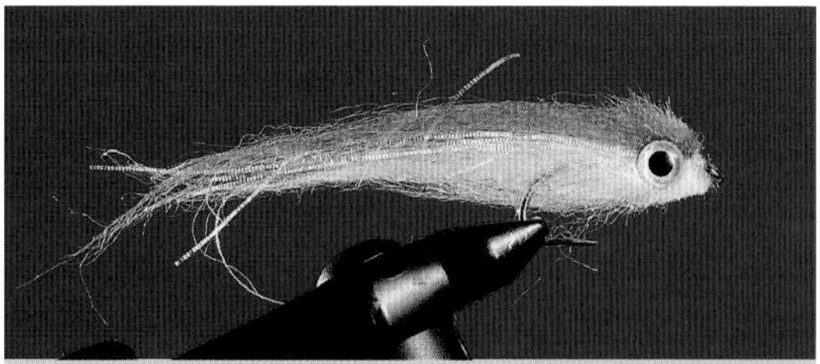

Furry Minnow (Steve May)

Hook: Tiemco 8089 or similar wet fly
Thread: White or black 6/0
Belly: White Craft Fur
Flash: Pearl Gliss 'N Glo
Back: Olive Craft Fur
Eyes: Silver 3D Epoxy Eyes

Note: Craft Fur minnows are quick to tie and have incredible action in the water. Use a sink tip to get them down in the water.

Red Neck Rabbit (Steve May)

Hook: #2 straight-eye streamer or steelhead hook
Thread: Black 6/0
Body: Pearl chenille to match wing color
Hackle: Red saddle hackle
Eyes: Hourglass or dumbbell, painted yellow with pupil
Wing: Zonker strip in black, white, pink, purple, or olive

Note: This is an excellent streamer that rides hook point up, has lots of action, and can be tied in any color combination to meet local conditions.

Clouser Minnow (Steve May)

Hook: Straight-eye short-shank streamer hook
Thread: Black 6/0
Belly: White bucktail or polar bear
Flash: Pearl Gliss 'N Glow
Overwing: Olive bucktail or polar bear
Eyes: Hourglass, painted yellow with pupil

Note: Dropback steelhead feed on minnows and are suckers for an olive-over-white Clouser. North of the border, where polar bear is legal to obtain and use, it does make a difference.

Golden Marabou Streamer (Ron McGraw)

Hook: #4 Tiemco 5263
Thread: White 3/0 Gudebrod
Tail: White marabou and silver Krystal Flash
Body: Pearl Chenille (medium), palmered
Collar: Gold UV Polar Chenille
Eyes: Red metallic dumbbell, 5/32

Psycho Sculpin (Kevin Feenstra)

Rear hook:	#10, 3-4XL straight-eye streamer hook
Front hook:	#4-6 heavy egg hook
Rear hook tail and wing:	Three clumps of Australian possum tail fur
Rear hook body:	Olive Ice Dub
Thread:	Color to match body
Overwing:	Small clump of Australian possum, tied to cover joint between the two hooks
Front hook body:	Thick clump of Australian possum body fur, tied as a clump
Pectoral fins:	Brown grizzly marabou feather, tied to either side of body
Eyes:	Bright pink, red, or blue bead chain eyes

Reaper (Kevin Feenstra)

Rear hook:	#10, 3-4XL straight-eye streamer hook
Front hook:	#4 or 6 heavy egg hook
Rear hook tail and wing:	Three clumps of Australian possum tail fur
Rear hook body:	Peacock Ice Dub
Thread:	Color to match body
Overwing:	Small clump of Australian possum, tied to cover joint between the hooks
Front hook body:	Peacock Ice Dub
Shellback:	6-10 strands of copper Krystal Flash, pulled over as a shellback and split to each side behind the eyes
Eyes:	Black bead chain eyes

Note: This dark nymph pattern is deadly for steelhead, whether used as a nymph or fished on the swing.

Kevin's Australian Possum Hex (Kevin Feenstra)

Rear hook:	#10, 3-4XL straight-eye streamer hook
Front hook:	#6 heavy egg hook
Rear hook tail and wing:	Three clumps of Australian possum fur
Rear hook body:	Yellow Ice Dub
Thread:	Color to match body
Overwing:	A small clump of Australian possum, tied to cover the joint between the hooks
Shellback:	Copper Krystal Flash or brown Antron
Legs:	Grizzly hen hackle, pulled over thorax
Thorax:	Bright orange Ice Dub
Eyes:	Black plastic bead chain

Note: Hex patterns can be used effectively as swung flies for steelhead.

Schmidt's Lunkergetter (Mike Schmidt)

Hook:	#1 Mustad 34007 or Daiichi 2546
Thread:	3/0 Danville monocord
Tail/wing:	Magnum rabbit strip
Body:	EP Sparkle Brush
Collar/ hackle:	Wool over top and bottom
Head:	Built-up thread head
Eyes:	Large painted lead barbell eyes

Barry's Pike Fly with a Twist (Mike Schmidt)

Hook:	#4 Daiichi 2340
Weight:	Lead wire wrapped on shank
Thread:	3/0 Danville monocord
Eyes:	3-D molded eyes
Tail/wing:	Rabbit strip and Mirage Flashabou
Body:	Rabbit strip

Note: Another variation on what has become a standby pattern for predator fish. The multicolored body is achieved by first wrapping the secondary color forward with space left between the wraps and then wrapping the primary color, leaving enough space for the first to show through.

Red and White Beadhead Zonker (Ron McGraw)

Hook:	#4 Daiichi 1710
Bead:	Red
Thread:	Red 3/0 Gudebrod
Tail and wing:	White Zonker strip
Body:	Silver UV polar chenille
Collar:	Red grizzly, Matuka style

Tan Beadhead Zonker (Ron McGraw)

Hook:	#4 Daiichi 1710
Bead:	Gold
Thread:	Tan 3/0 Gudebrod
Tail and wing:	Tan Zonker strip
Body:	Gold UV Polar Chenille
Collar:	Tan grizzly, Matuka style

Brown and Olive Zonker (Ron McGraw)

Hook:	#4 Daiichi 1710
Thread:	Brown 3/0 Gudebrod
Tail:	Olive barred Zonker strip
Body:	Copper UV Polar Chenille
Legs:	Rubber Hackle Speckle Flake, brown and orange
Throat and head:	Holographic Ice Dub
Eyes:	Red metallic, 5/32

Soft-Hackle Streamer, Hot Orange and Black (Ron McGraw)

Hook:	#6 Tiemco 5262
Bead:	Red 3/0
Thread:	Red 3/0 Gudebrod
Body:	Tip-dyed marabou, hot orange with black tip

Note: You can tie endless versions of this fly fisher's version of a deadly marabou jig using various colors of marabou, flash material, and beads.

Fruit Detector (Kevin Feenstra)

Hook:	#1/0-2 Daiichi 2461
Thread:	Color to match body
Tail:	Bright yellow/pearl and pink/pearl Krystal Flash topped with yellow Antron, pink and yellow phosphorescent Flashabou, and gold Flashabou
Overwing:	Orange and fuchsia bucktail above and below the body
Body:	Clump of yellow deer hair
Head:	Orange, pink, and chartreuse Ice Dub
Eyes:	Four small pink, gold, or silver bead chain eyes

Note: This bright variation of one of my favorite big predator flies works well for king salmon.

Fire Detector (Kevin Feenstra)

Hook:	#1/0-2 Daiichi 2461
Thread:	Color to match body
Tail:	Olive Krystal Flash, phosphorescent orange Flashabou, a clump of light olive Antron, and bright orange Flashabou above and below the tail
Overwing:	Olive bucktail above and below the body
Body:	Clump of olive deer hair
Head:	Olive, orange or pink, and chartreuse Ice Dub
Eyes:	Four small pink, gold, or silver bead chain eyes

Note: This is a good predator fly for salmon, steelhead, and lake-run browns. The color scheme is designed to take aggressive fish. It can be swung or stripped. Don't hesitate to throw in some natural materials such as marabou if you intend to fish it on the swing.

Bunny Minnow (Steve May)

Hook: Straight-eye streamer or steelhead hook
Thread: Fine monofilament
Wing: White Zonker strip
Flash: Pearl Gliss 'N Glo
Body: Pearl Mylar tubing
Eyes: Silver 3D Epoxy Eyes

Note: Minnows work especially well for fresh fall fish in the lower reaches of rivers or during the dropback phase in the spring when fish feed heavily before returning to the lake.

Black and Blue Electric Bugger (Karl Weixlmann)

Hook: Mustad 2XL streamer
Thread: Black 6/0
Tail: Black marabou
Body: Black Polar Chenille
Hackle: Black schlappen, finished off with a couple of turns of barred blue schlappen
Flash: Optional

Note: Buggers are steelhead and salmon standbys. You can tie numerous variations the same way. In some rivers, blue flash is a big help, while on others a peacock herl body is just the ticket.

Bead Sucking Leech (Steve May)

Hook: #2-10 streamer hook
Bead: Painted orange, chartreuse, or pink bead-head
Thread: Black, purple, or white 6/0 to match fly
Tail: Black, purple, or white marabou
Body: Black, purple, or white chenille
Hackle: Black, purple, or white
Rib: Optional
Flash (optional): Flashabou, pearl or accent color

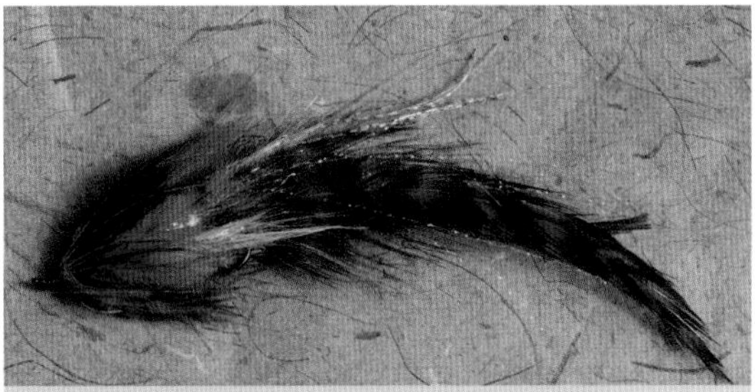

Senyo's Tall Tail Spey (Greg Senyo)

Hook: #4-8 upturned eye salmon hook
Thread: Black 6/0 Uni-Thread
Tail: 3- to 4-inch-long purple grizzly hackle feathers and purple Krystal Flash
Body: Holographic or prismatic tinsel
Wing: Hareline Ice Dub, pearl UV
Throat: Hareline Ice Dub, pearl UV
Collar: Black and purple schlappen

Note: This is my chocolate-water fly pattern. Its large profile and dark purple and black coloration provide a silhouette that is far easier to see under tough water conditions. Add a trailer hook to prevent missed strikes.

Senyo's Lake Erie ICE Spey Series, Egypt's Treasure (Greg Senyo)

Hook: #4-8 upturned-eye salmon hook
Thread: Black 6/0 Uni-Thread
Body: Silver or pearl holographic dubbing
Wing: Pearl or blue Hareline Ice Dub and Flashabou or Krystal Flash
Collar: Schlappen (various color combinations)

Note: This is a steelhead's breakfast! Best applications are swinging this pattern in early fall to fresh and aggressive fish or very late in the season for post-spawners heading back to the lake. It's one of my favorite Skamania patterns in the summer.

Greg's Spey Stone (Greg Senyo)

Hook: #4-8 upturned-eye salmon hook
Thread: Black 6/0 Uni-Thread
Body: Gray rabbit dubbing and black Larva Lace
Thorax: Pearl and blue Ice Dub
Wingcase: Black goose feather
Collar: Black and blue schlappen and two black goose biots

Note: Spey flies and fishing are very addictive, and so is drifting and tying stone fly nymphs for steelhead. This is my twist on the theme, mixing the two. This pattern produces extremely well when fished as a dropper off a marabou Spey or large minnow pattern.

Troutfitter Spey (Steve May)

Hook: #3 Bartleet
Thread: Black 6/0
Tag: Silver Mylar tinsel
Underbody: Silver Mylar tinsel
Abdomen: Chartreuse, fluorescent pink, or fluorescent orange Lazer Wrap
Body: Chartreuse, fluorescent pink, or fluorescent orange Estaz Chenille
Hackle: Mallard flank

Note: A high-water favorite. This one works well on rivers like the Saugeen and Maitland, when things are moving and there is about 1 1/2 to 3 feet of visibility in higher flows.

General Practitioner (Steve May)

Hook: Upturned-eye salmon hook
Thread: Black 6/0
Tail: Black bucktail
Body: Black seal fur dubbing
Hackle: Black rooster
Rib: Silver tinsel
Underwing: Golden pheasant tippet
Overwing: Black ringneck pheasant rump

Note: This pattern is a favorite swinging fly of many good steelheaders in Ontario.

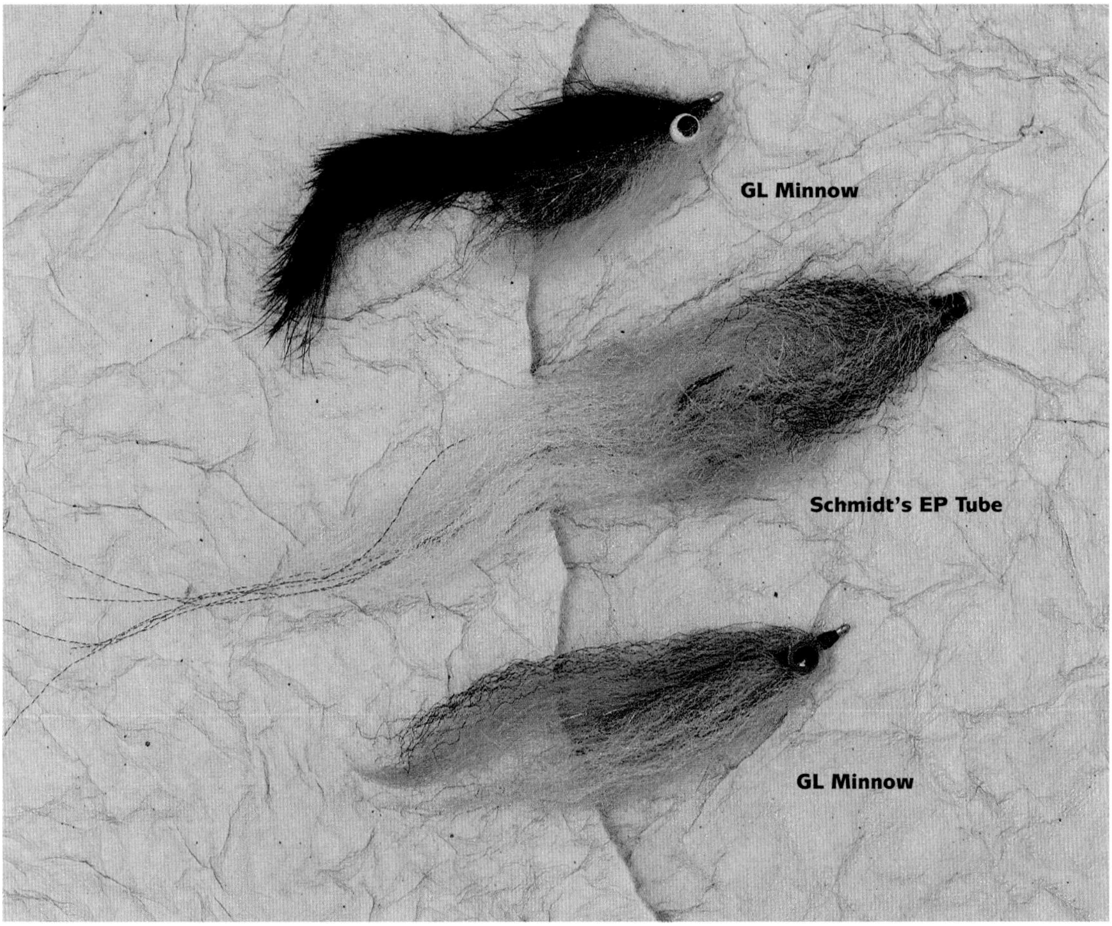

Schmidt's EP Tube (Mike Schmidt)

Hook: #4 red Eagle Claw, attached to tube
Thread: 3/0 Danville monocord
Tail/wing: Krystal Flash
Body: EP 3-D Fiber
Head: Built-up thread head

Note: This can be tied nearly weightless on a plastic tube or given significant weight by tying on a metal tube. Either way, the EP 3-D Fiber is tied in with the longest and lightest colored thread in the middle, out to the darkest and shortest threads on the outside.

Schmidt's GL Minnow (Mike Schmidt)

Hook: #1 Mustad 34007 or Daiichi 2546
Thread: 3/0 Danville monocord
Eyes: Large painted lead barbell eyes
Body: EP 3-D Fiber
Head: Built-up thread head

The EP Fiber is tied in with the lightest blend on the bottom, up to a dark blend for the back. This material sheds water on each backcast, so you can create a large fly that is light and easy to cast.

Big Black Tube (Steve May)

Tube:	$1^1/_2$ inch plastic
Bead:	Chartreuse Spirit River HotBead
Thread:	Black 6/0
Tail:	Black Zonker strip
Under Body:	Black Polar Chenille
Hackle:	Fluorescent blue, dark blue, or black marabou
Flash:	Purple Haze Flashabou
Collar:	Blue guinea

Note: In big water or dirty water this is a favorite to work deep down with a sinking tip.

Minnow Tube (Steve May)

Tube:	1 inch lined copper
Thread:	Fine monofilament
Body:	Pearl Angel Hair
Wing:	EP Fibers, gray over white
Hackle:	Grizzly on flank
Flash:	Angel Hair, pearl and silver
Eyes:	Silver 3D Epoxy Eyes

Note: A minnow pattern that has the advantages of a tube fly is a good addition to any steelhead box.

White Bunny Strip Streamer (Tom Harris)

Hook:	#8-12 Daiichi 1720 or equivalent
Bead:	Gold conehead
Thread:	White flat waxed nylon
Tail:	Eight to ten strands of pearl or gold Flashabou with rabbit strip over top
Body:	White Leech Yarn wrapped forward to one quarter of hook length
Thorax:	White Leech Yarn

Note: I push twelve wraps of wire into the back of the cone. After wrapping the body and tying off, form a loop with the thread and place some pulled-apart Leech Dubbing into it, and spin and wrap it forward to conehead. Then comb fibers back and trim if necessary. Do not make the rabbit strip too long or the fish will strike short, causing missed hookups. I also tie these in black, purple, and olive. This fly sinks quickly, while still retaining a lot of movement and attraction.

Muddy Water Streamer (Tom Harris)

Hook:	**#6-8 Daiichi 1720 or equivalent**
Bead:	**1/16-inch chartreuse HotBead**
Thread:	**Chartreuse**
Tail:	**Eight to ten strands of chartreuse or pearl Flashabou topped with chartreuse marabou**
Body:	**Cactus Chenille, medium pearl**
Hackle:	**Chartreuse Pseudo Hackle**

Note: Cut the hackle into a 3-inch tapered strip with the cross fibers removed, tied in, and wrapped forward. Place wraps one in front of the other. Do not wrap over or the fibers won't lie back properly.

Eggs

Fish eggs become a prime food source in rivers and streams when salmon, steelhead, and brown trout are spawning. Eggs from other species, such as suckers, also become food when they spawn. It seems that all lake-run species have a fondness for eating each other's eggs, and this behavior may also be attributed to imprinting when young.

Egg patterns duplicate a single egg or cluster of eggs and come in a wide range of neon and natural colors and sizes that can all catch fish. There are eggs made of silicone and other soft plastics, some made with colored beads, and still others made with hot-glue guns.

Larger egg and egg cluster patterns in sizes 8 and 10 are commonly used for salmon species, while sizes 10, 12, and 14 are more suitable for steelhead and brown trout. A size 14 Sucker Spawn is a staple fly along Lake Erie's south shore, and I even carry a few size 16s and 18s tied on Daiichi 1150 wide-gap, up-eye egg hooks for finicky steelhead.

The most common and commercially available type of egg pattern is the simple single-egg imitation, the common Glo-Bug, which probably catches more fish in the Great Lakes tribs than all other fly patterns combined. Available in all colors of the rainbow, Glo-Bugs carried in an array of sizes will let you match any Great Lakes egg hatch.

Omelets are Glo-Bugs tied with short rabbit strip tails, and Nuclear Eggs are basically Glo-Bugs that are veiled with another color. I categorize Glo-Spawns as an egg pattern tied Sucker-Spawn style using Glo-Bug material. Sucker Spawns are advancements of the old rug yarn fly, with the yarn material looped up the hook's shank to form a cluster of eggs. I like to mix colors and deviate from the solids found in most commercial patterns and fly shops.

Most Sucker Spawn–style flies are tied with strands of angora yarn, but a trip to a craft store can yield all types of acrylic and nylon materials that can be used to tie realistic, and not-so-realistic, egg patterns. The long fibers in angora yarn can cling to a fish's mouth, catching on teeth. You can sometimes watch the fish opening their mouths and shaking their heads trying to dislodge the fly. Time to set the hook, as steelhead can quickly engulf and spit out a fly. Angora can help you feel the take, however, giving you a better chance of sticking the fish.

Yarn balls are also used to tie single egg and egg cluster–type patterns. Some of the most realistic egg flies are fashioned with a hot-glue gun or using soft silicone rubber. The soft silicone eggs are also called Otter Eggs. Add beads to any egg pattern to increase sink rate and attraction.

Another popular style of egg pattern is the Blood Dot. A lot of steelheaders believe that a

A good selection of egg patterns should include small translucent and pastel colors for clear water, and large, bright, opaque patterns for stained water.

Blood Dot is just a Glo-Bug with another colored dot (or circle of color) in the middle of the egg. But the original, developed by Jeff Blood of Sewickley, Pennsylvania, is tied differently on a heavy wire scud hook, not an egg hook. Jeff stops the thread-wrapped base before the barb of the hook and splits strands of egg-colored Glo-Bug yarn to match the size of the hook being used. He makes what he calls two "bubbles" up the hook shank toward the hook eye with the strand of Glo-Bug yarn, before making a dot using a strand of apricot supreme Glo-Bug yarn that is lifted and snipped with scissors to form a yolk. The remaining strand of egg-colored yarn on which the yolk is tied is snipped off just behind the hook eye, saving the time needed to form more bubbles with the leftover material. The split material and tying sequence make a very translucent and realistic-looking egg pattern.

I let the current water conditions I'm facing that day determine what egg color and size I'm going to use. Big, bright, fluorescent colors, such as a combination of chartreuse and dark roe or hot pink and magenta, work great in low-visibility conditions, while softer, natural tones of cream and apricot work better in clear water conditions. You'll also catch more fish by matching the material density of the egg pattern to the current conditions. More material will give an egg pattern a denser, more opaque profile that is easier for fish to see in off-color conditions. A pattern using less material will give an egg pattern a lifelike translucency that is readily taken in clearer water conditions.

Many commercial egg patterns are tied with bright fluorescent pink or bright fluorescent orange thread, selling the angler but not the fish. These work when fishing higher water conditions, but I've found egg patterns tied with white, cream, tangerine, and other soft, pastel thread colors more productive when fishing clear water. The fish become conditioned to seeing the bright, commercially tied egg patterns flying by their heads and quickly become turned off by them.

In high water conditions with less than a foot of visibility, one of the first egg patterns I tie on is a size 8 or 10 chartreuse and dark roe Glo-Spawn, or a Nagy Glo-Bug Half & Half. When facing clear water conditions I prefer an egg pattern with more translucency. Using small amounts of Glo-Bug yarn looped onto a hook shank allows light to pass through the material, much like a real fish egg.

My go-to egg pattern, which has caught salmon, steelhead, and lake-run browns throughout the Great Lakes, is a simple Three-Loop Pink Lady (see pattern below) tied on a Tiemco 2488H egg hook, with chartreuse thread for dirty water and cream thread for clear water. By varying the amount of material, I can create a dense, opaque pattern that fish can see in stained water, or with smaller amounts of material, a translucent pattern that, when wet, looks just like a real glob of fish eggs.

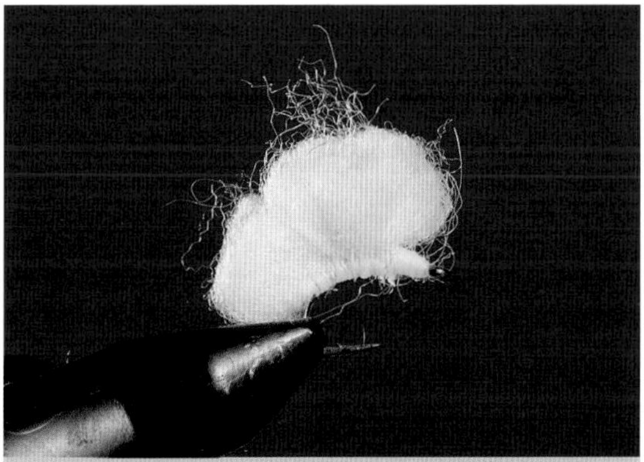

Three-Loop Pink Lady (Karl Weixlmann)

Hook: #10-16 Tiemco 2488H

Thread: Chartreuse 3/0 or 6/0 Danville

Body: Two strands of Pink Lady Glo-Bug yarn, stripped from skein and rolled or twisted, then looped three times up the hook shank. Use pieces of Glo-Bug yarn with the most orange coloration.

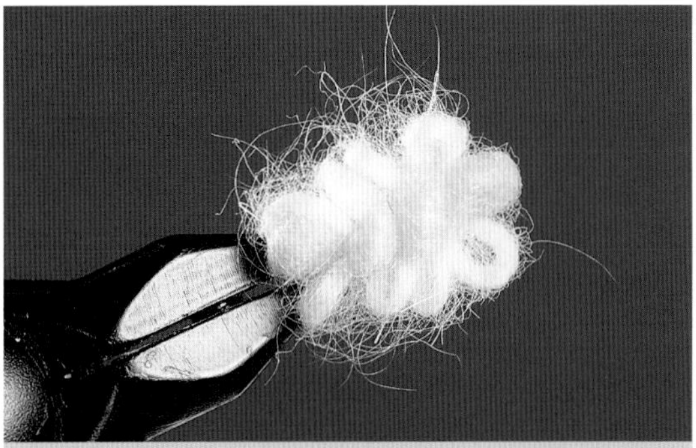

Cream, Orange, and White Sucker Spawn (Karl Weixlmann)

Hook: #10-16 Tiemco 2488H

Thread: Cream 3/0 or 6/0 Danville

Body: One strand of cream angora and one strand of white angora on the outside of one strand of apricot supreme micro Glo-Bug yarn, looped three times up hook shank

Note: A pearl Flashabou tail can be added to larger flies. These color combinations of angora and Glo-Bug yarn bleed together when wet, creating a realistic egg pattern.

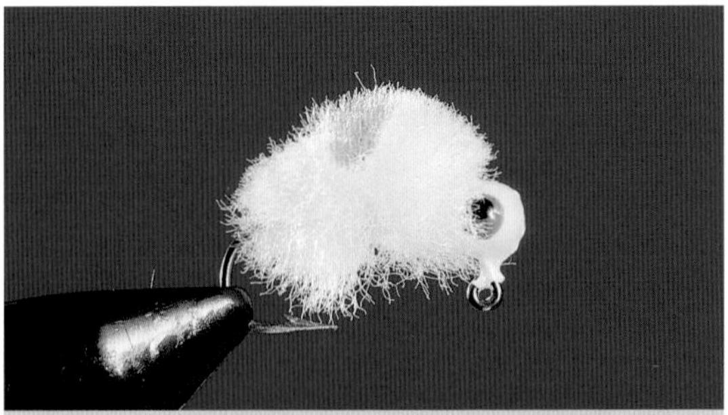

McMullen's Better Glo-Bug (Karl Weixlmann)

Hook: 1/32- 1/60-ounce painted or unpainted jig

Thread: To match egg color

Body: Glo-Bug yarn tied to shank and cut with scissors to form egg

Note: This egg, which I learned about from Pennsylvanian guide Joe McMullen, rides hook-point up when fished under an indicator, preventing snags. The light jighead gives the fly better depth penetration. You can vary jighead and body colors. After wrapping a thread base, use three loops of thread to attach material to shank, then circle thread around base of material. Next, wind thread in front of and behind material to keep it from sliding along hook shank. Lift material and clip with scissors to form egg.

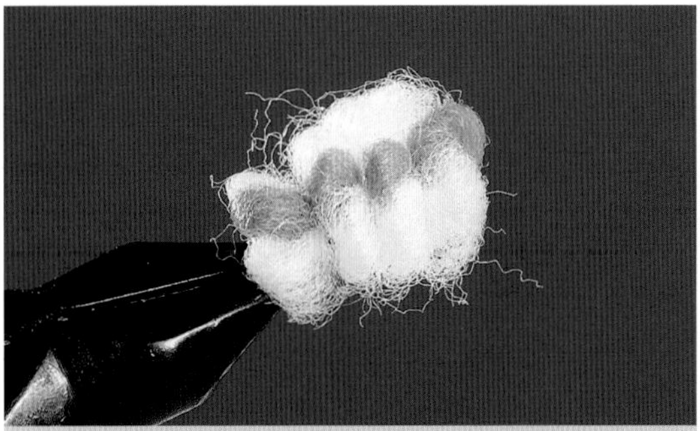

Half & Half Glo-Spawn (Karl Weixlmann)

Hook: #8-14 Tiemco 2488H

Thread: Chartreuse flat waxed nylon

Body: Two strands of chartreuse Glo-Bug yarn on the outside of one strand of Alaskan Roe Glo-Bug yarn, looped up the shank

Note: This is John Nagy's deadly dirty water combination tied like a sucker spawn egg fly.

Canadian Nuke Egg (Steve May)

Hook: #10-14 Daiichi 1150 or similar egg hook

Thread: Fluorescent orange 6/0

Wing: Oregon Cheese and Steelhead Orange Glo-Bug yarn

Note: This is a clear-water standout. It is great for fall fish but really shines in clear-water dropback fishing on rivers like the Saugeen and Maitland.

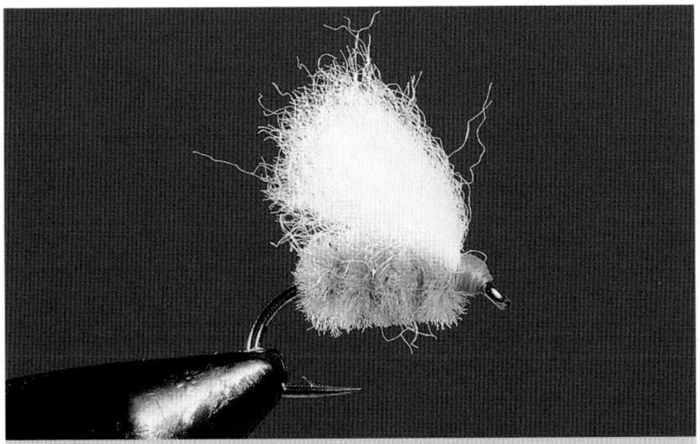

Flea (Steve May)

Hook:	#10-16 Mustad 3399 or equivalent
Thread:	To match chenille body
Body:	Orange, pink, or chartreuse chenille
Wing:	White or Oregon Cheese Glo-Bug yarn

Note: The Flea is a simple fly, and one that beginners can tie perfectly with even less practice than Glo-Bugs.

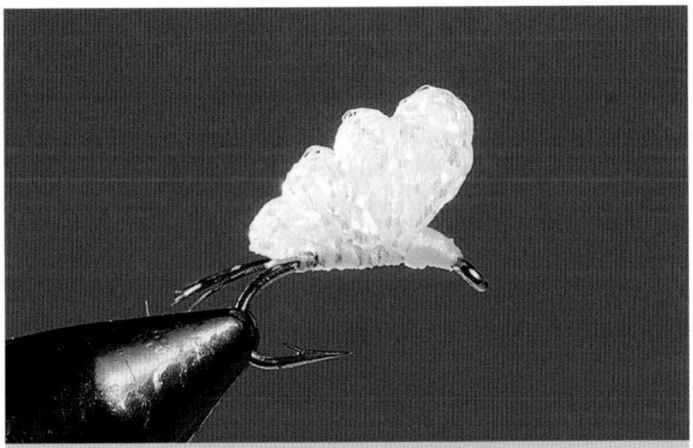

Crystal Meth (Todd Kaday)

Hook:	Daiichi 1150 or equivalent
Thread:	6/0 to match body
Tail:	Holographic Flash or Krystal Flash
Body:	Pearl, orange, chartreuse, or pink Diamond Braid, looped up hook shank

Note: Kaday, who now lives in the state of Washington, says that the steelhead were addicted to the fly when he first tried it, hence the name.

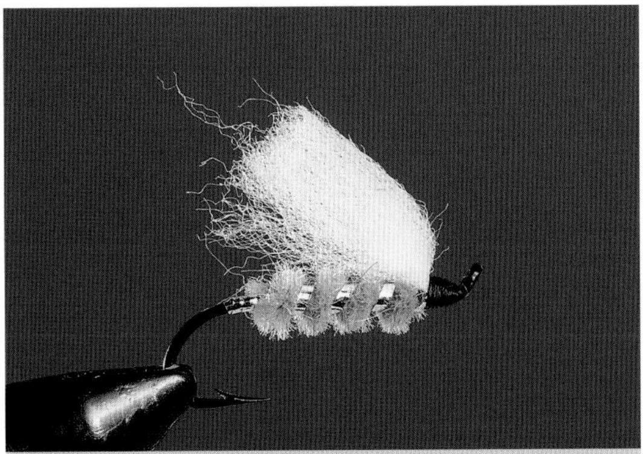

Frammus (Steve May)

Hook:	#8-14 wet fly hook
Tag:	Mylar tinsel (silver)
Body:	Orange, pink, or chartreuse chenille
Rib:	Mylar tinsel
Wing:	White or Oregon Cheese Glo-Bug yarn

Note: For those who look down on all egg flies, this one has a wing, body, and rib. It is effective in higher flows when you need more attracting power and visibility than a Glo-Bug offers.

Nymphs

Stoneflies, caddisflies, and mayflies are common invertebrates found throughout Great Lakes tributaries. After learning of an increase in wild steelhead propagation found in the Cattaraugus system in 1996 and the ability of juvenile steelhead to imprint on various invertebrate food forms, I started sampling invertebrates along south shore Lake Erie tributaries, from Cattaraugus Creek in New York to the Grand River in Ohio. Of all the tributaries I sampled in the region, the Catt had the largest population of invertebrates, including golden stoneflies, *Isonychia* mayflies, and several species of caddis.

The largest invertebrates I have found in local tributaries were golden stoneflies and hellgrammites, primarily on the Catt, but also appearing in good numbers on both Conneaut Creek and the Grand River in Ohio, with the hellgrammites much fewer in number than the goldens in these

Nymph patterns work great on pressured fish that are used to seeing bright egg patterns.

locations. Some of these stonefly nymphs were almost as long as my thumb, with a dark, mottled brown back and a light, creamy yellow abdomen. The Catt Gold Nugget was born of these samplings. I've also found golden stones that have a lighter-colored exoskeleton and back, due to molting.

In addition to stoneflies, caddis are also abundant. Imitations of green-bodied caddis species should be in every Great Lakes fly box. Crooked Creek, near the Ohio border, turned up a lot of these green caddis that have black heads, and I've since found them in just about every tributary that I've fished. The abdomen color of this net-building (noncased) caddis looks like a combination of olive and chartreuse, not the insect-green usually seen in other caddis patterns. The Crooked Creek Caddis was inspired by this sampling and produces fish throughout the Great Lakes.

Many Pennsylvania tributaries are sterile by comparison with others in the Great Lakes area. Shale bottoms and seasonal ice scouring do not bode well for invertebrate habitat, though there

Mayfly nymphs are easy to imitate with a Pheasant-Tail Nymph. ALAN CARTER PHOTO

Black and blue are effective color combinations for streamers and nymphs, like this Black and Blue Electric Stone.

The metabolism of lake-run species slows down during the winter. Nymph patterns duplicate food sources that are found in the tributaries. STEVE MAY PHOTO

are good winter and early spring hatches of tiny black stones that make nearby snowbanks look as though they were sprinkled with a pepper shaker. Black stones ranging in sizes from 8 to 18 are essential components of any Great Lakes nymph box. I substitute a simple black Axxel Flash Hare's Ear for most of my dark stonefly imitations.

Greg Senyo's stonefly patterns are designed to more accurately represent the natural. According to Senyo, "Standard patterns fail to mimic a stonefly's movements and only key on the natural in color and size. Stoneflies, once dislodged from the riverbed, do not just suspend and float in the river's current. In fact, they frantically wiggle side-to-side and up-and-down in search of any structure to grab onto. Picture yourself falling from a 100-story building, trying desperately to grab for anything to stop your fall. You are not just calmly falling to the ground, are you? A stonefly, caught in the current of one of our tributaries or western rivers is no different. I developed this pattern to be universal across the Great Lakes and its tributaries, along with our frontier streams to the west, and our famous New York and Pennsylvanian trout streams. With its impressionistic looks and natural movements even the most lethargic and dormant steelhead and trout are instinctively triggered to react. And by simply changing the pattern's color and size, it becomes effective in all seasons and streams conditions." (See Senyo's patterns on pages 116, 118, and 121.)

The importance of midges, specifically chironomids, or bloodworms, is generally overlooked by most Great Lakes fly fishers, but I've had great success fishing with these tiny patterns in the dead of winter when a steelhead's metabolism slows to a standstill.

I almost always incorporate weight into a nymph pattern with either a bead or lead or wire wraps, or both. Even with a bead, I wrap lead wire around the front half of the shank and shove it into the bead opening, adding bulk to the thorax section. I probably use a beaded pattern for 95 percent of my nymphing. When fishing tandems with an egg above the nymph, the weight of the bead helps sink the nymph under the egg during the drift. An unweighted nymph will swirl the nymph around the egg during the drift. You need that added depth penetration to keep the nymph drifting near the stream bottom. In ultraclear water conditions, switching to a beadless nymph can generate hookups on wary fish.

Axxel Flash Hare's Ear (Karl Weixlmann)

Hook:	#8-16 Mustad Signature R72
Thread:	Black 3/0 or 6/0 Danville
Tail:	Black rabbit guard hair
Rib:	Two split strands of black Axxel Flash, twisted
Wingcase:	Two lengths of black Axxel Flash
Legs:	Picked-out black rabbit
Head:	Black or gold bead, sized to hook

Note: The Hare's Ear has always been a universal fish catcher. In the black version, I substitute black Axxel Flash for the rib and wingcase. This is a synthetic multistrand material that comes in spools. This fly can be tied with a variety of flash and dubbing colors.

Catt Gold Nugget (Karl Weixlmann)

Hook:	#8-14 Mustad Signature R72
Thread:	Brown, tan, or chartreuse 3/0 or 6/0 Danville
Tail:	Pheasant biots splayed over pre-dubbed abdomen hump, or brown speckled Hungarian partridge
Rib:	Gold, brown, or chartreuse wire
Back:	Mottled turkey, lacquered and folded
Abdomen and thorax:	Orvis Antron blend, golden stone or cream angora mix
Wingcase:	Mottled turkey, lacquered and folded
Legs:	Folded or wrapped partridge, speckled brown
Head:	Gold tungsten bead, sized to hook

Note: I developed this golden stonefly pattern to imitate the many nymphs I sampled in 1996 on both Cattaraugus and Conneaut Creeks and on the Grand River. The actual bug has a thorax section with three segments, but I don't waste time duplicating that, preferring a representative pattern that has a dark brown, mottled back and a light, cream-colored belly. I don't think fish count thorax segments. It works throughout the Great Lakes region wherever goldens are found and even where they're not. I also tie a Chartreuse Nugget, substituting chartreuse rabbit or similar chartreuse dubbing for the abdomen and thorax, for greater visibility in stained water. To ease the process and shorten the time required when tying some stonefly patterns, I substitute a dark, soft-hackled or rabbit-fur tail instead of using cumbersome goose biots that are often hard to align. This also gives the nymph more movement in the water.

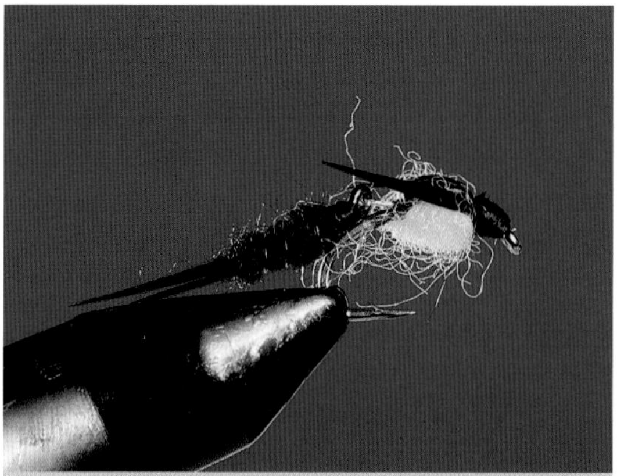

Senyo's Wiggle Stone (Greg Senyo)

Front and thorax

Hook: #10-16 Daiichi X120

Thread: Black 6/0 Uni-Thread

Tail: Two black goose biots

Thorax: Hareline Ice Dub in blue, orange, chartreuse, purple, pink, peacock, flashback, or cream

Wingcase: Pearl Flashabou or black electrical tape

Legs: Two black goose biots

Tail section

Hook: #12-16 Mustad 3906 cut at the bend

Body: Black seal or rabbit dubbing

Rib: 4-pound monofilament

Note: This is my go-to nymph, and number-one steelhead producer, mimicking the natural movements that steelhead key in on. I always carry a wide selection of them in different colors, and my largest steelhead each year is usually caught on this pattern. Connect tail to thorax by forming a loop with 12-pound Fireline or 8-pound fluorocarbon. Make sure to leave loop just wide enough to give tail free swimming motion.

Senyo's Steak and Eggs (Greg Senyo)

Hook: #10-14 Daiichi X120

Thread: Black 6/0 Uni-Thread

Tail: Two black goose biots

Body: Black Larva Lace (medium)

Thorax: Peacock Ice Dub

Legs: Two black goose biots

Head: Any color egg yarn or McFly Foam

Yoke or post: White or cream egg yarn and pearl Krystal Flash

Note: I developed this fly for when water conditions are very low in the spring. I like to fish this pattern for steelhead in swift water, with my favorite size 14. Tie in the yoke long with Krystal Flash and hold tightly to the side with hackle pliers. Once the egg has been trimmed, pull the yoke back to the top and trim, leaving 1/4 inch or higher than egg, and fan out material.

EZ Hex (Jerry Darkes)

Hook:	#8-10 Daiichi 1710 or TMC 200R
Thread:	Brown 3/0
Tail:	Gray ostrich herl; do not trim long end
Rib:	Gold or copper wire
Body:	Dirty yellow dubbing with long ends of ostrich herl pulled over top
Hackle:	Two to three turns of pheasant rump
Eyes:	Small plastic bead chain

Note: This is a quick and easy Hex pattern that works. In smaller sizes, this pattern also imitates brown drakes.

JQ Caddis (Jerry Darkes)

Hook:	#10-14 Daiichi 1120
Thread:	Chartreuse 3/0 or 6/0 Danville
Body:	Chartreuse stretch tubing or Jelly Cord
Head:	Black dubbing
Bead:	1/8 or 3/32 inch

Note: This imitates any of the green-bodied caddis larvae. The larger sizes are more productive in the western Great Lakes; use smaller sizes in eastern Great Lakes.

Crooked Creek Caddis (Karl Weixlmann)

Hook:	#10-18 Tiemco 2457
Thread:	Chartreuse 6/0 Danville
Body:	Dubbed chartreuse and olive rabbit, mixed
Hackle:	Dark, webby soft-hackle on larger sizes
Thorax/ head:	Black dubbed rabbit
Bead:	Black, sized to hook

Note: This is a good, all-purpose, olive-and-green-bodied caddis imitation. Naturals assume a curved shape when tumbling downstream. No need for a soft-hackle on smaller sizes.

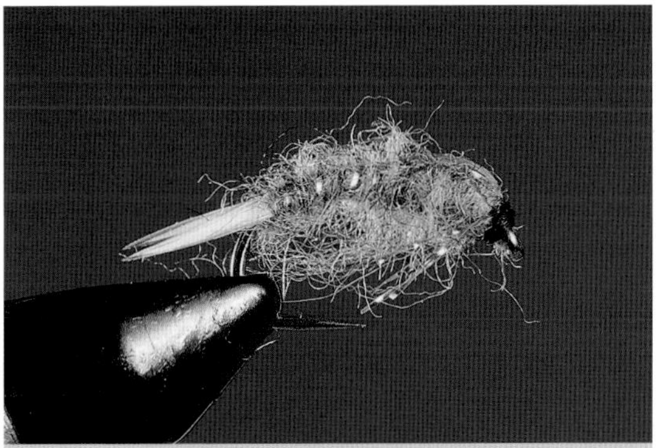

Rolling Stone (Jerry Darkes)

Hook:	#10-14 Daiichi 1120
Thread:	Black or light brown 3/0 or 6/0 Danville
Tail:	Black, brown, or amber goose biots
Rib:	Root beer or olive Krystal Flash
Body:	Black, brown, or golden stonefly blend
Wingcase:	Root beer or olive Krystal Flash
Legs:	Several Krystal Flash fibers from wingcase, tied back and trimmed short

Note: This is a good, general stonefly pattern with some extra flash for off-color water.

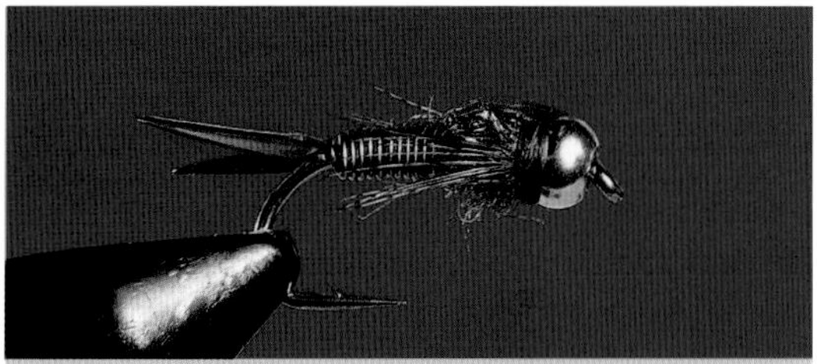

Steely John (Steve May)

Hook: Mustad R72 or equivalent heavy nymph
Thread: Black 6/0
Bead: Brass
Tail: Goose biots (olive, black, brown, or chartreuse)
Abdomen: Ultra Wire (olive, copper, black, or chartreuse)
Wingcase: Thin Skin and pearl Mylar
Thorax: Peacock herl
Hackle: Hungarian partridge

Note: A steelhead version of the ever-popular Copper John. I have used this with success around the lakes and on both shores. This fly can save the day in pocketwater holes that require you to get the fly down pronto.

Full Motion Hex (Steve May)

Hook: 2XL streamer
Thread: Black 6/0
Bead: Brass, matched to hook size
Tail: Cream Zonker strip
Rear hackle: Hungarian partridge
Rib: Pearl Flashabou
Body: Tan or ginger Antron-blend dubbing
Front hackle: Hungarian partridge
Collar: Black rabbit dubbing

Note: This is my favorite steelhead nymph. This versatile performer with movement catches fish when other flies fail.

Terminator Nymph (Steve May)

Hook: 3XL streamer
Thread: Black 6/0
Bead: Brass
Tail: Black goose biots
Underbody: Lead wire
Body: Black chenille or peacock herl
Hackle: Black saddle, trimmed
Flash: Holographic Mylar

Note: A heavily weighted nymph can substitute for split-shot and is especially effective in pocketwater on rivers like the Bighead. This fly can be tied in olive, purple, and peacock as well.

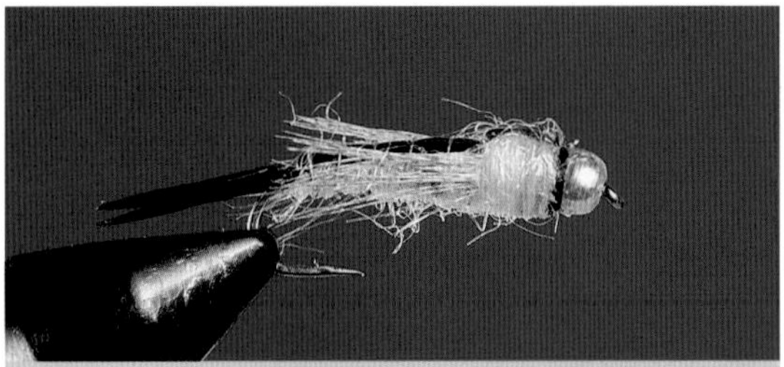

Senyo's Steely ISO (Greg Senyo)

Hook: #12-16 Daiichi X710
Bead: Silver or black, matched to hook size
Thread: Black 6/0 Uni-Thread
Tail: Two black goose biots
Body: Pearl UV Ice Dub
Rib: Fine silver wire
Wingcase: Black electrical tape and holographic tinsel
Legs: Gadwall feather tips

Note: I created the In Stead Of (ISO) nymph to offer high-pressured steelhead a new look instead of all the standard patterns used traditionally, day-in and day-out, on our tributaries. This has been one of my save-the-day patterns for the past few years.

Steelhead Prince (Steve May)

Hook: Mustad Signature R72 or equivalent
Thread: Black 6/0
Bead: Brass
Tail: Brown goose biots
Rib: Pearl Krystal Flash
Body: Peacock herl
Hackle: Brown hen
Wing: White goose biots

Note: This fly is especially effective on pressured fish sulking in fast water.

Antron Bug (Steve May)

Hook: Tiemco 2487
Thread: Tan 6/0
Body: Small tan Estaz
Wingcase: Tan Antron yarn
Eyes: Black monofilament

Note: This fly is a good Mysis imitation or a general light-colored attractor nymph. The mono eyes seem to attract attention when other nymphs are ignored.

Steelhead Pheasant Tail (Steve May)

Hook: Daiichi 1150 or similar egg hook
Thread: Black or brown 6/0
Tail: Pheasant tail fibers
Rib: Fine copper wire
Body: Pheasant tail fibers, wrapped around hook shank
Thorax: Peacock herl

Note: This fly works in a variety of conditions. A flashback and bead are good additions to this fly, and the larger hook helps with hooking and holding steelhead.

Black and Blue Electric Stone (Karl Weixlmann)

Hook: #10-14 Mustad Signature R72
Thread: Black 6/0 Danville
Tail: Black goose biots, splayed over pre-dubbed abdomen; or substitute black soft-hackles
Rib: Two strands of electric blue Fire Fly Tie, twisted
Abdomen: Dubbed black rabbit
Thorax: Dubbed black rabbit
Wingcase: Electric blue Fire Fly Tie, folded and epoxied
Legs: Two turns of black, soft hackle
Head: Black bead, sized to hook

Gold-Bodied Beadhead Stonefly (Tom Harris)

Hook:	#12-16 Daiichi 1260 or equivalent
Bead:	Gold
Thread:	Tan
Tail:	Tan biots
Body:	Gold D-Rib
Wingpad:	Turkey tail
Thorax:	Tannish dubbing
Legs:	Partridge, or any mottled soft-hackle, tied out the sides

Note: The D-Rib tubing stretches (no bulk at the tie-in) and gives great body segmentation.

Gold Caddis Goo Bug (Tom Harris)

Hook:	#12-14 Daiichi 1120 or equivalent
Bead:	Gold
Thread:	Tan
Body:	Gold D-Rib, with pearl Flashabou underbody
Thorax:	Gold/rust Super Brite dubbing or equivalent
Hackle:	Gold Pseudo Hackle

Note: The Flashabou underbody gives the D-Rib body a little flash, and the Pseudo Hackle, with its trilobal fibers, gives a bright sheen to it. This fly works great in deeper water or when the streams are getting off-colored.

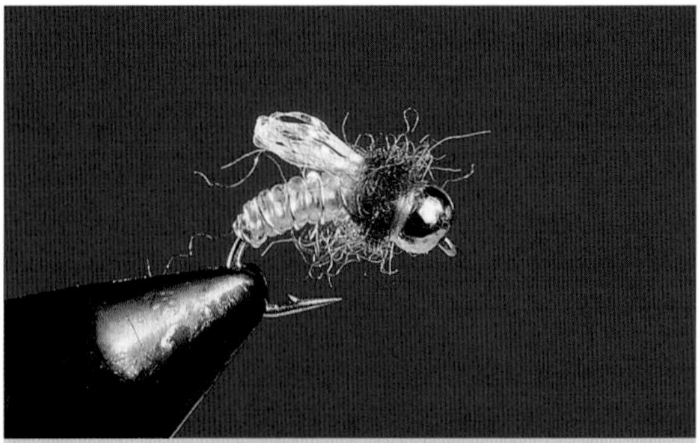

Zebra Midge (Tom Harris)

Hook:	#12-16 Daiichi 1120 or equivalent
Bead:	Gold
Thread:	Brown
Tail:	Pearl Krystal Flash
Rib:	Silver or gold wire
Body:	Brown midge tubing
Wingcase:	Three to four strands of pearl Krystal Flash
Collar:	Brown Super Brite dubbing

Note: You can tie this in various colors. My favorites are a black with silver bead and a pheasant-tail abdomen with gold bead.

Viagra Caddis (Steve May)

Hook:	#12-14 Daiichi 1150
Bead:	Brass
Thread:	Black 6/0
Tail/ abdomen:	Olive, chartreuse, or brown Ultra Chenille
Thorax:	Black seal fur dubbing or peacock Ice Dub

Steelie Soft-Hackle (Karl Weixlmann)

Hook:	#10-16 Mustad Signature R72
Thread:	Olive 6/0 Danville
Tail:	Five or six speckled Hungarian partridge fibers topped with two strands of olive Krystal Flash
Rib:	Two strands of olive Krystal Flash, twisted
Body:	Dubbed olive rabbit
Hackle:	Two or three turns of speckled Hungarian partridge

Notes: This great low-water fall and cold-winter-water pattern can be tied in various shades and colors for different water conditions. The pulsating, webby soft-hackles provide movement. Effective when swung, dead-drifted under an indicator, or bottom-bounced. It can also be tied with a bead, but I don't use the bead when fishing over pressured fish.

Senyo's Shrimp Scampi (Greg Senyo)

Hook:	#10-14 Daiichi X120
Thread:	White 6/0 Uni-Thread
Body:	Pearl UV Ice Dub
Case:	Olive Midge Flash
Tentacles:	UV Pearl Ice Dub, tied as a wing and brushed out, and two strands of olive/chartreuse Krystal Flash
Eyes:	Mono eyes, large to medium, or bead chain

Note: This is my spin on a Mysis shrimp imitation, which is tied much larger than the natural. This pattern fishes best as a tandem rig, running two Scampi between 8 and 12 inches apart, on the swing or drifted through fast water and pools. Wrap light wire around middle of eyes and twist until tight to eyes, then tie onto hook half the width of hook away. Dub the wire before you add the Krystal Flash tentacles.

Steelhead Woolly Worm (Steve May)

Hook:	#8-12 nymph hook
Thread:	Black 6/0
Tail:	Red hackle fibers
Tag:	Hot red chenille
Body:	Chartreuse chenille
Hackle:	Grizzly
Back:	Peacock herl

Tiny Winter Black (Steve May)

Hook:	Tiemco 2487
Thread:	Black 6/0
Tail:	Black hackle fibers
Body:	Black rabbit dubbing
Wingcase:	Black hackle
Thorax:	Black hackle

Note: This fly is effective on clear-water streams in winter and early spring.

Peacock Nymph (Steve May)

Hook:	Daiichi 1150 egg hook
Thread:	Black 6/0
Body:	Peacock herl
Rib:	Copper wire
Hackle:	Starling or small black hen neck

Note: This clear-water stonefly is especially good in cold water and for lethargic fish.

Possum Nymph (Steve May)

Hook:	#8-14 nymph
Thread:	Black 6/0
Bead:	Brass, sized to hook
Tail:	Australian possum
Rib:	Mylar tinsel, pearl
Hackle:	Hungarian partridge
Collar:	Black rabbit dubbing

CHAPTER FIVE

Techniques

Matching the technique with the water type and conditions to get a good drift is the primary challenge of all Great Lakes dead-drift nymph presentations, including sliding a slinky, indicator nymphing, and high-sticking. For streamer and swinging presentations, angle and depth are critical. The following methods of fly presentation will catch all lake-run species in a variety of water conditions.

Sliding a Slinky

A deep- and fast-water dead-drifting technique can work wonders on large or medium-size rivers and during high-water conditions on smaller streams.

The effectiveness of a slinky rig fished dead-drift was emphatically driven home for me one overcast November morning on Cattaraugus Creek in southwestern New York, by Dr. Evan Morse from Cleveland, Ohio. Evan gave me a

Above: Learning how and when to mend the fly line is essential for tributary fly-fishing success.

Steer fish away from underwater obstructions by moving the rod to the side. Then drop the rod tip perpendicular to the water to reduce the upward angle of the leader as it slices through the water. This will help reduce abrasion on the tippet material should the fish run under a boulder or a downed tree.

look of despair when viewing the high water that had only 6 inches of visibility, but I assured him that steelhead could still be caught.

The high water had fish on the move, and I chose a run of heavy water just upstream from a large bend pool in which to start fishing. With his extensive Michigan steelheading background, Evan broke out the running lines and slinky rigs and proceeded to pound the steelhead moving up through the run with a Worm Fly, which looks like a neon San Juan Worm.

The Rig

Michigan steelheaders developed running-line rigs to obtain optimal depth penetration when presenting a fly, and these are rigged with lead shot, pencil lead, or slinkies (shot placed and sealed in parachute cord) on the leader. They can really save the day during high water and have become a staple of fly presentation on larger watersheds, like the Salmon River in New York and the Muskegon River in Michigan, where the fly needs to get down into deep pockets and runs that contain short drifts.

Dry-line steelheaders may have an aversion to handling so much lead (hence the chuck-and-duck nickname for this method), and you can rest assured that the technique has nothing to do with conventional fly casting, in which the weight of the line carries the fly. In this case, the weight on the leader carries the line, as in conventional spinning or baitcasting.

Running lines (also called shooting lines) are thin, nontapered lines manufactured in several dif-

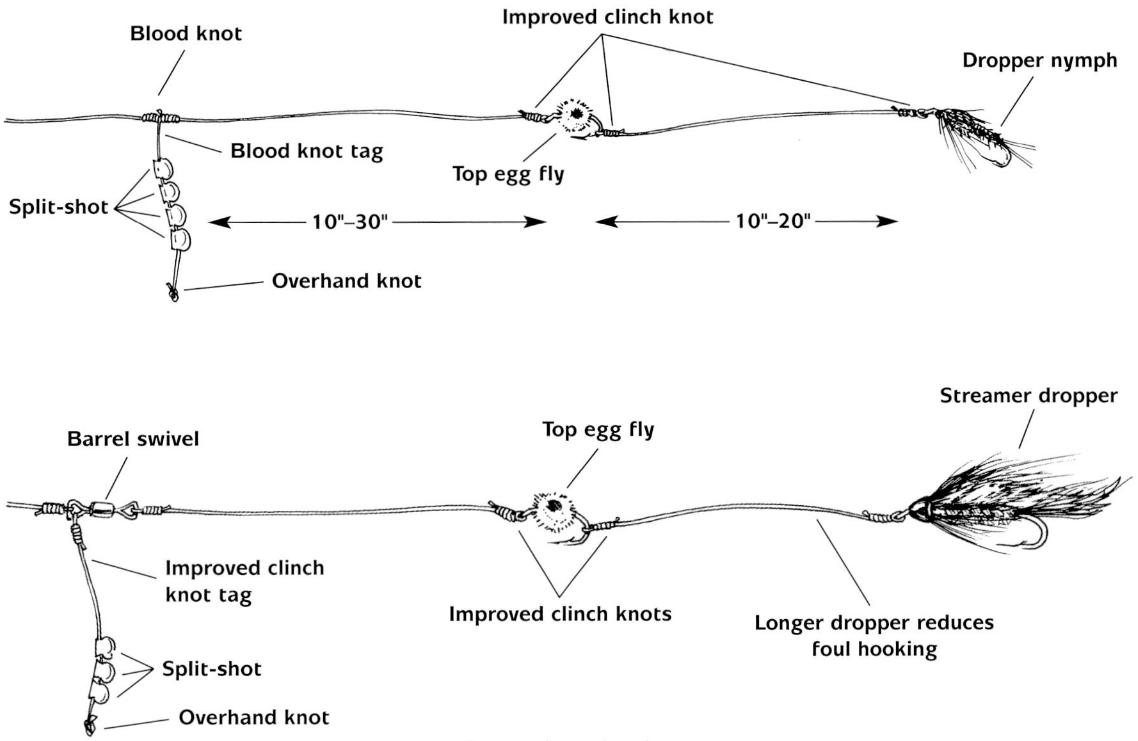

Bottom-bouncing rigs

ferent forms. Heavy, 20- to 30-pound colored nylon line called Amnesia is one variety. Single-strand mono core with a nylon coating is another. Some anglers use Dacron backing as a running line. I prefer a thin, level floating fly line with a braided nylon core that can double as an indicator line when used with long, noodle-type fly rods. They handle a little more like a real fly line and do not tangle as much.

3M Scientific Anglers makes several great products for these applications that are designed for casting with split-shot into the deep, fast runs in which steelhead and salmon hold. Diameters range from .031 to .042. Shooting lines with hard PVC coatings and braided cores are slightly stiffer, tangle less, and handle more like traditional fly lines. Fewer tangles mean less downtime, leading to more hookups. This 100-foot line can also be reversed on the reel for several added years of use.

This buck ate a chartreuse and orange Glo-Spawn in high water conditions.

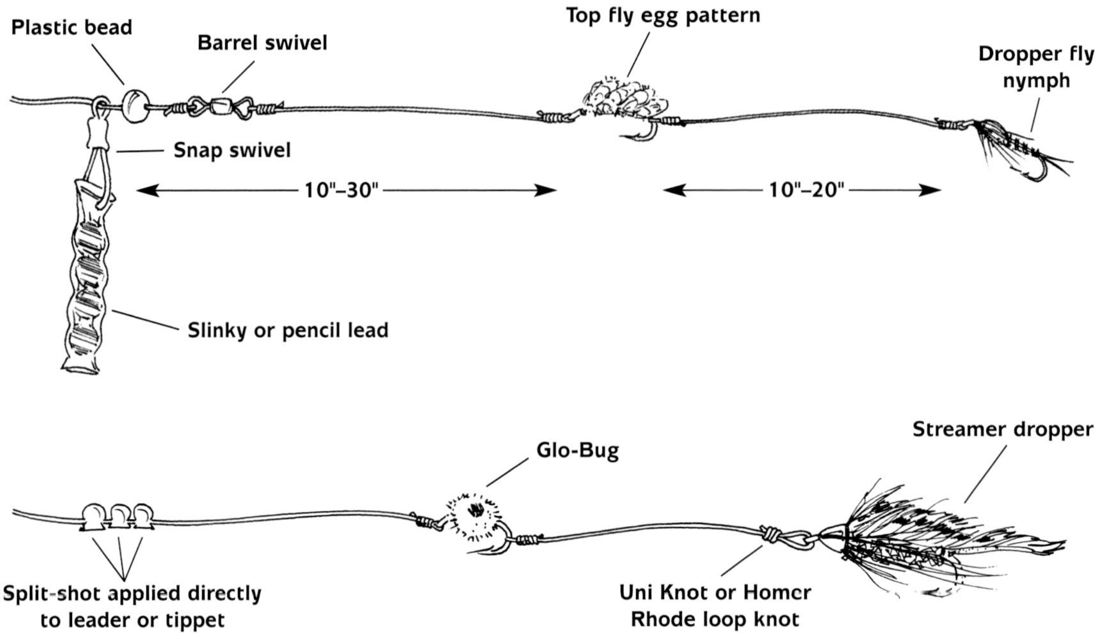

Bottom-bouncing rigs

Nail knot 8 to 12 feet of 0X nylon (monofilament) or fluorocarbon to the end of the running line, and tie it to a two-way barrel swivel with an improved clinch knot. A stiff, abrasion resistant material, like Maxima Green or Chameleon, is good for bottom-bouncing techniques. Some anglers like to use a 24- to 36-inch length of 20- or 25-pound fluorescent red Amnesia as a butt section to help follow the drift and detect strikes.

You can then attach split-shot to the knot's tag end, which should be left about 3 inches long. An overhand knot at the tag end of this dropper helps prevent the shot from easily sliding off. Then knot a 2- to 3-foot length of lighter tippet to the other end of the barrel swivel, and add to it one or two flies. One advantage of this method is that if you are snagged on the bottom, the shot will sometimes pull off, saving the flies.

Another method is to attach a slinky to the leader before tying it to the barrel swivel and attaching the tippet material. Place a small bead on the leader to keep the slinky from fouling and subsequently weakening the knot at the barrel swivel. The slinky slides freely up and down the leader, with a swivel clip or eyelet. Similar pencil-lead attachments can also be used.

Weighting is simple in principal, and you should constantly adjust it. Determine the size of the slinky by the water depth and speed: more weight for deeper, faster water and less weight for slower, shallower water. I still laugh when I think of the day Bill Belden and Mike Brenner used common washers when we ran out of heavy shot. It was the only thing that could get us on the bottom in a deep, fast run that plunged into a corner pool, and we did not want to leave the river. We hung the washers from the leader with a mono dropper. This rig worked wonders. We had fewer hang-ups, and the takes were hard and aggressive—at least with this particular pod of fresh-run chromers.

Technique

Start by positioning yourself slightly upstream and across from the section of water you want to cover. Strip enough line off the reel to accomplish the cast and feed the drift. Cast far enough upstream to start making bottom contact as the drift comes in front of you. Immediately after the cast, feed slack into the drift, and mend upstream to sink your fly.

Lift the rod and come tight to the drift. As the drift comes in front of you, you'll want to start feeling contact with the bottom and start the slide, feeling the ticking on the bottom with your rod tip. By reaching out with the rod and high-sticking, you'll remove drag and snag less often. The drift speed should be two or three times slower than the surface current speed, giving fish holding tight to the bottom time to inspect the presentation.

Lifting and dropping the rod will help slide and maneuver the slinky rig into likely holding areas on the river bottom. Most takes come at the end of the drift because this is where the fly obtains maximum depth and also a perfect dead-drift. Takes can be rod-dropping savage or as light as a pause in the drift. Set the hook downstream if the drift feels unnatural, pauses, or throbs, and if you no longer feel that tick, tick, tick on the rod. Sometimes a steelhead will suddenly, and surprisingly, just be there at the end of the drift. You can extend the drift by bending your body at the waist and bowing downstream while feeding line into the drift. With this technique, fly fishers have the opportunity to catch Great Lakes steelhead, salmon, and trout previously untouched with traditional fly-fishing techniques.

Learning how the weight responds to the rod takes time, and softer-tipped rods can help. With this much weight on the leader, a cast is really nothing more than using the rod tip to propel the weight. Letting the weight touch the water's surface behind me, I like to throw a little line out downstream over my left shoulder and toward the bank when the current is moving from right to left (being right-handed) and then use the weight and water behind me to load the rod and propel the cast up and across. For longer casts you might have to double-haul.

A Note on Lead

Lead is toxic, and its use or purchase has been banned in some Great Lakes regions, notably New York and Canadian national parks and wildlife areas.

Some interesting new substitutes are available for fly fishers looking for environmentally friendly alternatives, such as tin, tungsten, and lead-free soft weights. The Toobies Shot System from Skip's Original Products incorporates steel shot inserted into a clear plastic tube that you slide onto the leader. Orvis, BossTin, Dinsmore, and Innovative Angler all have lead-free weight products. Attach lead-free putties and soft weights to the leader at the tippet knot to prevent sliding. By removing or adding a pinch of putty, you control the speed and depth to which the fly sinks.

Indicator Nymphing

This is a moderate to deep dead-drifting technique for large and small tributaries in various water conditions.

A hot Indian summer had settled down upon the Salmon River in upstate New York. The river was low and clear, and the hoped-for cold front and wet weather never arrived. The famed Douglaston Salmon Run, a pay-access area on the lower river, yielded no sign of the whitewater explosions that would indicate a run of king salmon coming in. An earlier run of king salmon and Skamania steelhead had already run the river and settled in

Indicator Nymphing: Creating a Dead-Drift

Get into position slightly up- and across stream from where the fish is holding. Make a quartering up- and across-stream cast.

Lift the rod between the 9 and 10 o'clock position and mend upstream, with a lift and flick of the wrist and forearm.

The end of the mend places the fly line upstream from the indicator, reducing drag and allowing the fly to sink before the start of the dead-drift. The indicator is now pointing downstream and lying on its side.

As the indicator drifts in front of you, recover slack line with your left hand. Mend upstream as needed to sink the fly, especially in fast water. (continued on page 130)

Indicator Nymphing: Creating a Dead-Drift (continued from page 129)

Extend the rod and follow the indicator with the rod tip. The indicator should start to go vertical as your body pivots to follow the drift.

Continue to follow the indicator with the rod tip as it drifts downstream from you. The indicator has now gone completely vertical, with the fly drifting just off the bottom and at a 90-degree angle beneath it. Takes are most likely to occur from this point on. The indicator should drift smoothly through the holding water without line manipulation.

Start to drop the rod tip as your body continues to pivot, and follow the drift downstream. If the fly line ever gets even with, or downstream from, the indicator, you may need to mend upstream to ensure a drag-free drift. You may also need to check the indicator, stopping or slowing its progress during the drift with the rod tip to ensure that the fly hangs beneath the indicator at a 90-degree angle.

Drop your rod tip to the water as you follow the indicator. Mend the line downstream onto the slower water closest to you to extend the drift. Slack-line stack mending—where the line is fed and flipped off the end of the rod tip and onto the water's surface—can also help extend the drift.

(continued on page 132)

Indicator Nymphing: Creating a Dead-Drift ((continued from page 131)

The current pulls and straightens out the belly in the fly line made by the downstream mend. Another series of downstream mends can continue the drift until you run out of current and the fly swings below your position. The longer the fly is in the water, the more likely a fish will have a chance to see it. Often the fly will be taken as it rises off the bottom at the end of the drift.

to the flies-only zone upstream of the Altmar bridge, so my fishing buddy Alan Carter and I drove up the river.

Sure enough, we spotted some steelhead holding in the deep tailout of the Cemetery Pool, in the upper end of the lower flies-only zone. The pool immediately above the bridge was lined with fly anglers giving the ol' heave-ho with running lines and lead and occasionally foul-hooking kings holding in the deep, slow center of the pool.

Walking up the east bank with an 8-weight rod set up for dry-line steelhead nymphing, I was surprised to find no one fishing at the head of the pool, where the water plunged in through several deep troughs. I had at least 30 feet of streambank to work with—almost unheard of on the Salmon River. I thought I'd give it a try here before moving upriver to the tailout of the Cemetery Pool. If there were steelhead holding just upriver, there might also be some holding here.

Nymphal shucks covered the rocks near the water's edge, so I set up with a size 12 Catt Gold Nugget nymph on a 10 1/2-foot leader with a 3X, 8-pound tippet. Using a large high-density foam indicator to float the amount of shot needed for depth penetration in the deep slot, I lobbed a cast, quartering up- and across stream. Three mends and a lift of the rod later, I watched the float plunge near the end of the drift.

I swung the rod hard downstream over my right shoulder and felt a thumping, shaking head. Visions of my first Skamania danced in my head as I fought the fish downriver, landing it near another angler who happened to have a scale. I reached down and pulled the nymph from the corner of the mouth of a 17-pound king salmon!

Just to make sure it wasn't a fluke, I went back to the head of the hole and hooked five more fish. Most simply beat me up on the light tackle. All of them gave a good dunk and were hooked firmly inside the corner of the mouth. All were king salmon. I was shocked, but it made sense. It was a totally different presentation with a totally different fly pattern that the fish had not seen before. The lesson is that an angler should make technique alterations according to the conditions—in this case, low water and pressured fish. Most anglers were bombing away with lead and bright, neon-colored egg patterns. The finesse presentation of a nymph on a light leader drifted drag-free is what triggered the bite that day. And whoever said that king salmon wouldn't eat a nymph fished under a bobber?

Over the past decade, 90-degree angle, dry-line nymphing has seen an explosion, probably because it's one of the easiest methods to learn, and many a Great Lakes guide has weaned first-time fly fishers on this technique. The best way to get someone to pay attention to your instruction is to get them hooked up on fish within the first five minutes, and indicator nymphing can make that happen in short order. Watching the drift can be mesmerizing—at any moment, you can get a dunk. Steelhead stupor, the state of mind that shuts out the rest of the world while you're concentrating on the indicator's drift, occurs when you have everything set just right, you're dialed in, and you know you're going to get a hit.

Let's be honest: strike indicator systems are just a refined form of bobber fishing but with a fly rod and a fly tied on the end of the leader. Some fly-fishing purists may scoff at the idea of attaching a bobber to the leader, but it's one of the deadliest techniques you can master. And mastering it is definitely not as easy as it seems. It's a little more

Dead-drift streamers under indicators to imitate a wounded or crippled bait fish.

complicated than just putting an indicator at the end of the leader and setting the hook when it dunks. It's all about precision in creating a perfect 90-degree-angle drift directly beneath the indicator; precision in setting the depth; precision in placing and sizing the shot; precision in selecting the proper indicator, and in creating a smooth, clean, drag-free drift that imitates a free-drifting nymph, egg, egg cluster, or stunned baitfish.

I got sick of watching center-pin anglers crushing steelhead with flawless, 100-yard-long, drag-free drifts. "Pinners," as jealous fly fishers call them, use monofilament line on a free-spool, center-pin reel (that looks a lot like a fly reel), coupled with very long rods, 14 feet or longer. The free-spool reel allows the angler to smoothly feed line into an extremely long drift. Because the reel has no drag system, it has to be palmed.

The long rod gives the center-pin angler the ability to lift great lengths of line off the water to maintain direct contact with the float. This minimizes drag on the drift that would be caused by line lying on the water. Even thin monofilament can create drag when left on the water where current can push and pull it. The long rod allows you to glide, feed, and check the float as it drifts downriver.

A large wood or plastic float in a pear or pencil shape is positioned at the approximate depth of the water being fished, and split-shot are staggered heavily down-leader beneath the float. Staggering and spacing the shot eliminates any curve or belly in the leader beneath the float, and keeps the float completely vertical during the drift, suspending the bait at a perfect 90-degree angle to the float. This totally drag-free, dead-drift presentation is so deadly that I started adapting these presentation principles for fly-fishing replication in 1996 by using lighter and less terminal tackle for my indicator nymphing techniques.

Floats and indicators are available in a huge variety of shapes, sizes, and colors, including yarn indicators; colored tubes that slide onto knotless leaders; pinch-on foam; round, oval, and teardrop-shaped high-density foam and polystyrene floats; and balsa pencil- or pear-shaped floats. Matching the right style, size, and shape to the current conditions is important in generating more hookups. For most indicator fishing, I like the high-density polystyrene indicators that hold up various amounts of staggered shot without sinking. These indicators are nearly indestructible and extremely buoyant, and grooves won't form on the inside of the indicator from leader friction, as they will with some foam models.

A variety of indicators in different sizes and shapes helps you adjust to changing water conditions.

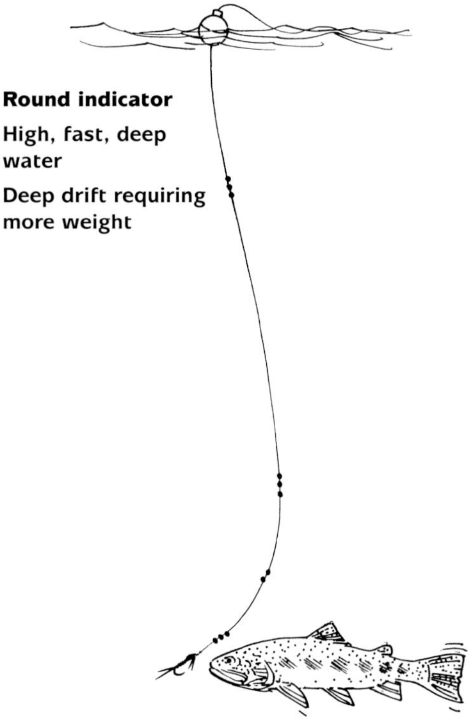

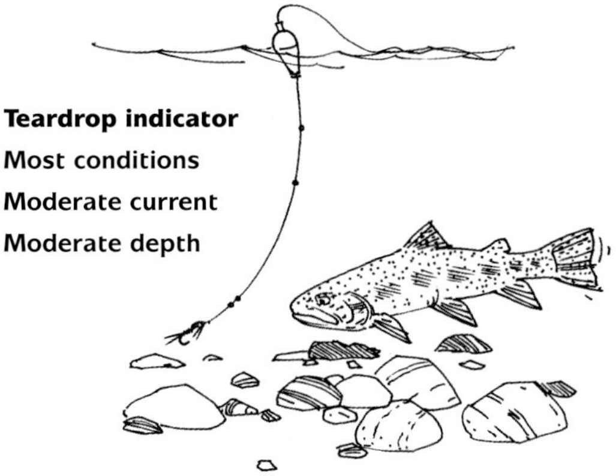

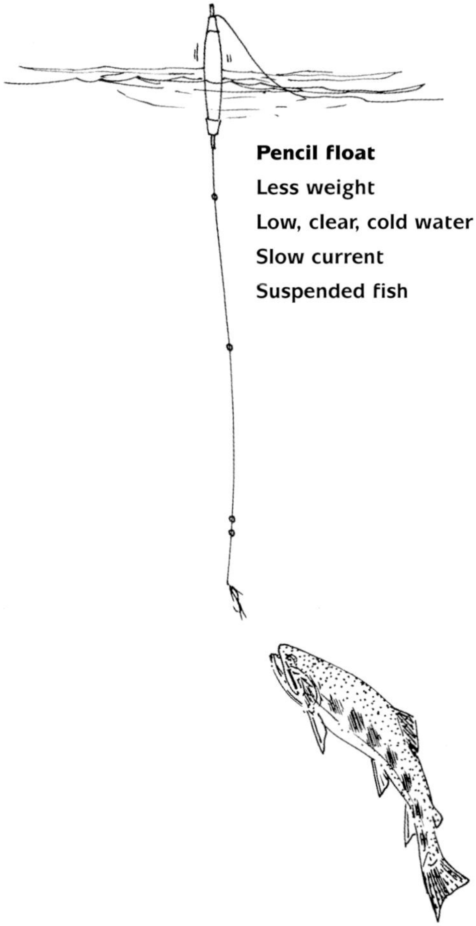

They come in a variety of solid and two-toned fluorescent colors and sizes. Most foam and polystyrene models are manufactured in various shapes with a slit in the side for the leader and a plastic peg or toothpick that inserts through the top of the indicator, pinning the leader in place. They're easily removed from the leader when switching from indicator nymphing techniques to high-sticking and bottom-bouncing techniques as you fish through different water types. I prefer peg models over toothpick models, which can weaken tippets.

Float Master Products (of Brunswick, Ohio) manufactures a great indicator system for perfect 90-degree-angle nymphing that uses a piece of surgical tubing for leader attachment, is easily removed, and slides up and down the leader for immediate adjustment while still retaining its position without sliding. A loop in the leader is pushed up through the bottom of the float with the tubing placed through the leader loop, which is then pulled snug into the indicator.

I also use the cylindrical wood floats manufactured by Thill, which are meant to be attached to the leader with rubber sleeves for low, clear water and for winter, when takes can be subtle. With proper weighting, this indicator type is nearly invisible and will give little resistance to a taking fish. I also have some custom-made indicators, lathed from balsa wood by Tom Harris, which have lasted through years of use.

Round indicators create more surface tension, making them harder for a fish to pull below the water's surface. Countless times, I've watched steelhead eat drifting flies with only a short hesitation in a round indicator's drift, followed by an immediate rejection of the fly by the fish. The angler doesn't even know that a fish has eaten the fly until a shout of "set the hook" rings out, much too late by then for an effective hook-setting effort. Round indicators work better in higher water or when the fish are taking aggressively.

Teardrop-style indicators have a tapered bottom that reduces resistance to a taking fish, giving a more pronounced dunk. Under most stream conditions, I use the 5/8- and 3/4-inch sizes, while the 1/2-inch size works well for smaller streams or lower water, when less weight is needed. The 1-inch size gives better visibility on big water and when more weight is needed to get the fly down. With large indicators and an increase in staggered shot to slow the drift, even deep, fast runs and deep pool throats can be fished effectively.

One of the most critical aspects of indicator nymphing is where the indicator is placed on the leader. Too far up the leader and the fly will drag unnaturally across the bottom, which is the leading cause of foul-hooked fish. The shot and fly can

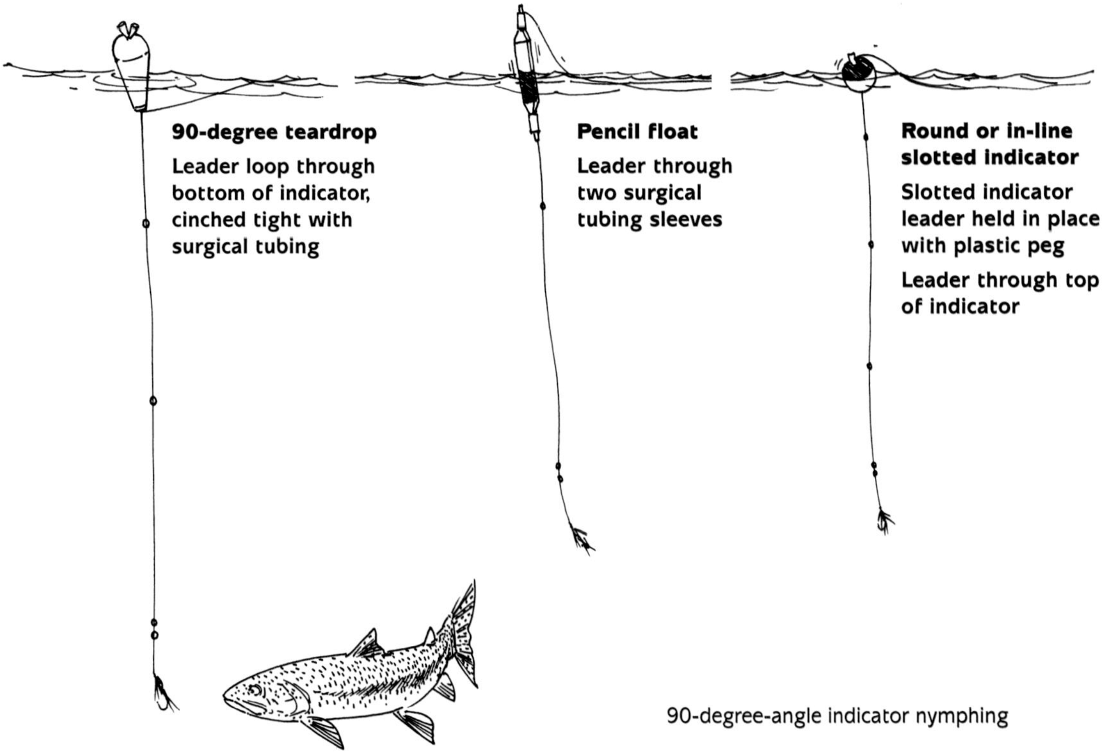

90-degree-angle indicator nymphing

No-snag indicator nymph rig

also hang on the bottom, making the indicator dunk and resulting in false bites and the ensuing hook-sets that tangle the leader.

If you place the indicator too close to the fly or too shallow, the fish are just not going to see the fly and you're not going to get the bite. The general rule is to place the indicator at the approximate depth of the water being fished, not the 1½ times the water depth that I've been reading about in trout books most of my life. In most cases you want the fly to be drifting within inches of the bottom, but I'd rather be a little too shallow than a little too deep, since on many occasions I've watched steelhead rise off the bottom to eat a fly.

If you're not constantly adjusting your terminal tackle (meaning depth, indicator size or shape, shot placement and size, or tippet material) for each spot you fish, you're not catching as many fish as you could be. You can make several steps up- or downstream and may have to make an important adjustment to get hooked up. Several inches can make a big difference in getting—or not getting—the bite.

Proper weighting is also extremely important, and smaller shot sizes (called dust shot) are used near the fly, with larger shot placed farther up the leader and spaced out under the indicator. Too much weight, and the float sinks; too little weight, and the float doesn't go vertical. You also need to consider the weight of the fly itself in this calculation.

In deeper, faster-moving water where fish are holding tight to the bottom, you're going to need more weight to get near the bottom quickly and a larger indicator to float and hold this added weight off the bottom. Staggering shot beneath the indicator slows down the drift, eliminating the curvature (or belly) in the leader or tippet material beneath the indicator, and quickly transmitting a take of the fly with a good, visual dunk. Shallower, slower water requires less weight and a smaller indicator.

Smaller shot should be placed near the fly to minimize the visual disturbance of the drifting fly. This is especially important in low, clear water and when fishing over pressured fish. I use naturally dull dust shot and Blackbird Split Shot (manufactured by RedWing Tackle) in sizes BB-1, BB-2, BB-3, and BB-4. Blackbird shot won't slide up or down the leader. I also use Thill soft shot and Anchor Double Cut Micro Shot as well as Water Gremlin size 3/0, B, and BB. Larger shot should be placed farther up the leader, away from the fly and the fish and closer to the float.

A ⅝-inch teardrop indicator will hold up two BB, three B, or four BB-3-size shot. A ¾-inch teardrop indicator will hold up two 3/0, three BB, four B, or five BB-3-size shot. Smaller indicators require less shot and larger ones require more shot, logically enough, in order to obtain a perfect 90-degree-angle drift.

There is no doubt in my mind that fish spook from shiny new split-shot, especially in clear water. Dull dust shot is less invasive, but you can easily dull down bright, new split-shot by adding a few drops of water and vinegar to the shot pouch and then shaking it up and letting it sit for a day or two. Oxidization occurs, dulling the shot by removing the shiny patina of lead. Rinse and use as normal.

Shot can be placed as close as 3 or 4 inches away from the fly, or as much as 18 to 24 inches away, depending upon current velocity, water clarity, depth, and where the fish are in the water column. Proper weighting occurs when enough weight has been added to the leader to make the indicator stand up and go vertical during the drift. Proper weighting is also best learned through trial and error while fishing through different water types and with different size floats. You can check weighting by flipping the rig in front of you before fishing, to make sure you have enough depth for the fly to drop straight beneath the indicator. If the indicator is lying on its side and the fly is not touching bottom, you need to add more weight.

Steelhead often suspend in the water. Make sure to set your indicator at the proper depth.

Many Great Lakes fly fishers don't realize that steelhead, salmon, and trout suspend throughout the water column, mostly in long sections of slower moving water. Although getting to the bottom is often necessary when fishing many sections of a tributary, this is not the case when fish are stacked up in layers or hovering close to the surface. I've caught a lot of early fall steelhead on south shore Lake Erie tributaries with a soft-hackle fly suspended only 10 to 24 inches below the indicator.

Fish normally suspend in pool flats where you can see them layered throughout the water column. Set the depth of the indicator at approximately the same depth you see the fish. Picking them off from the top and working your way down through the water column will increase your catch rate and decrease the chances of foul-hooking, which occurs when you fish your fly too deep.

Indicators that have pegs, toothpicks, or tubing riding above the water's surface also provide visual clues as to what the fly is doing beneath the surface. Straight up and down means the drift is drag-free, with the fly directly beneath the indicator. An indicator leaning downstream means the fly is still upstream of the indicator. You'll need to mend the line upstream to get the fly down through the water and beneath the indicator. An indicator leaning upstream means the fly is drifting downstream ahead of the indicator, creating drag without depth penetration. You may need to make a downstream mend to correct the drift.

I have found up- and across-stream positioning from the fish and the targeted area to be the single best position for presenting a fly and can change my presentation angle by moving out into the current or by backing up. Close positioning to the fish and precision casting allow the fly angler to obtain a better drag-free drift. Less fly line on the water equals less drag on the fly. In clear water where I can see the fish, I'll frequently get down low or even crawl into position, kneeling in or out of the water as needed.

Use a nice, slow casting rhythm and an open loop for casting indicators and weight on the leader. An elliptical style of casting is useful when throwing all that terminal tackle. The rod pulls (*not* jerks) the fly line, leader, and weight smoothly around in a low oval with an upward-moving backcast. The forward stroke should accelerate slowly before power and speed are applied so that the leader doesn't snap back into itself, resulting in a pile up and the dreaded downtime.

Keep the loop nice and wide on the forward stroke, and picture following the drop of the cast with the tip of the rod. As the line and leader unfurl, lift the rod to slow down the energy transfer and weight of the terminal tackle on the leader. Then drop the tip of the rod, and extend it to follow the end of the cast, essentially holding the cast above the water for a brief moment, while the terminal tackle unfurls without tangling. A fast, high, and abruptly stopped forward cast can pile and tangle the leader, especially when using indicators, staggered shot, and tandem fly rigs.

Roll casting is useful when obstructions prevent an overhead forward cast, and today's long-belly, weight-forward steelhead tapers perform the task well and allow for easy line mending. When roll casting indicator setups with added weight on the leader, you must lift the weight and flies and skid them across the surface in order for the rod to transfer enough energy into the line and leader and shoot them forward.

I use a relatively forceful lift and pull of the line with the rod, smoothly pulling the leader, weight, and fly to the water's surface, and then I skid the rig across the surface as the rod comes back. By moving the rod back and parallel to the water's surface, I can continue the skid, forming a low oval of fly line behind me. The lift of the rod to the 2 o'clock position is a brief but short stop, or else the weight will sink and ruin the forward cast. The stop occurs on the back end of the skid as the

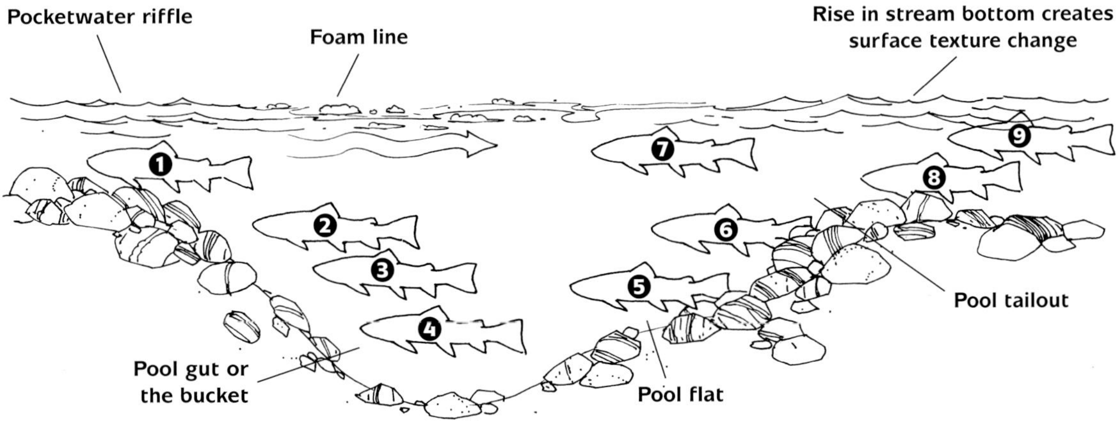

Fish location. Fall holding: 2, 3, 8, 9; Fall running/spring running: 1, 2; Winter holding: 4, 5, 6, 8; Spring holding: 2, 3, 6; Spring/fall spawning: 9; Fall/spring suspending: 7

Roll Cast Skid: Casting with indicators and weight

To effectively cast weight and terminal tackle with indicators, staggered shot, or tandem fly rigs on the leader, lift them to the water's surface with a backward and upward sweep of the rod, forming an oval or D-loop in the line. Here, the start of the roll cast skid brings the terminal tackle to the surface, and starts the skid.

Bring the rod back parallel to the water's surface with a sideways sweep, continuing the skid. The terminal tackle sliding along the water's surface forms a bubble trail.

The rod loads as the D-loop forms in the fly line to the side and behind you.

The D-loop is now fully formed, just before the start of the forward stroke and a brief stop of the rod at the top of the sweep. (continued on page 142)

Roll Cast Skid: Casting with indicators and weight (continued from page 141)

Accelerate to an abrupt stop on the forward cast, moving the rod through a relatively wide arc to form a wide loop and prevent tangles.

The terminal tackle is lifted from the water's surface and propelled up- and across-stream on the forward cast.

The end of the cast drops the rig upstream along the current seam entering the pool.

rod comes vertical before the forward stroke and check of the rod that propels the cast forward.

Cover a wide expanse of water with a systematic approach, breaking down prime holding water into a series of drifts. Start close to the bank and work your way out to cover fish that could be holding in front of you in deeper water, where you can't read the bottom. Cover specific zones like current seams, foam lines, drop-offs, and bottom depressions. These compressed areas can hold a lot of fish and require repeated casting in the same general vicinity. Get as close as possible to minimize the number of currents you cast across and reduce drag.

You should cast well upstream from a deep target so the fly can sink to the desired depth by the time it drifts in front of you. A common mistake is to cast into or just upstream from the fish's holding position, causing the fly to float over and behind the fish rather than into it.

Immediately mend upstream of the fly line after an up- and across-stream cast, to place the indicator upstream of the fly's position, giving the fly time to sink before the indicator begins its float. Make an upstream mend when the fly line catches up to the drifting indicator. If the fly line sits on the water downstream of an indicator, the current can push it and pull it downstream, creating a belly in the line and causing drag.

Where, when, and how to mend the fly line is important to obtaining a drag-free drift and is a skill mostly learned through trial and error on various water types. A lot of fly fishers mend the fly line by extending the arm to lift the line off the water and loop it in a half circle upstream. Instead, execute a mend of the line with a forearm lift of

By getting on the far bank, this angler was able to get a better drift through the current seam leading into the pool.

the rod and an upstream wrist flick that snakes the line and leader upstream, right to the indicator. To achieve a long drift that allows your fly to sink deep, you must mend the line and leader all the way to the indicator. Most anglers do not mend the line enough, mend the line while the fly travels through the strike zone, or set the indicator at the wrong depth.

Depending on current speed and surface current flow, you may need to make another mend upstream to give the fly more time to sink. In heavy, fast water, like the head of a plunge pool, use three or more upstream mends to sink your fly before it starts to drift into the strike zone. If necessary, make an upstream mend to eliminate drag whenever the fly line gets downstream of the indicator. To reduce drag, cast into the same tongues or speeds of current in the drift. This may require wading into fast water to ensure a clean drift on the slower water found on the other side, or vice versa.

Some spots require creative line-mending sequences in order to get a drag-free drift in front of the fish. Try upstream and immediate downstream mending when fish are found holding along fast and slow water seams. Downstream mending works for the start or continuation of the drift when you have slow or nonmoving water in front of you. Fly line lying on slow water tends to hang there and must be mended downstream for the drift to start or continue.

When steelhead are holding behind current breaks like shale ledges or in stream bottom depressions, you want the fly to fall into the hole before the indicator does. An upstream or reach mend needs to be made just before the fly reaches the upstream edge of the drop-off, letting the fly drop into the depression before the indicator. If the indicator drops in first, the current will push it downstream, immediately creating drag on the drifting fly and pulling it out of the strike zone.

After the initial series of mends or line placements, you want to start the dead-drift of the fly at the beginning of the strike zone, making sure the fly rod is lifted to the 10 o'clock position with rod tip pointed at the indicator to follow its downstream drift in high-stick fashion. Fly line is thick and heavy. Its tension on the water's surface creates drag. Even when using triangle tapers and running lines, the more line you can get off the water by extending and lifting the rod, the better drag-free drift you're going to have.

Slack is one reason for missed strikes, so you have to quickly take it out of your line. I tuck the fly line under the middle finger of my rod hand and pull in the slack with my left hand. To feed slack into the drift, I open my middle finger; to come tight to the line (such as when I want to set the hook), I pinch the line with my middle finger. A lot of dry-fly trout guys hold the line with the left hand away from the rod, in the same way as

Dead-drifted egg patterns will probably catch more lake-run species than any other presentation.

executing a cast, after the cast has been made and while following the drift. Think of all that slack you need to take out of the line when lifting the rod to set the hook. It often results in a couple of head shakes and an "Oops, I missed another one." The fly line should be tucked under the rod hand's middle finger after the cast has been made. The hands should naturally come together at the end of the cast.

It's extremely important that your fly floats drag-free. A common mistake is to mend the line as it drifts through the fish. The rod tip should be slowly dropped as it follows the drift and indicator downstream from your position. You can also move the rod tip slightly upstream during the drift, to hesitate or stall the indicator's drift, allowing the fly that is drifting deeper and slower to get underneath the indicator. This is called "checking the float" and helps maintain that 90-degree-angle drift. Again, anytime the fly line drifts downstream of the indicator, an upstream mend is needed to remove the belly in the line that causes drag. If the fly line is not catching up to the indicator because it is laying on slow water, you may need to mend downstream to continue the drift.

After the rod tip nears the water's surface at the end of the drift, slack-line stack mending extends the drift even further. Feed fly line from the left hand through the right rod hand, and flip the loose line onto the water with the tip of the rod in a series of stacks. These are upward flips of the rod tip that pile the line on the surface of the water as the current removes the slack. Keep the rod tip low and pointed at the indicator while tucking the line under the middle finger of the rod hand after each stack mend. This gives you a better chance of setting the hook on a fish that takes far downstream. Lean at the waist and extend the rod, mending downstream near the end of the drift to extend the drift.

Any dunk or hesitation of the indicator requires an immediate downstream hook-set, and I often refer to the hook-set as just another extension of the drift. There is a fine line between a good, solid hook-set and one that breaks the tippet. Eager, first-time steelheaders easily get excited as a guide hollers, "Fish, fish, fish!" and as a result, may set the hook too hard by wildly yanking on the rod and line. Or they set the hook upstream, pulling the fly right out of the fish's mouth. A fish faces into the current, and setting the hook upstream can, at best, give a tenuous purchase in the upper lip. Always set the hook downstream and toward the bank, with a smooth, hard, lift and snap of the forearm, to bring the hook into the corner of the fish's mouth.

Another method for 90-degree-angle indicator nymphing is to place shot on a dropper beneath the fly. This allows the shot to penetrate the water first and get deep fast, requiring less mending. It's an effective fast-, deep-, or high-water technique, where the fly has to be super-tight to the bottom, but ineffective for suspended fish and in slower-moving pools with broken bottom depressions, where the shot can hang on the bottom, resulting in false dunks and foul-hooked fish.

West Coast steelheaders who need to cover large expanses of water also use downstream nymphing techniques. First, make a down- and across-stream tuck cast, and then make a series of stack mends to feed fly line into the drift, allowing a heavily weighted fly to get deep before the drift even begins. Then feed line continuously to maintain a dead-drift presentation. Areas of conflicting surface currents and textures need creative mending techniques in order to get a drag-free drift. Set the hook with the rod pointing downstream and sweeping toward the bank.

High-Stick Nymphing

This is a dry-line, bottom-bouncing technique without an indicator, used for moderate to shallow depths with swift- to slow-moving currents.

One of the harder techniques to master, high-stick nymphing is just a fancy way to describe

High-Stick Nymphing

Make a slack line cast, quartering up- and across-stream to the current seam along the far side of the boulder. Make an immediate upstream mend if fishing in fast or deep water.

After letting the fly sink, tuck the fly line under the rod hand and lift the rod between the 9 and 10 o'clock position, coming tight to the drift. At this point, the weight on the leader should hit the bottom.

As the fly drifts downstream of you, drop the rod tip to extend the drift and keep the fly deep. The weight on the leader should be constantly ticking bottom. To get a longer drift, stack mend or feed line into the drift.

bottom-bouncing a fly with a traditional full-floating fly line without an indicator and with less weight than you would use with running-line techniques. The name of the technique comes from keeping the rod high and extended at the 10 o'clock position through most of the drift.

I don't like moving the rod much higher than the 10 o'clock position, as this makes for ineffective hook setting. Wading close to your target gives you a better drift because you can lift more fly line off the water. A common practice is to attach several size BB split-shot directly to the leader 6 to 24 inches above the fly, closer when fishing deeper, faster water, farther when fishing slower and shallower water. The amount of weight depends upon the depth and speed of the current. Running lines combined with droppers or slinky rigs may be better choices in deeper and faster water types that require more than two or three size 3/0 shot.

When you are executing this technique properly you can feel contact with the bottom during the drift through the rod tip. Bottom composition types can be revealed through different "ticks" of the rod. A steady tick, tick, tick is likely to be an even graveled bottom with stones of similar size. A tick, pause, tick, pause could be the weight on the leader hitting the tops of large boulders in a deep run. A steady downward dip in the rod is likely to be the weight snagging the bottom or a ledge.

Snags, common when bottom-bouncing, can be freed by walking upstream and out into the current before pulling back on the line. A quick strip-strike and line release can sometimes free the snag, or you can also do this by roll casting forcefully over and away from the snag and lifting quickly with the rod tip.

In any case, you want to set the hook downstream with a sharp lift of the rod and snap of the forearm on any pause, throb, stop, or hesitation of the drift. Any unnatural feel during the drift can indicate the soft take of a fish in cold water. In warmer water, the take can be unmistakable—a sharp rap or pull on the line as the fly drifts downstream from you.

This technique works in places where indicator techniques fail because the current speed is too fast and would quickly push the indicator and fly out of the strike zone. Shallow riffles and runs, pocketwater, and spots where broken bottom contours hold fish in tight spaces are all water types where this technique excels. Longer, 12½- to 14½-foot tapered leaders give a deep drift on big water with a minimum amount of line interference, creating a smooth, drag-free drift. Shorter, standard 9½- or 10½-foot leaders work well on smaller streams.

Place split-shot on the leader or a dropper, anywhere from 6 to 24 inches away from the fly. Shot size, amount, and placement are determined by depth and current speed. Place shot closer to the fly when you need to sink it quickly in fast water with compact holding areas. If more than three or four size 3/0 shot are needed to get to the bottom, consider using running line and slinky rigs. Any more weight makes fly casting with traditional fly lines cumbersome.

Another method for rigging terminal tackle is to tie the end of the leader to a small barrel swivel with a clinch knot, leaving a 3-inch tag end to crimp on a split-shot. (You can also crimp shot onto the tag end of a blood knot.) Knot the tippet section and fly to the other end of the barrel swivel.

Positioning up- and across stream from the targeted drift zone enables the fly to reach the desired depth. The same line-mending techniques used when indicator nymphing also apply to high-stick nymphing. An upstream mend or a series of upstream mends are usually needed immediately after an up- and across-stream cast. Visualize the drift of the fly, and make fly-line adjustments during the drift to get the fly where you want it to go.

Take up slack line with your left hand and lift and extend the rod to about the 10 o'clock position until the fly drifts in front of you. Drop the rod tip as the fly travels downstream of you to feed line into the drift and extend it. After dropping the rod tip to the water's surface, you may need to make downstream or stack mends to continue to extend the drift when slow water is in front of you with faster current farther out.

Standard weight-forward floating lines work, but modern nymphing lines work even better. Lines like the Wulff Triangle Taper have won rave reviews because the thinner front taper of the fly line creates less drag on the water's surface during the drift. As with indicator nymphing, floating running lines work well with long noodle-type fly rods, though they won't cast far with a small amount of weight.

Tracking the Fly

The best way to learn how to properly place, mend, and manipulate a fly line during a drift is to visually track the fly through the water until you can no longer see it. You can usually decipher whether or not the fly is on the right course before it drifts out of sight. By tracking the fly, I mean observing what the fly is doing and where it is going as it falls through the water column. When you can see the fly, you can make any necessary corrections to the drift to get the fly in front of the fish. You can also learn how a variety of water types, currents, and current speeds affect the drift or swing of the fly.

It can be hard to follow a fly's descent and drift visually, especially when using a small, dark pattern. I'll often use a white Zonker or a large cream egg pattern as a teaching tool in order for the angler to see the fly as it descends through the water. If you watch the fly during its descent, you'll quickly learn several things. One is that you are probably not mending the fly line far enough upstream. A mend made with several feet of fly line still on the water does not put the fly at the proper depth. The mend needs to made right through the leader and to the indicator.

Foul-Hooking

Playing a foul-hooked fish (one that is not hooked in the mouth) can ruin the fishing for others around you and spook all the other fish that you'd like to catch. It can also result in tangled lines as the fish goes berserk, or leave a beautiful fish looking like a pincushion. Because good fly-fishing technique tells you to set the hook when a drift feels unnatural or an indicator hesitates or dips, sooner or later you're going to foul-hook a fish, and what you do will help give a better impression of all anglers.

First, learn to tell on the hook-set whether a fish is foul-hooked or not. A good downstream hook-set firmly plants the hook in the corner of the fish's mouth where everyone wants it to be, and the fish will come up shaking its head. An upstream hook-set will either miss the fish or hook it in the top of the mouth. Either way, you get a head shake. These head shakes are the hard jolts and thumps felt through the rod. If you set the hook and feel the rod tip wobble without the sharp thumping, the fish is probably hooked near the tail. The fly line will move back and forth where it cuts the surface, revealing the infamous tail wag.

Here's how to get your fly back and leave the fish unscathed. Immediately drop the rod tip to create slack. If you keep pulling back with the rod, the fish will only bolt or you will further embed the hook where you don't want it to be. Creating immediate slack lets the fish continue to hold in position because it's not feeling that much pressure or resistance.

Next, step slowly downstream of the fish and try to get behind it. Once you are below the fish, tighten the line slowly while still pointing the rod tip at the fly. When you feel the tension of the fish, tuck the fly line tight to the cork under your index finger, and give the rod a quick, straight pull downstream to pop the hook off. This works nine times out of ten when done correctly. The key is to not put too much pressure on the rod if you feel a tail wobble.

Fishing with tandem-fly setups where fish are concentrated and compacted into small areas is one of the main reasons foul-hooking occurs. This method is deadly when using an egg attractor pattern as the top fly and a nymph as the dropper. As the drift comes downstream, a belly forms in a fly line that swings a tandem rig through the water with the flies hitting the side, backs, or tails of the fish. The indicator dips and you set the hook, foul-hooking the fish accidentally. Slack-line stack mending reduces this swing while extending the drift, but sometimes it's better to fish just one fly correctly where fish are concentrated. Another way to reduce foul-hooking and still retain the effectiveness of a tandem setup is to clip the top fly's hook point off at the bend, attaching the dropper fly and length of tippet to the eye of the hook on the top fly.

Swinging Techniques

Getting crushed at the end of the swing is one of the ultimate thrills for a Great Lakes fly fisher. I mean really getting ripped, when the rod is almost yanked from your grasp by the vicious slam of a charged-up steelhead, salmon, or brown trout. They can absolutely unload on a fly, much like the violent hit of a muskie.

The technique may not always put as many fish in the net as some of the other methods because you're searching for those aggressive fish that are fewer in number, but once the hammer drops a few times, your search for another swing fix will continue. The allure of catching fish on a swung fly is ancient within fly-fishing history.

Runs and pool buckets from 3 to 6 feet deep, the speed of a slow to brisk walk, make good swing water. Boulders there are likely hold to fish just in front of and behind the rock. Traditional dry-line (floating line) swinging, also called greased-line swinging, presents the fly broadside to the fish at or just under the water's surface in channels, depressions, and runs shallow enough to give fish lying on the bottom a chance to see your fly.

Water temperatures of 45 degrees or more are considered productive for swinging techniques. Below this temperature fish metabolism drops and predatory chase instincts are therefore reduced. Swinging can still work in lower temperatures, but you have to work harder for the fish and slow down the swing. For fish that won't take a fly near the surface and when water temperatures are cooler, add a couple of size B or BB shot to the leader 12 to 18 inches from the fly, use heavily weighted flies for depth penetration, or use tapered sinking and tungsten-based leaders with 3.9, 5.6, and 7.0 inches-per-second sink rates.

I also use custom-made 3- to 12-foot T-14 sinking tips with loop-to-loop connections, or type 3 and type 5 10- to 15-foot sink-tip fly lines, for swinging in deeper water, such as the pool's bucket where the water sweeps in and drops, deep pool flats, or deep pool tailouts. To sink your fly to the right depth, you may need to cast at an up- and across-stream angle. Pool flats containing less current and depth may require down- and across-stream casting.

Pool tailouts that retain enough current speed to maintain a swing are other classic locations. Tailouts that have a reduction in current speed and depth may be better suited to greased-line swinging techniques. The large surface window that a tailout provides makes it more likely that near- and subsurface presentations will be seen by the fish. Slow-moving tailouts may require you to mend downstream or strip the line to give the fly more action.

I prefer a fast-action rod for casting heavier sink-tip lines. Changeable sink-tips that connect to the fly line loop-to-loop allow you to change sink

The Down-and-Across Wet Fly Swing

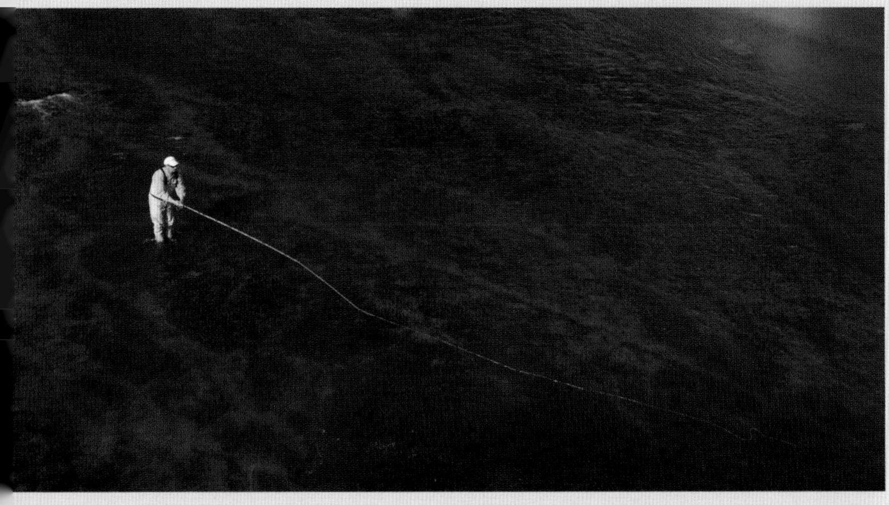

Cast down- and across stream, above the anticipated holding water. JAY NICHOLS PHOTO

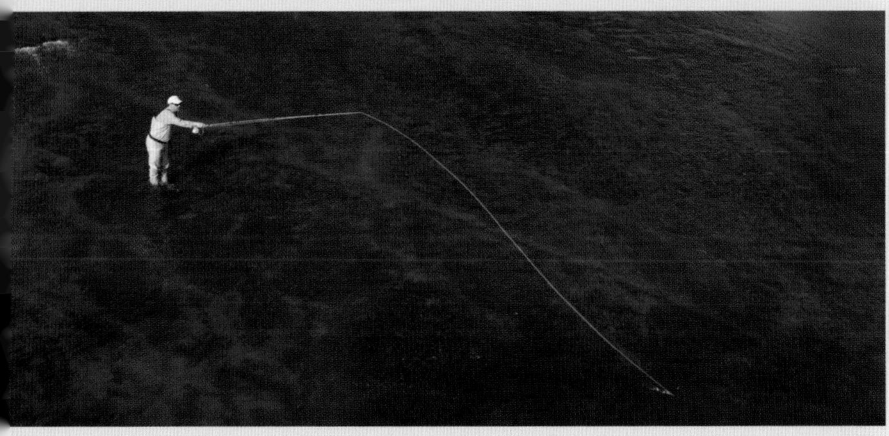

Mend the line upstream to give the fly time to sink before it starts to swing. JAY NICHOLS PHOTO

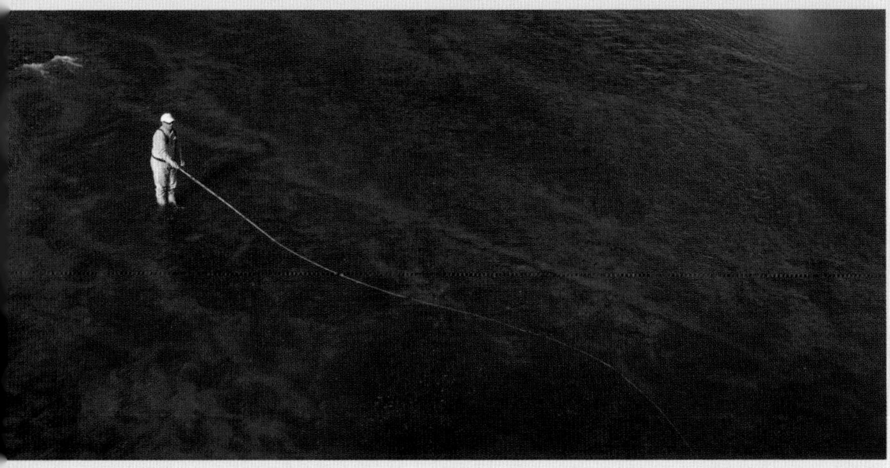

Drop the rod tip and point it at the fly as it starts to swing into the holding water. The swing occurs as the current begins to push on the belly of the fly line. JAY NICHOLS PHOTO

(continued on page 152)

The Down-and-Across Wet Fly Swing (continued from page 151)

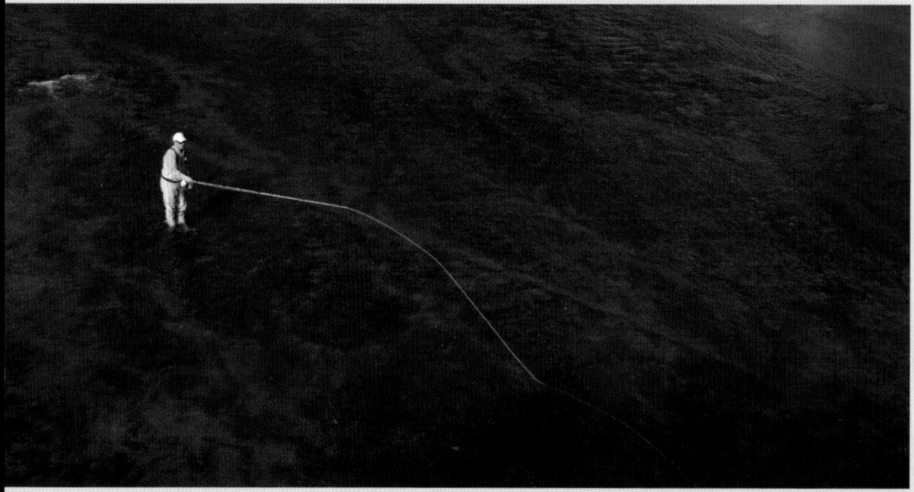

Mend upstream again when the belly in the fly line reaches the fly's position for added depth penetration. JAY NICHOLS PHOTO

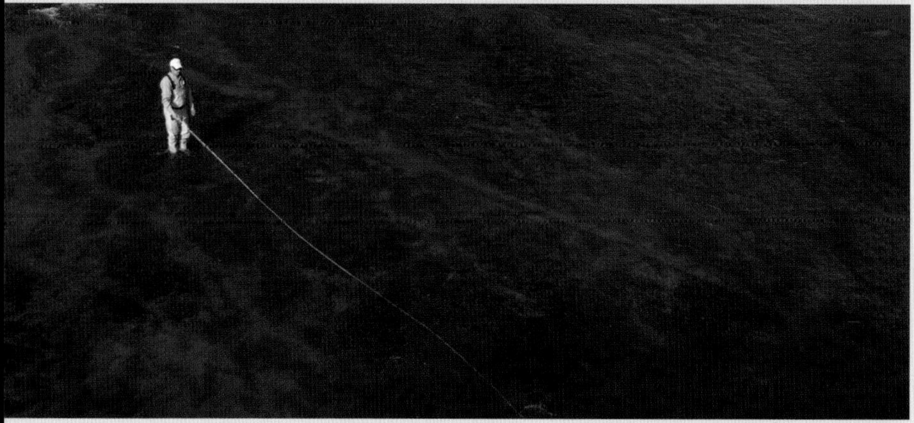

Drop the rod tip after the mend, pointing it at the fly as it swings downstream. JAY NICHOLS PHOTO

Follow the fly with the rod tip through the lower end of the swing. You may need to mend downstream to continue the swing. JAY NICHOLS PHOTO

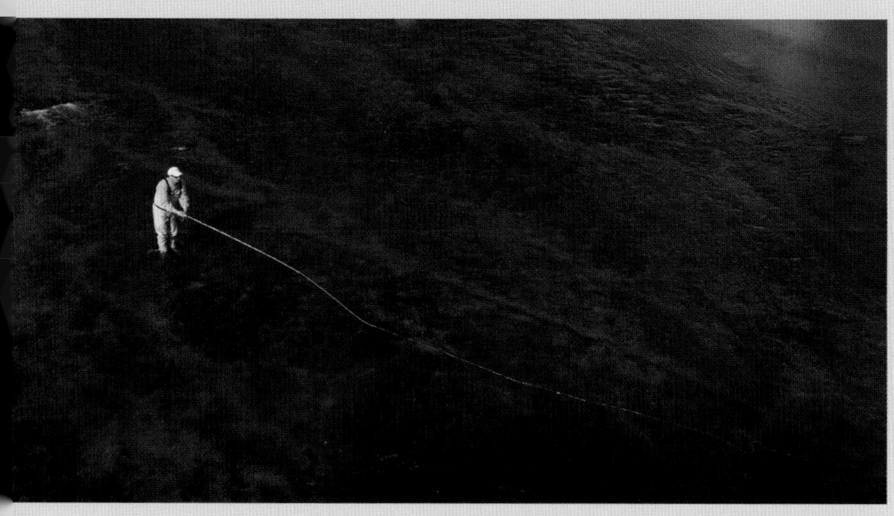

You can extend the swing by bending at the waist. The fly can be left to hang at the end of the swing or stripped to entice any following fish.
JAY NICHOLS PHOTO

rates for varying conditions. Terminal tackle is simple, with a short 3- to 5-foot leader nail knotted to the end of the sink-tip line. A straight length of 12-pound mono or fluorocarbon works just fine for steelhead under most fishing conditions. I like to use a Uni-knot or Duncan loop when attaching the fly to give it a free swinging action.

The Technique

Classic swinging presentation is a down- and across-stream cast made at a 45-degree angle upstream from the targeted area. I prefer a "softer" swing, where positioning entails moving farther out in the current and farther upstream from the targeted area. Fast current can cause the fly to swing harshly at a 45-degree angle. This can spook fish out of the holding area or foul-hook them if your swing is too long.

Cast down- and across stream, yet far enough upstream from the swing zone to allow time for your fly to sink. Make an initial upstream mend, or series of upstream mends, and feed slack into the drift to sink your fly. Constant mending during the swing may be needed to slow the fly, get it deep, and keep it in front of fish for as long as possible. Remove any slack in the fly line after mending to detect strikes as the fly dead-drifts before the start of the swing.

As the fly swings downstream from you, drop your rod tip and point it at the fly, with the rod held to the side and following the fly, after coming tight to the swing. After dropping the rod tip to the water, tuck the line under your index finger and follow the swing of the line with the tip of the rod. A loop of loose line between the reel and the index finger can be fed into the swing or to a hooked fish. At the end of the swing leave the fly hanging in the current below you, or strip a few times to induce takes from fish that have followed the fly.

In fast, deep, heavy water, such as the top end of a pool, you may need to cast up- and across

In tailouts with minimal current, you may need to mend downstream to initiate a drift or start a swing. In this case, the angler mends through a depression and underneath overhanging vegetation along the far bank.

stream and mend upstream several times to get the fly down. As you follow the drift and swing of the fly, you may have to mend upstream to continue to sink the fly and slow the swing, keeping the fly in front of fish-holding positions for as long as possible. In slower, shallower water, you may need to mend downstream immediately to get the fly moving and prevent hanging up. However, a downstream belly that is too large will cause the fly to swing too fast.

Fighting the Fish

If you want to land that fish, you better run, buddy. That's what you're here for, and that's why you made the trip. The first ten seconds and the last ten seconds of any battle are the most important times to be on your toes when fighting lake-run species—and I mean literally on your toes. After the hook digs in and that head starts slashing back and forth, most fish turn tail in the current and make a beeline right back to the big lake.

Current seams created by boulders make excellent choices for fly presentation. A deeper pocket is often formed where the current is forced to one or both sides of the boulder.

Make a downstream mend over a boulder to continue the drift.

Spey Casting

Spey casting was developed in Scotland centuries ago to eliminate the need for a backcast and create a change of direction from the end of the swing back to the target. Spey casting with a two-handed fly rod allows you to deliver the fly to the strike zone quickly, repeatedly, and with less effort; cover large bodies of water more effectively; lift and mend long lengths of fly line; and keep the fly in the strike zone for a longer period of time. Spey casts can also be made with a single-handed fly rod.

Those new to casting two-handed rods may find them difficult to use, just as it probably was with your very first attempts at fly casting. Hooking salmon and steelhead with the two-hander is the cure for getting over the hump. There are so many varieties of casts that I recommend you hire a professional instructor to get hands-on experience. Double Spey, single Spey, snake roll, switch, oval, and snap-T Spey casts can all seem overwhelming and confusing to those who are new at this. Books and DVDs are good teaching tools, but nothing beats an instructor who can scrutinize your cast and make corrections.

Spey casting methods are named after specific rod motions that are implemented to set up the forward cast. Using one motion of the rod to create an anchor and form a D-loop is called a single Spey cast. Two motions of the rod, one to create an anchor and a separate motion to form a D-loop, is called a double Spey cast. A double Spey cast also incorporates a change of direction, gener-

Two-handed fly rods are gaining in popularity on larger Great Lakes tributaries. Spey casting techniques allow anglers to cover wide expanses of water with minimal effort.

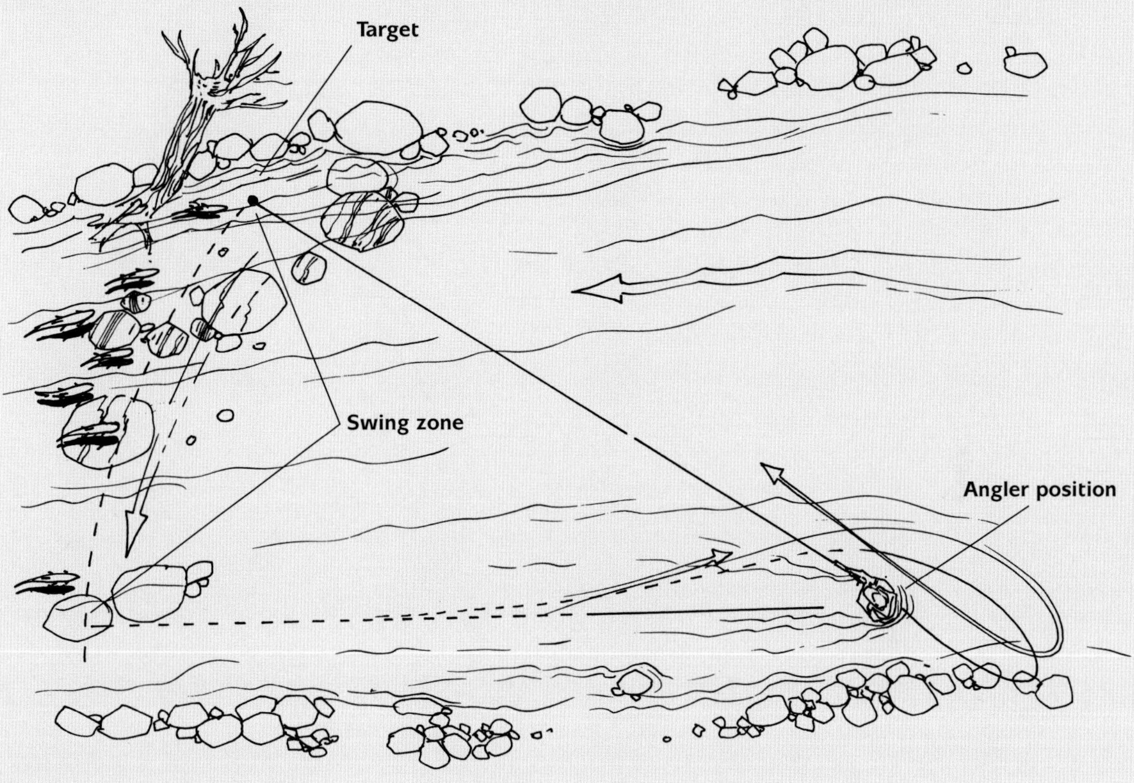

Spey cast, overhead view: 45 degree angle change of direction from bank to target

ally from 30 to 90 degrees from the bank to the target. A good book on the subject is Simon Gawesworth's *Spey Casting,* published by Stackpole Books.

The Spey method of casting uses the tension of the fly line on the water and the formation of a D-loop in the line to load the rod, never lets the fly get behind the caster, and is accomplished with two sequences—a contrived cast and a forward cast. The contrived cast is the movement of the rod that creates an anchor (the portion of fly line left on the water, either upstream or downstream of the angler) and forms a D-loop of fly line underneath the rod tip during the backcast. The forward cast creates an aerialized loop of fly line similar to a roll cast, but there is much less anchor line left on the water. The D-loop must be formed 180 degrees to the target on the backcast and to the outside of the rod tip to avoid collision on the forward stroke.

Two-handed fly rods now have multiple applications for Great Lakes fly fishing. Indicator nymphing techniques can be used with floating lines and two-handed rods to reduce the amount of time spent false casting while maintaining constant control and tension of the fly line during the drift. You can cover larger pieces of water more effectively and access areas that have little to no room for overhead casting. Because of

(continued on page 158)

Spey Casting

(continued from page 157)

these benefits, "switch" or "two-hand assist" rods have been developed for use with either one or two hands for overhead or Spey casting.

Two-handed fly rods can also be used for overhead casting on Great Lakes shorelines and beaches where distance is needed. With today's modern Spey tackle, fly fishing with a two-handed fly rod has never been easier and has become an essential component in Great Lakes fly-fishing technique. (For more on choosing a rod, see Spey Rods in chapter 6.)

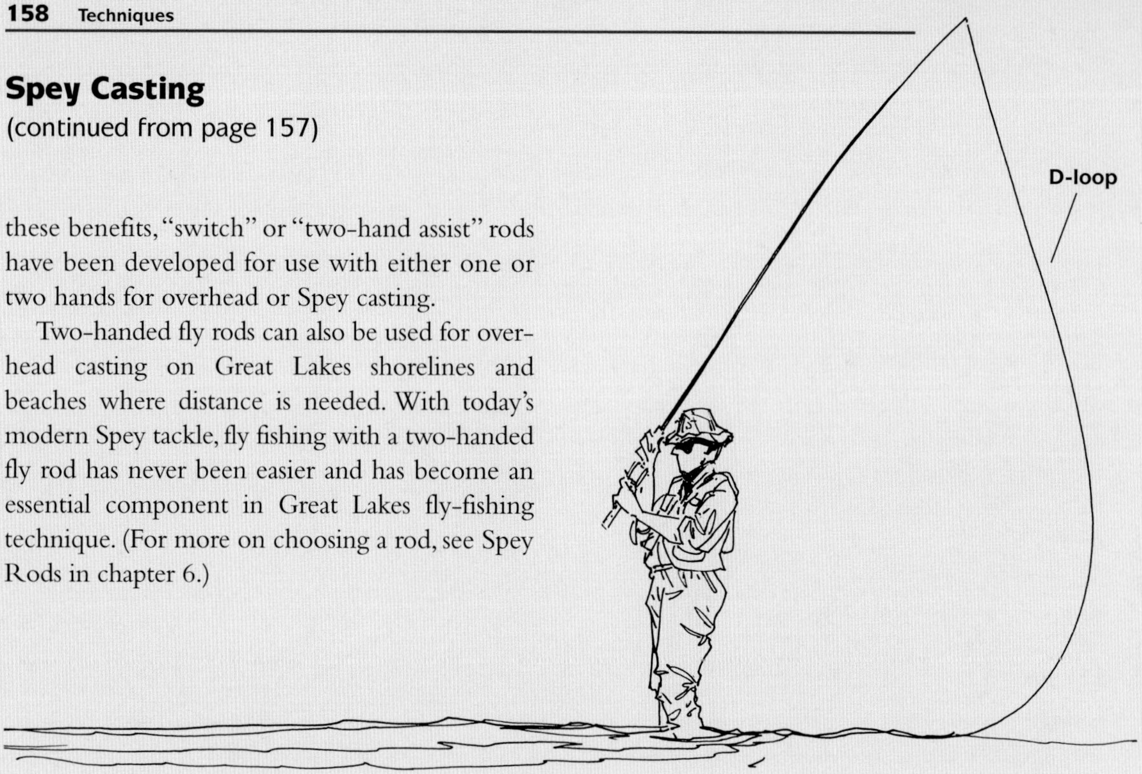

Spey cast, side view: rod in ready position to start forward stroke

What you do on that first initial run usually makes or breaks your chances for landing a trophy-size fish. You simply cannot stand there and watch line melt from your reel (not for very long, anyway) or expect to haul a heavy fish upstream through heavy current, especially when using light leaders and tippets. During those first ten seconds, you must remove any slack in the line while keeping the line taut, get the fish on the reel, and let that fish go. The initial surge and run of a steelhead or salmon can happen so fast that it can leave you with a broken leader and a broken heart. A lot of inland trout and first-time tributary fly fishers are not used to the extreme power and weight of these fish. On the first surge of the fish, the line can get hilariously tangled around the rod butt, reel, arm, or hand. Once the line is clear, the reel's drag will be engaged and you can palm the spool to help slow down the run.

After that, you're probably going to have to follow the fish. Most lake-run species turn their bodies into the current and head downstream, though some may go up. Either way, the farther you are from the fish the less control you have, and chances are greater that something will go wrong. Try to get even or slightly downstream of the fish so that it has to work against the rod and the current. Whenever the fish runs, lift the rod to help prevent the line and leader from scraping against obstructions and to prevent a belly of line from forming that can break your tippet.

You can drop the rod tip and apply side pressure when the run stops. Now is the time to get down-and-dirty with the fish, applying alternating

Switch rods, which can be used with one or two hands, and two-handed fly rods are gaining in popularity throughout the Great Lakes.

pressure against the fish and current with the rod. Making the fish work against the current and the rod helps tire it out more quickly. As you bring the fish closer, be prepared for more runs and surges.

The last ten seconds, when you think a fish is beaten, give it another opportunity to get off. It won't want to come into shallow water and often makes another screaming run or heads for any nearby obstruction. Be ready for any such last-second maneuvering by the fish. Once the fish is exhausted, you can back up and beach it or reach down with a pair of hemostats to remove the

Alternating side pressure with various rod angles helps tire the fish and keep it off balance.

To reduce harm to the fish, and to take the best pictures, pinch your thumb and forefinger around the base of the tail, using your other hand to support the weight of the fish under its belly.

hook while the fish is still in the water. If the fish is beached, it doesn't need to be dragged up on the bank where it could flop around and possibly cause itself injury. Once the fish is on its side, lead the fish to slower current at the edge of the bank to allow easy hook removal. After the hook is removed, take the fish where the current can help to resuscitate it, and face it into the current. You can watch the fish gulp water, recuperate, and in return get a nice cold splash in the face from a tail slap as you let it go. I carry a net only when I'm guiding.

Some states where coldwater fisheries have been artificially created through stocking efforts promote their fisheries as "put-grow-and-take" propositions where substantial harvest has historically occurred. A good example of harvest being detrimental to a put-grow-and-take fishery occurred recently on Pennsylvania's Walnut Creek. Low water persisted throughout the fall season, preventing upstream migration, and the fish stacked by the hundreds in the lower section of the creek, where they were subsequently harvested. When good water levels arrived by late fall, fewer fish were available to make the run upstream, resulting in poor fishing in the middle to upper sections of the creek.

But many tributary anglers, whether bait, lure, or fly fishers, now realize the value of a carefully released steelhead, salmon, or brown trout. The thrill of landing one of these species is passed along to another angler, far outweighing its value as food.

Face the fish into the current so it can gulp water and replenish oxygen. The fish will eventually gain strength and swim away on its own.

CHAPTER SIX

Tackle

Modern fly-fishing tackle has come a long way, and its refinement has been well-suited for Great Lakes fly fishing. At one end of the spectrum are noodle-type fly rods, capable of handling huge fish on extremely light tippets. On the other end, we have super-fast, saltwater-style rods, capable of throwing the line into the backing when fishing from beaches and piers. Reels are now available with hermetically sealed drag systems that perform smoothly in harsh conditions and with large-arbor spools designed for quickly taking up line. Fly lines and leaders are now manufactured for specific uses and presentations. It can be difficult making tackle decisions and purchases when presented with all these choices. You should consult your local dealer or

Above: Steelheaders dish out a lot of abuse on equipment. Fly reels should function properly during harsh conditions. STEVE MAY PHOTO

Size your tackle to the tributary you are fishing and the size of fish you expect to catch. Both 5- and 6-weight fly rods can easily handle 4- to 6-pound steelhead on small tributaries. KARL WEIXLMANN PHOTO

destination fly shop to find out what tackle is best suited for that particular fishery.

Fly Rods

Fly rods are tools, and you want to use the right tool for the job. Rod weight and length should be determined by the physical characteristics of the tributary you are fishing, the size and species of the fish you expect to catch, and the technique being used. Small to medium-size tributaries with steelhead or coho salmon averaging from 4 to 10 pounds can be easily handled with a 6- or 7-weight rod. Larger rivers with heavy current that have the potential for steelhead or brown trout weighing over 10 pounds require a 7- or 8-weight rod. King salmon require nothing short of a 9- or 10-weight rod for fish that can weigh up to 30 pounds or more. I prefer a 10-weight, which gives you more control with these massive fish.

A 9 1/2-foot long rod is the standard length for most tributary fly fishing, but today's trend is to use longer 10- to 10 1/2-foot rods that enable the angler to mend, lift, and direct long or short lengths of fly line. Longer rods enable the angler to cover greater amounts of water, provide better reach when short-line indicator nymphing or tight-line bottom-bouncing, and make it easier to roll-cast with shot and indicators.

By choosing the rod size to suit the size of the tributary I'm fishing, I've been able to catch a lot of steelhead using short, 7 1/2- to 8 1/2-foot, 4- and 5-weight rods on tiny tributaries with lots of brush on the banks, where there's no room for a

9-foot rod. I've never had a steelhead break one of these tiny rods, but a heavier weight rod in a short length would probably be a better choice, where there are a lot of blowdowns and logjams. My largest fish, caught on a 7 1/2-foot 4-weight, weighed 9 1/2 pounds.

Modern, fast-action fly rods are good for swinging techniques with sinking or sink-tip fly lines and large flies with heavy tippets, but they are ineffective when nymphing with small flies and light tippets. I've watched a lot of steelhead get snapped off on the hookset when using today's super-fast, high-modulus graphite rods. There is no shock absorption or give during the hook-set. Nymphing techniques require a shock-absorbing medium- to medium-fast-action fly rod with a light tip to hook and play large fish with small tippet diameters. Ultrathin, ultralong leaders tapering to 4X or 5X are sometimes needed to hook Great Lakes salmonid species under increasing water clarity and fishing pressure.

Custom-made semi-noodle or noodle fly rods built on St. Croix Wild River spinning rod blanks are made for protecting light tippets when using indicator nymphing or bottom-bouncing techniques. Steelhead weighing over 18 pounds have been landed on 2-pound-test tippet using this specialized tackle, but these rods make poor cast-

Custom-built noodle fly rods that are 10 to 10 1/2 feet long have great shock absorption capabilities when using light tippets during low and clear water.

ing tools with traditional fly lines and are best suited for triangle taper lines or running lines.

I like a compromise that can do it all—a medium-fast rod that can ably perform all the techniques used in Great Lakes tributary fly fishing, indicator nymphing with light tippets, swinging streamer patterns, and bottom-bouncing. A rod with a stiff enough butt section should easily lay out 60 feet of line, while still adding shock absorption capabilities when setting the hook. Scott Fly Rod company, for example, manufactures an A3 series of fly rods in a 10-foot length that is ideal for most steelheading conditions and techniques, carries a lifetime warranty, and currently retails for less than $335. Steelheaders break rods, and whether you slip and fall, step on it, trip over it, or throw weight on the leader into it, it's just the nature of the beast. Having a couple of lifetime warranties on fly rods helps keep you on the water. For king salmon I like a fast rod with a soft tip that can handle casting weight on the leader and lets you put the stick to the fish.

Spey Rods

Three factors should be considered when choosing a two-handed rod for tributary fishing: weight, length, and action. Weight and length should be determined by the size of the river and the size of the fish. Rod action—fast, medium, or slow—should be determined by the fishing technique used, the particular Spey-casting style being employed, and the associated fly lines that perform these different tasks.

Traditional two-handed rods with slow to medium actions load easier and have better feel (or feedback) for beginning casters. They are better suited for full-floating fly lines that contain long, 60- to 80-foot head sections, and traditional Spey-casting techniques. Medium to medium-fast, two-handed rods are better suited for floating and sinking fly lines that have short to mid-length heads from 27 to 65 feet long. Fast two-handers are good when using large, heavy flies and fast-sinking lines with short, heavy head sections from 27 to 45 feet long, and a shooting or running line for distance.

Using modern technology and materials, many rod manufacturers now build 6- to 8-weight, 10½- to 12½-foot switch rods that are ideal for fly fishing on medium-size Great Lakes rivers and streams with one or two hands. Large rivers require longer rods, up to 14 feet or more for the wading angler, while those elevated and fishing out of a boat can get by with shorter rods.

Reels

As a kid, I learned that the fly rod was more important than the fly reel. At the time, the reel was considered just a line-holding device that could be palmed if a fish took line. Not anymore. These days, a quality fly reel with a quality drag system is even more important than the rod when fly fishing Great Lakes tributaries for steelhead and salmon. I'd rather be using a cheap rod and a good reel than a cheap reel and a good rod. These are not fish that can be stripped in.

The most important consideration when purchasing a reel for Great Lakes fly fishing is the drag system. It should have a low startup inertia that instantly engages the drag to eliminate leader or tippet breakage when fish take off. It must also handle the abuse and weather that Great Lakes tributaries dish out and still perform properly in subfreezing weather.

In cold weather, I've watched many reels completely lock up or go into complete free spool, which is unacceptable when a trophy fish is on the end of the line. The drag system on a fly reel should be airtight and waterproof. Not all sealed drag systems can make that claim, although they may perform well in good weather. Consult and question the manufacturer or dealer before making a choice. Fair-weather fly fishers find that most of today's reels are great performers when element exposure is not an issue.

Reels with smooth drags are needed for tackling steelhead with light tippets.

Fly reels machined from aluminum bar stock are lightweight and cause you less fatigue over the course of a long day on the water. Large-arbor spools are a must for rapid line retrieval when a hooked fish charges directly at the angler and for retrieving loose line when getting a hooked-up fish on the reel. Once the fish is on the reel, you'll want to be able to easily find and adjust the drag control if needed. The drag should be preset to provide just the right amount of resistance to a running fish, without breaking the leader or tippet. It may seem wise to err on the light side here and palm the reel, but most drags on good reels can be cranked down farther than you might expect and still function properly. Setting the drag too light can result in overrun on some models, causing the fly line to tangle upon itself in the reel spool.

Lines

You can certainly catch a lot of fish with a traditional, standard, weight-forward floating fly line, but many of the new fly lines can enhance your technique and increase your performance and are manufactured specifically for steelhead and salmon fly fishing. Scientific Anglers and RIO Products produce steelhead and salmon long-belly weight-forward fly lines with long back tapers developed for roll casting, overhead casting, and single-handed fly rod Spey casting. The long rear tapers excel at mending and line control as the fly swings or drifts through a pool. Wulff Triangle Tapers have a longer and thinner front taper for less line tension on the surface of the water, which reduces drag during the drift.

For sink-tip swinging, integrated sink-tip fly lines or interchangeable tip systems allow you to adjust to various conditions by employing various sink-tip lengths and sink rates. Running lines used for deep-drifting techniques should have braided nylon cores, which have less tangling and less stretch when compared to level mono-core running lines with thin PVC coatings. Your local fly shop can make recommendations based upon the fishing that is available.

Leaders

I try to keep it simple when it comes to leader selection and use 9 1/2 to 10 1/2-foot 1X to 4X tapered, knotless steelhead leaders for most of my guiding, adding or subtracting tippet material as

Fly reels for Great Lakes steelhead should have smooth drags with a low startup inertia for protecting light tippets. This chromer buck ate a size 14 Catt Gold Nugget nymph fished on 4X fluorocarbon.

needed. I like a stiff butt with a supple tip for most indicator and high-stick nymphing techniques. It helps turn over the junk and produces less tangles, while the supple tip allows for a free-drifting fly. Some anglers prefer a supple butt and supple tip to help further reduce drag.

Nylon leaders tapered to 3X work just fine for most steelheading conditions, using shorter (8 1/2- to 9 1/2-foot) leaders on smaller streams and longer (12- to 14-foot) leaders on bigger water or when facing clear water. Tippet material can be added as the leader becomes shortened from changing flies, hanging up, or "tree-branch fish." I use 0X, 1X, or 2X for swinging streamers, fishing stained water, or for coho and king salmon. Clear water may require dropping to 4X or 5X when small flies are needed to get the take from steelhead.

For those who like to build their own leaders, stiff butt and middle sections that are approximately 8 1/2 feet long and tied with Maxima or other hard nylon materials, with a 3- to 5-foot tippet section of softer, flexible material like Frog Hair, work well. In clear water, the use of fluorocarbon leaders and tippet material can greatly increase your hookup rate.

Accessories

Chest packs are becoming more common, but I still like to have everything right in front of me and generally use a traditional fly-fishing vest with a large back storage area for raingear or water bottles. Four main outside pockets and four inside pockets have all the room required to hold at least four fly boxes, a Ziploc bag of indicators, leaders, and all the terminal tackle that I'll need for that day's fishing.

Polarized glasses are an absolute must for tributary fly fishing and cutting glare from the water. I feel like I'm fishing blind without them. Dark lenses work best on bright sunny days, and lighter

QuickShot split-shot dispensers make shot selection and placement a breeze.

The fly angler on foot needs a fully stocked vest with important accessories and tools immediately at hand.

amber-colored lenses work best during overcast days. Polarized glasses are now available that change lens color according to the amount of sunlight on that given day. I've lost or dropped so many pairs of expensive glass-lensed polarized glasses, even when using a lanyard to hold them around the neck, that I now buy less expensive models with polycarbonate lenses.

A stream thermometer can help the angler deduce fish-holding positions and run-timing stages for lake-run salmonids. In warmer weather, find spring seepages that attract lake-run species. Tributary temperatures from the mid-40s to upper 50s coincide with active, migrating runs of coldwater species that will take flies readily from classic holding positions as they move upstream. When tributary temperatures fall below 45 degrees, migration starts to slow down as fish move to slower and deeper tributary sections, although runs of steelhead and brown trout can still occur in colder water.

Tippet spool dispensers should be easily accessible and hold at least 4 spools, from 1X to 4X. Some people like the accessory lanyards that hang around your neck and carry an assortment of tools, such as line nippers, retractors, hemostats, leather leader straighteners, or tippet material dispensers, but for me everything gets tangled or in the way so I just keep these items separated with clip-on hooks on the left- and right-hand side of my vest.

Frog Hair QuickShot dispensers are one of the best accessories ever made for the tributary angler who needs quick and easy access to various sizes of tin, tungsten, or lead shot. These pin to the vest and have three containers that easily open and close without spilling. A hook sharpener is probably the single most important accessory to help you catch more fish. Even though modern manufacturing methods produce chemically sharpened hooks that are super-sharp right out of the package, wear and tear on the hook point caused by bottom-bouncing flies eventually results in dull hooks and the head shake of a lost fish. Keeping hooks sharp throughout the day helps you hook and land more fish.

CHAPTER SEVEN

Economic and Environmental Issues

Sport fishing on Great Lakes tributaries provides a huge economic boost to local, lakeshore communities. Local governing bodies need to be made aware of these positive economic impacts in order to sustain Great Lakes coldwater fisheries into the future. With many manufacturing sectors along the Great Lakes corridor closing or moving out of the country, many lakeshore communities now rely upon tourism and sportfishing for major economic benefits.

The power of the almighty dollar is one of the only ways to gain fisheries recognition from local legislators and government agencies. Economic impact studies have shown the importance of the Great Lakes fisheries in benefitting economic growth and potential. The future and long-term sustainability of coldwater fisheries is further dependent upon green-space preservation along the tributary corridors that give lifeblood to the Great Lakes. Individuals and groups who take the time to

Above: Local economies thrive where coldwater fisheries are protected, preserved, and enhanced.

Many Great Lakes tributaries offer spectacular scenery and exceptional fly-fishing opportunities. Green-space buffer zones and protection from development are needed for future fishery enhancement and sustainability along these beautiful arteries that feed the Great Lakes.

lobby for quality Great Lakes tributary fishing can positively influence managing and governing bodies. The least we can do is give our children the same or better opportunities than we have had.

Angling Pressure

There are days when it seems like everyone showed up at the same time to fish the same tributary that you're on. Lots of big fish draw lots of big crowds, and on the more popular tributaries, fishing alongside another angler is common—with common courtesy, unfortunately, sometimes left at home.

Show common courtesy to the anglers fishing nearest to you. Ask if they mind you fishing in the vicinity. You should get out of the way for anybody playing a fish and not take his spot when he moves to follow the fish downstream.

Rotating a pool is a common practice on West Coast steelhead fisheries and one which allows everyone to fish through productive water, but it is virtually unheard of on Great Lakes tributaries.

Crowding is common on the lower ends of many Great Lakes tributaries. Using a *DeLorme Atlas & Gazetteer* can help you get away from the crowds.

The future is passed to another generation as a steelhead clears a set of falls on its journey upstream to the spawning grounds. This steelhead hit the rush of current three-quarters of the way up and powered itself through the raging whitewater and into the next upstream pool, exemplifying the power of the fish and its urge to migrate.

On larger watersheds, I've asked other people to join in doing this. Some have obliged, others have not—but it never hurts to ask.

Communal fishing has its rewards, but I'll sacrifice numbers of fish for solitude and a chance at still hooking up. I go fishing to get away from people, not to become one in a crowd. When seeking solitude, look to the less heralded waters. Many of the lesser-known streams can provide world-class fly fishing under the right conditions. A good map is invaluable in pointing you in the right direction.

Common courtesy should also be shown to private property owners. If a section of tributary is posted as private property, you should seek out the owner and ask for permission to enter and fish. Access and navigability laws change from state to state, and it's up to the angler to find out what the local laws are. Native Americans own substantial lands on Great Lakes tributaries where special fishing permits may be required.

Access

Access points can change from year to year, and many states have different access laws pertaining to their watersheds. Some states like Ohio have realized the positive economic impact that tributary fishing provides for local economies and have increased public access. Some states like New York have historically protected and enhanced public access to the tributaries, while others like Pennsylvania are currently implementing tributary access programs.

With access and regulations being local issues, fly anglers should seek local answers. Many of the more popular tributaries in the Great Lakes region have public access and fishing access points throughout their entire length. Public water abounds throughout the Great Lakes, and quality experiences can still be found within the boundaries of public water. Local fly shops can also help point you in the right direction. Tributary and watershed maps indicating popular fishing spots are readily available and can also be found on the Internet. Your research can be further enhanced by utilizing programs such as Google Earth. It's pretty cool being able to zoom down on unknown water and wonder what promise it may hold.

I prefer to expand my steelhead horizons using traditional techniques, and on a yearly basis, I try to land a steelhead where I've never before caught one. Half the fun of planning any fishing trip to any location is pulling out a *DeLorme Gazetteer* and researching the area. Roads that cross or parallel the tributary of choice are obvious points of

Even though it's getting harder, chrome can still be caught far away from crowded access points. You might not catch as many fish, but you can still have a quality Great Lakes experience.

reference, though sometimes these may not lead to actual access. Plain old gumshoe-style footwork and thoroughly driving around an area I've wanted to fish (or hunt), along with the simple act of knocking on a door, has resulted in some of the best outdoor experiences I've ever had in my life. I learned respect for private property at a young age, as I rode around with dad on bright, early fall mornings and watched as he knocked on local farmers' doors, seeking places to hunt. Always ask permission before entering private property, and respect the property owner's wishes. This helps to maintain a decent, working relationship with landowners, keeping those doors open for all of us, into the future.

Some regional biologists have provided information for accessing the tributaries in their regions, and many tributary access points can now be found on the Internet, though this information is subject to change.

Resources

For stream maps, tributary access points, fishing regulations, and guides

Indiana
http://www.in.gov/dnr/fishwild/
For access, regulations, and maps, click on Fishing-Overview.

Michigan
http://www.michigan.gov/dnr
For access, click on Fishing, click on Inland Trout and Salmon Guide, click on Maps.

Minnesota
http://dnr.state.mn.us/index.html
For access, go to Fishing page and click on Public Water link at bottom of page.

New York
http://www.dec.ny.gov/outdoor/fishing.html
For access, click on Places to Fish.

Ohio
http://www.dnr.state.oh.us
For access, click on Wildlife, click on Fishing, and click on River Fishing Maps.

Ontario
http://www.mnr.gov.on.ca/MNR/fishing
For access, click on Trib Maps.
View the Annual Report for stocking numbers and locations at: http://www.glfc.org/lakecom/loc/mgmt_unit/homepage2006.htm. or go to the GLFC homepage, click on About the GLFC, choose the Annual Reports link.

Pennsylvania
http://www.fish.state.pa.us
For access, click on County Guide.

Wisconsin
Fishing access maps available on the DNR's web site at http://dnr.wi.gov/fish/lakemich/TributaryAccess.htm

Real-time tributary flow data
Up-to-the-minute water flow in cubic feet per second and gauge height is provided by the United States Geological Survey at: http://water.usgs.gov/realtime.html.

References and Required Reading

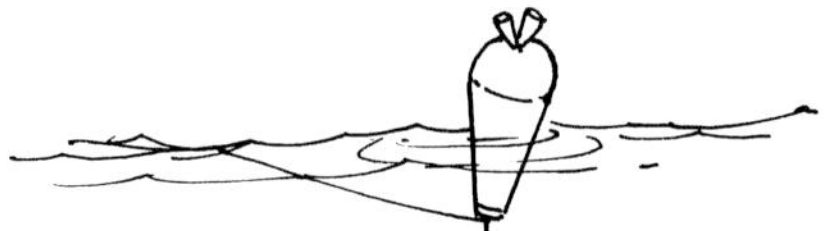

A Steelheader's Way: Principles, Tactics & Techniques, Lani Waller, Headwater Books, 2009.

Fishing the Great Lakes: An Environmental History, Margaret Beattie Bogue, University of Wisconsin Press, 2000.

Fly Fishing For Great Lakes Steelhead: An Advanced Look at an Emerging Fishery, Jerry Kustich and Rick Kustich, West River Publishing, 1999.

Steelhead Dreams: The Theory, Method, Science and Madness of Great Lakes Steelhead Fly Fishing, Matt Supinski, Frank Amato Publications, 2001.

Steelhead Guide: Fly Fishing Techniques and Strategies for Lake Erie Steelhead, John Nagy, Great Lakes Publications, 2008 (rev.).

The Complete Steelheader: Successful Fly-Fishing Tactics, John Larison, Stackpole Books, 2008.

The Orvis Pocket Guide to Great Lakes Salmon and Steelhead: Tips, Tactics, and Techniques, Matthew Supinski, The Lyons Press, 2004.

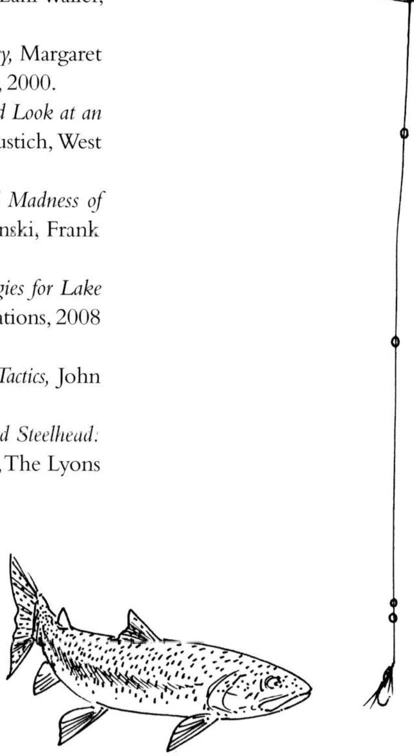

Equipment and Tackle

High-density polystyrene indicators

Float Master Products
1167 Potomac Drive
Brunswick, OH 44212-3141
440-669-9928
www.floatmasterco.net
info@floatmaster.net

Foam indicators

Weldon Slotted Bobbers
Weldon Tackle Mfg.
18613 St. Clair Avenue
Cleveland, OH 44110
www.weldontackle.com

Leaders, tippet material, indicators, and accessories

Gamma Technologies/Frog Hair
200 Waterfront Drive
Pittsburgh, PA 15222
1-800-437-2971
www.froghairfishing.com
info@froghairfishing.com

RedWing Tackle
Blackbird Shot/Floats
905-683-8989
www.redwingtackle.com

Rods

Scott Fly Rod Company
2355 Air Park Way
Montrose, CO 81401
1-800-728-7208

Fly lines

3M Scientific Anglers
St. Paul, MN 55144-1000
www.scientificanglers.com

RIO Products
5050 South Yellowstone Highway
Idaho Falls, ID 83402
1-800-553-0838
www.rioproducts.com

Royal Wulff Products
7 Main Street, Box 948
Livingston Manor, NY 12758
1-800-328-3638
845-439-4060
www.royalwulff.com

Flies

Greg Senyo
Jag Fly Company & Steelhead Alley Outfitters
419-466-9382
www.steelheadalleyoutfitters.com
www.jagflyco.com

Mike Schmidt
Angler's Choice Flies
5560 Little Falls Drive
Dublin, OH 43096
614-638-6727
www.anglerschoiceflies.com

Index

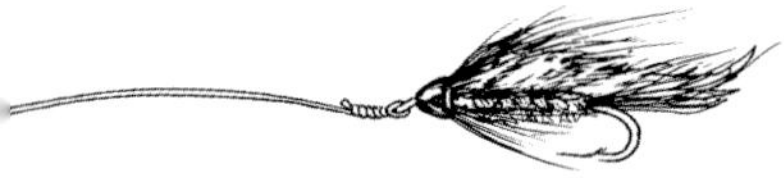

Fly names refer to page with recipe.

Accessories, 167–168
Ahnapee River, 11
Angel Hair Alewife, 92
Antron Bug, 119
Aquatic Nuisance, 97
Arcola Creek, 11
Ashtabula River, 11, 84
Atlantic salmon, described, 18–20
  fisheries list, 21
  fishing characteristics, 21
  life cycle / run timing, 20–21
Au Sable River, 6, 11, 16
Axxel Flash Hare's Ear, 115

Baptism River, 11, 18
Barry's Pike Fly with a Twist, 100
Bayfield River, 11
Beaches/shoreline, 46–48, 50–54
Bead Sucking Leech, 103
Beaver River, 11, 84
Betsie River, 11, 16, 18, 45
Big Black Tube, 106
Big Creek, 11, 84
Bighead River, 11, 16, 84
Big Huron River, 11, 16, 84
Big Manistee River, 11, 16, 18, 45, 46, 84
Big Otter Creek, 11
Black and Blue Electric Bugger, 103
Black and Blue Electric Stone, 119
Blackhoof River, 11
Black River (Lake Huron), 11
Black River (Lake Ontario), 18, 19, 21, 26, 45
Black Sturgeon River, 11
Boardman River, 11, 45
Boats, 77, 80, 82–83
Bois Brule River, 11, 16, 18, 84
Bowmansville Creek, 11
Boyne River, 11
Branch River, 11, 84
Bronte River, 11
Brown and Olive Zonker, 101
Brown trout, described, 21–23
  fisheries list, 26
  fishing characteristics, 24–26
  life cycle / run timing, 23–24
Buffalo Creek, 11
Bunny Minnow, 103

Canadaway Creek, 11
Canadian Nuke Egg, 110
Carp River, 11, 16
Cascade River, 11
Cattaraugus Creek, 7, 11, 26, 65, 72, 80, 84, 111, 113, 115, 123–124
Catt Gold Nugget, 115
Chagrin River, 11
Chambers Creek, 5
Chaos Maker, 97
Chautauqua Creek, 11, 26
Chinook salmon, described, 11–13
  fisheries list, 16
  fishing characteristics, 15
  life cycle / run timing, 13–15
Chocolay River, 11, 16, 18, 84
Clear Creek, 7
Clothing, winter, 35, 37–38
Clouser Minnow, 98
Coho salmon, described, 16–17
  fisheries list, 18
  fishing characteristics, 17
  life cycle / run timing, 17
Coldwater River, 11
Conneaut Creek, 11, 84, 111, 113, 115
Cowles Creek, 11
Cream, Orange, and White Sucker Spawn, 110
Credit River, 11, 16, 18, 21, 45
Crooked Creek, 11, 113
Crooked Creek Caddis, 117
Cross River, 11
Crystal Meth, 111
Cypress River, 11, 18

Devil Track River, 11, 18
Don River, 11
Douglaston Salmon Run, 14, 127
Dowagiac River, 11, 43, 84
Dry-fly tactics/techniques, 78–79
Duffins Creek, 11

East Branch Au Gres, 11
East Twin River, 11, 84
Environment, 169, 171–174
Eggs
  fishing with, 107, 109
  recipes, 109–111
18 Mile Creek (Lake Erie), 11, 26
18 Mile Creek (Lake Ontario), 10, 16, 26, 32
Elk Creek, 11, 26, 29, 70, 79, 90
Emerald Bunny, 95
Emerald Candy, 94
Emulator with Flash, 97
Erie Canal, 22
Erie-sistable, 79
EZ Hex, 117

Fall, fishing in, 28–31
Falls River, 11
Fighting the fish, 154, 158–160
Fire Detector, 102
Fishers Creek, 11

Flea (fly), 111
Flies, described, 85–86
  dry, 78–79
  eggs, 107, 109–111
  nymphs, 111, 113–122
  recipes, 79, 91–95, 97–105, 109–111, 115–122
  streamers, 87–88, 90–91–95, 97–105
Float fishing
  boats, 77, 80, 82–83
  where to go, 83–84
4 Mile Creek, 59
Frammus, 111
Fruit Detector, 102
Full Motion Hex, 118
Furry Minnow, 98

Ganaraska River, 11, 16
General Practitioner, 104
Genesee River, 6, 10, 16, 18, 26
Georgian Bay, 45
Gold-Bodied Beadhead Stonefly, 120
Gold Caddis Goo Bug, 120
Golden Marabou Streamer, 98
Grand River (Michigan), 11, 16, 18, 84
Grand River (Ohio), 11, 72, 84, 88, 111, 113
Grand River (Ontario), 11, 42, 45, 46, 84
Grand River Special, 92
Grapefruit Head Leech, 93
Gratiot River, 11
Grease Stain, 94
Greg's Spey Stone, 104
Grindstone Creek, 10, 26

Hackle Flash Zonker, 92
Half & Half Glo-Spawn, 110
HF Sculpin, 95
Highland Creek, 11
Humber River, 11
Huron River, 11
Hurricane River, 11

Irondequoit Creek, 10

Jackpine River, 11, 18
Johnson Creek, 10, 26
Jordan River, 11
JQ Caddis, 117

Kalamazoo River, 11, 84
Kevin's Australian Possum Hex, 99
Kewaunee River, 11, 16, 18, 46, 84
Knife River, 3, 11, 16, 18

Lake Erie, 57
  brown trout, 1, 21, 23–24, 26
  Chinook salmon, 1, 11
  coho salmon, 16
  steelhead, 4, 5, 7, 9, 11, 45, 46, 48, 50, 111, 138
Lake Huron
  Atlantic salmon, 20, 21, 45
  brown trout, 26
  Chinook salmon, 11, 16
  steelhead, 6, 7, 11, 45, 46
Lake Michigan
  Atlantic salmon, 19, 20
  brown trout, 21, 26, 47
  Chinook salmon, 11–12, 16
  coho salmon, 16, 18
  steelhead, 5, 11, 42, 45–46
Lake Ontario
  Atlantic salmon, 18–21, 45
  brown trout, 26, 47
  Chinook salmon, 11, 12, 16
  coho salmon, 16–18
  steelhead, 3, 5–7, 10, 11, 39, 45
Lake Superior
  Atlantic salmon, 19–21, 45
  brown trout, 26
  Chinook salmon, 16
  coho salmon, 16–18
  steelhead, 3, 4, 7, 11, 45, 46
Lead, substitutes for, 127
Leaders, 165, 167
Lines, 165
Little Calumet River, 11, 45
Little Manistee River, 5, 6, 11, 16, 18, 84
Little Salmon River, 10
Little Sandy Creek, 39

Mackenzie River, 11
Maitland River, 11, 16, 18, 84, 104, 110
Manistee River, 32
Manitowoc River, 11, 84
Marabou-Tailed Clouser Minnow, 95
Marsh Creek, 26
Maxwell Creek, 10
McMullen's Better Glo-Bug, 110
Menominee River, 11
Michipicoten River, 11, 16, 18, 46
Milwaukee River, 11, 16, 18, 46
Miner River, 11
Minnow Tube, 106
Moby Goby, 92
Mosquito River, 11
Muddy Water Streamer, 107
Muskegon River, 6, 11, 16, 18, 42, 77, 84, 124

Nemadji River, 11
Niagara River, 10, 11, 16, 26, 84
Nine Mile River, 11
Nipigon River, 16, 18, 46
Nith River, 11
Normandy Creek, 11
North Sandy Creek, 10, 16, 21, 26
Nottawasaga River, 11, 16, 18, 84
Nymphing techniques
  high-stick, 146–150
  indicator, 127–146
Nymphs
  fishing with, 111, 113–115
  recipes, 115–122

Oak Creek, 11
Oak Orchard Creek, 10, 16, 18, 19, 21, 22, 26, 45
Oconto River, 11, 16, 18, 46, 84
Ocqueoc River, 11, 16
Ontonagon River, 11, 16, 18, 84
Orange Bomber, 79
Orwell Brook, 60
Oswego River, 10, 16, 18, 22, 26, 84

Palisade Creek, 11
Peacock Nymph, 122
Pentwater River, 11
Pere Marquette River, 6, 11, 16, 18, 21, 45, 84
Peshtigo River, 11, 16, 18
Pigeon River, 11
Pike River, 11

Platte River, 11, 18
Poplar River, 11
Possum Nymph, 122
Potter's Creek, 11
Psycho Sculpin, 99

Raccoon Creek, 11
Reading the water
  adjusting to conditions, 70–77
  current seams, 63–64
  depressions, 64–66
  high-water strategies, 73–74
  low-water strategies, 74–77
  overview of, 55–59
  pocketwaters, 62–63
  pools, 66–69
  riffles, 62–63
  runs, 66
  surface structures, 69–70
  tributary sections, 59–61
Reaper, 99
Red and White Beadhead Zonker, 101
Red Neck Rabbit, 98
Reels, 164–165
Rifle River, 11, 16, 84
River Chicken Emulator, 97
Rocky River, 11
Rods, 162–164
Rogue River (Lake Michigan), 11
Rogue River (Lake Ontario), 11
Rolling Stone, 117
Root River, 11, 16–18, 45, 46

Salmon Fly, 95
Salmon River, 3, 7, 10, 13–19, 21–23, 26, 32, 40, 45, 59–60, 84, 124, 127, 132–133
Salt Creek, 11, 45
Sandy Creek, 10, 22, 26
Sauble River, 11
Saugeen River, 11, 16, 46, 84, 104, 110
Sauk Creek, 11
Schmidt's EP Tube, 105
Schmidt's GL Minnow, 105
Schmidt's Lunkergetter, 100
Senyo Sculpin, 91
Senyo's Egypt's Treasure, 104
Senyo's Shrimp Scampi, 121
Senyo's Steak and Eggs, 116
Senyo's Steely ISO, 118
Senyo's Tall Tail Spey, 103
Senyo's Wiggle Stone, 116
7 Mile Creek, 11
Sheboygan River, 11, 16, 18, 45, 46
Shoreline/beaches, 46–48, 50–54
16 Mile Creek, 11
Slinky rigs, 123–127
Soft-Hackle Streamer, Hot Orange and Black, 101
Soper Creek, 11
South Sandy Creek, 10, 16, 21, 26
Spey casting, 156–158
Split Rock Creek, 11
Spring, fishing in, 38–40, 42
Spring Creek, 6
Steelhead, described, 3–6
  fisheries lists, 10–11, 45–46
  fishing characteristics, 10
  history, Great Lakes, 6–7
  life cycle / run timing, 6, 8–10
Steelhead Pheasant Tail, 119
Steelhead Prince, 119
Steelhead Woolly Worm, 122
Steelie Soft-Hackle, 121
Steel River, 11, 16, 18, 45, 46
Steely John, 118
St. Joseph River, 11, 16–18, 43, 45, 46, 84
St. Lawrence Seaway, 16, 20
St. Mary's River, 11, 16–18, 20, 21, 45, 84
Stony Creek, 10
Streamers
  fishing with, 87–88, 90–91
  recipes, 91–95, 97–105
Sucker River, 11
Summer, fishing in, 42–46
Swinging techniques, 150–154

Tackle, 162–162
  accessories, 167–168
  leaders, 165, 167
  lines, 165
  reels, 164–165
  rods, 162–164
Tahquamenon River, 11
Tan Beadhead Zonker, 101
Techniques and tactics
  dry-fly, 78–79
  fighting the fish, 154, 158–160
  high-stick nymphing, 146–150
  indicator nymphing, 127–146
  slinky rigs, 123–127
  Spey casting, 156–158
  swinging, 150–154
Temperance River, 11, 16, 18
Terminator Nymph, 118
Three-Loop Pink Lady, 109
Thunder Bay, 45
Thunder Chicken, 93
Tiny Winter Black, 122
Trail Creek, 11, 45
Troutfitter Spey, 104
Trout Run, 60
Tubular Smelt, 94
12 Mile Creek, 11
20 Mile Creek, 11, 26, 70, 79
Two Hearted River, 11, 16, 18

Vermillion River, 11
Viagra Caddis, 120

Walnut Creek, 1, 7, 11, 23, 26, 160
Welland Canal, 16
West Twin River, 11, 84
Wheeler Creek, 11
White Bunny Strip Screamer, 106
Whitefish River, 11
Whiteman's Creek, 11
White River, 11, 16, 18
Wilmot Creek, 11, 16, 21
Winter, fishing in, 31–35, 37–38
Wolf River, 11

Young's Creek, 11

Zebra Midge, 120